LIAM CO

The
DARK SIDE
Of
CELEBRITY

Irish Courtroom Scandals of the Rich and Famous

MENTOR
BOOKS

First published in 2009 by

Mentor Books Ltd.,
43 Furze Road
Sandyford Industrial Estate
Dublin 18
Republic of Ireland

Tel: +353 1 295 2112/3
Fax: +353 1 295 2114
e-mail: admin@mentorbooks.ie
www.mentorbooks.ie

A catalogue record for this book is available from the British Library.

ISBN: 978-1-906623-38-8

Cover: Kathryn O'Sullivan
Typesetting and layout: Mary Byrne
Editor: Treasa O'Mahony

Printed in Ireland by ColourBooks Ltd

The Publishers would like to thank the *Irish Independent*, *The Irish Times*, Getty Images and *Phoenix* magazine for permission to reproduce images.

The Publishers have made every effort to trace and acknowledge the holders of copyright for material used in this book. In the event of any copyright holder having been omitted, the Publishers will come to a suitable arrangement at the first opportunity.

Contents

1.   Flowers for Michelle   1

2.   Twink and the Fink 34

3.   The Battle for the Rock 55

4.   The Sex of Bono's Baby. 79

5.   The Merchant Prince and the German Chattel . . . 97

6.   Goldin's Disappearing Act 122

7.   The Ambassador's Daughter 151

8.   The Man in the Silver Shadow 173

> *There is a crack in everything*
> *That's how the light gets in.*
>
> **Leonard Cohen**

Acknowledgements

Thanks to Danny and Treasa at Mentor Books.
Photographs courtesy of Independent News & Media,
sourced by Andrea Byrne and Willie Brennan.
Also thanks to the many court reporters whose work is quoted in these
stories and who do such a fine job.

Liam Collins
September 2009

Chapter 1
Flowers for Michelle

He knew he was in trouble the moment he saw her walking into the party that Saturday night. She was wearing a tiny black cocktail dress, her mane of lush black hair cascading over her cleavage. Her long tanned legs tapered into red designer shoes and she turned every male eye in her direction. Michelle Rocca, the one-time Miss Ireland and Eurovision Song Contest presenter, stood out like a beauty queen in a hay barn.

As he watched her enter the room filled with his casually-dressed friends in their designer jumpers tied around their shoulders and their jeans, he wished once again that he hadn't slept with her just three days earlier. He knew that was a big mistake. It had rekindled all the old fire he had worked so hard to dampen down. It had also left him seriously compromised with his present girlfriend, who was standing at the other side of the room oblivious to the drama about to unfold around her.

Cathal Ryan was rich and apparently successful. He was accustomed to getting what he wanted when he wanted it, and at one time he had wanted Michelle so badly he had begged her on O'Connell Bridge in Dublin to throw all the rings from her other lovers into the swirling waters of the Liffey below.

Then he, the dashing pilot turned aviation tycoon, would give her the one ring that would bind them together forever. Of course she hadn't done it. Love was one thing but Michelle was quite attached to her diamonds. Michelle Rocca had been through the false glamour of beauty pageants and television studios. She had clawed her way through the bitchy corridors of the modelling world, and she was wise enough to know that if a man gave you a nice piece of jewellery, you didn't cast it into the deep, dark swirling Liffey water.

But all that was long before this evening. Long before their headlong pursuit of each other had turned bitter and twisted; long before distrust and fear had crept between them.

Cathal had taken a long time to extricate himself from the poisonous relationship that had developed between them. But then, just a little more than 48 hours before the dramatic events of the party began to unfold, he had foolishly shared his bed with her again. More for old time's sake than passion he told himself, and because he had been brought up to appreciate the finer things in life – fine wine, fine paintings, fine houses and all the beautiful things with which he and his family surrounded themselves. Michelle was a heady mixture of beauty and intoxication. But that's not how Michelle viewed their most recent encounter. No, she had seen the old flame rekindling and so here he was caught in a love triangle that spelled nothing but trouble.

Now, as he sipped another gin and tonic, he looked nervously at his date for the evening, his 'girlfriend' even, although she wasn't aware of his assignation with Michelle just two days earlier. Sara Linton was standing at the other side of the room tossing her long blonde hair as she chatted away about horses – as if she hadn't a care in the world. And she hadn't. They had left his father's stately home earlier that afternoon laughing together, and they headed out for the pleasing prospect of a weekend with good friends, good food, fine wine and a bit of banter. But now, like so many other times, life was turning sour on him again. As he looked across the room Cathal Ryan could already see trouble brewing in those big, dark, dangerous eyes of Michelle Rocca, the beauty queen, his one-time lover and the mother of his beloved baby daughter.

That Saturday night in 1992, socialite June Moloney was celebrating her 30th birthday party. About 20 close friends, mostly from the horsey world, had gathered for a party at Blackhall, a stud farm of 320 acres near Clane, County Kildare that she and her husband Brian managed for the fabulously wealthy ruler of the Gulf state of Dubai, Sheikh Mohammed. They were well known 'party-people' and most of the guests were from the same racing circles in which the Moloneys moved.

Blackhall, with the imposing look of a minor stately home, its immaculate lawns and white-fenced gallops, was the ideal setting for a girl to celebrate her good fortune, and June Moloney and her friends knew how to celebrate in style.

Some of the guests were staying overnight in the guest rooms of the imposing old ivy-clad mansion which had once been the home of Theobald Wolfe. It was he who had built the seven-bay Georgian mansion with a flat roof and a fantastic cupola rising from the centre of the house under which the guests now toasted the birthday girl with pink champagne and cocktails.

Indeed Wolfe had left a mark on Irish history after one of his tenants named their son Theobald Wolfe Tone in his memory. But such historic niceties were probably lost on the guests who mingled in the grand salon that night. They were more interested in social gossip than history.

The stud farm had passed through several owners before falling into the hands of Sheikh Mohammed who owned thousands of acres of the lush limestone-rich land of Kildare. He bought it because it adjoined his even more famous and sumptuous Kildangan Stud where he stayed on his infrequent visits to Ireland to attend the Derby or to inspect his extensive bloodstock interests.

At Blackhall the Moloneys enjoyed the run of the old mansion, most of which was converted into offices, apart from the chaotic bedrooms upstairs, and the estate. They had previously lived in Tipperary, where they knew the wealthy Ryan family, particularly Cathal, the son of Tony Ryan, founder of GPA and Ryanair and one of the wealthiest men in Ireland. It was from this wealthy racing set that most of the guests for the evening were drawn.

June Moloney had scented trouble right from the moment Michelle Rocca had asked for the invitation to the party. June had even consulted Cathal, asking him if he could deal with it. But the devil-may-care pilot and deputy chairman of Ryanair couldn't see the danger, or wouldn't. He could be so bloody arrogant sometimes.

His upbringing at Clongowes Wood College and his privileged life as the eldest son of one of Ireland's richest men had given him the nonchalant attitude of an Irish squire: Let's stir everything into the mix, see what happens and to hell with the consequences. It was an attitude that had already led to a broken marriage and a custody battle over his two young children. As the guests toasted the birthday girl in the grand salon, they did so unaware that before the night was over the girl in the black cocktail dress and Cathal Ryan would between them make it one of the most infamous parties of that era.

*   *   *

3

June Moloney first met Michelle Rocca with Cathal Ryan and his father Tony Ryan in a pub in Dublin after an All-Ireland hurling final in September 1991. The two women had since become quite good friends – and this friendship even survived Michelle's turbulent relationship with Cathal Ryan.

But while June was friendly with Michelle in a 'girly' kind of way, visiting each other's houses and attending concerts together, she was much closer to Cathal than she liked to let on. So when the tumultuous relationship with Michelle broke up, it was June who 'played cupid' and introduced Cathal to his current girlfriend, Sara Linton, a friend of hers from the horsey set in which she moved. That was just one of the secrets she kept from Michelle, and one of the reasons she had only reluctantly invited her to the birthday party in Blackhall Stud that Saturday night in March 1992.

The previous Wednesday, Cathal had booked into Tulfarris House Hotel in County Wicklow. He invited his mother Máiréad, long separated from his father Tony, and his younger brother Shane to join him for dinner and stay the night in the luxurious hideaway on the borders of Wicklow and Kildare. Cathal, the eldest in the family, was 'very fond' of a drink it would later emerge. He was also gregarious and good company.

During the evening he phoned his friend June at nearby Blackhall and asked if she and her husband Brian wanted to join the Ryans for dinner. It would liven things up and make it more than just a few members of a family getting together.

June was in a bit of a quandary, and she explained why. She would love to join them for dinner, but his one-time lover Michelle Rocca, their daughter Claudia and her cousin had arrived unexpectedly at Blackhall that afternoon and were planning to stay the night. She couldn't just leave Michelle like that, she explained. But Cathal, always up for a party, said 'no bother'. Despite their turbulent past, he told June to bring Michelle to join the dinner.

The atmosphere around the table was 'cordial and quite relaxed' they all agreed. They knew each other reasonably well and Michelle, as the mother of Máiréad Ryan's granddaughter, got the respect she deserved. With some fine wine to aid the dinner and the sparkling conversation, it was about 12.30 a.m. before they got up from the table.

By that time most of the other guests staying at the country house had already retired for the night. Brian and June Moloney said they were going home to Blackhall but Michelle was in good form and she said she would have another drink and follow them later in a taxi – although the chances of getting a taxi in that part of the country at that hour of the morning were extremely remote, as they all knew. As his mother and brother made their way to their own rooms, Cathal ordered another bottle of champagne and he and Michelle went upstairs to the ornately-decorated suite, with its gilt furniture and its Georgian ambience. What happened that Wednesday night would later become a matter of some dispute between the glamorous couple.

According to Michelle, 'we made love that night' in the big double bed and their tempestuous relationship was rekindled to such a degree that Cathal asked her to marry him. According to Cathal, they sat up most of the night talking intensely about their daughter, the long-running saga of their troubled relationship and, beautiful and wealthy as they were, sipping champagne in one of the country's most exclusive hotel rooms, trying to figure out where it had all gone so badly wrong.

Such was the intensity of their relationship that they had often done that kind of thing before, he maintained. When they fell asleep at dawn, collapsing onto separate sides of the big double bed, he protested that they were both too exhausted to embrace, let alone have sex. And he 'most certainly' had never proposed marriage to her, he would later declare.

In the morning after a leisurely breakfast Cathal drove Michelle back to Blackhall where he spent some time talking with his daughter Claudia. He then left to go back to Kilboy, his father's mansion in the foothills of the Silvermines Mountain near Dolla in County Tipperary, where he was living at the time.

But the midweek episode left June in some difficulty about her 30th birthday party which was arranged for the following Saturday night. She had invited Cathal and her friend Sara Linton as a 'couple'. In the days that followed the dinner at Tulfarris, Michelle, who knew about the party, dropped a couple of hints that she would also like an invite. When Michelle rang later in the week and said she was going to 'come down' with a birthday present, June found herself, as host, in an unbearable position. If she didn't invite Michelle, their friendship might be over. If she did invite her, there was the distinct possibility of an ugly encounter between the former lovers.

Moloney decided to be upfront with both of them.

'You're more than welcome to come . . . but only if you can handle seeing Cathal with his girlfriend and you promise to behave yourself,' June told Michelle on the phone, knowing a lot about the hot-tempered relationship that existed between them for several years and hoping that Michelle might get the hint and stay away.

'I always behave like a lady,' replied Michelle haughtily.

Cathal didn't object either. So the die was cast. That's how Michelle came to make such a grand entrance to Blackhall that night.

At first everything seemed to go as smoothly as the host had hoped. Michelle said a quick hello to Cathal and, champagne cocktail in hand, began to mingle with the other guests.

But before the night was over Cathal Ryan and Sara Linton would flee from the house leaving Michelle Rocca covered in blood and wailing like a banshee. June Moloney's party came to an abrupt and disastrous end. But all this almost pales in comparison with the lurid court case that would drag the whole tawdry episode into the public domain and along the way enthral the general public with a glimpse into the world of privilege and wealth that most of them couldn't even imagine at that time.

It was a legal case that threw up celebrity names like the guest list of a charity ball. As well as the Ryans – Cathal and his father Tony – there was the celebrity hairdresser David Marshall. There was Michelle Rocca, her gaggle of beautiful sisters and her friend Marian Gale. There was her current boyfriend, the rock singer Van Morrison. And the bit-players included Michael O'Leary, the Ryanair boss, who didn't appear as a witness but was certainly mentioned in dispatches.

Even the lawyers were celebrities – solicitor-to-the-stars Gerald Keane acted for Michelle while his willowy blonde wife at the time, Clodagh, carried the legal files. Even the barristers for the opposing sides, Garrett Cooney SC and Nicholas Kearns SC, were more that just professionals doing a job. They became such passionate advocates for their respective clients that the judge – who himself would later attain much celebrity as chairman of the Moriarty Tribunal – had to intervene to implore them to cool down.

And there, among all the beautiful people who were either called as witnesses or came to gloat at the lurid details, was Cathal Ryan himself, cutting a lonely figure as personal details of his private life were laid bare, with allegations of domestic violence and excessive drinking echoing around the wood-panelled walls of Court No 4 in the Four Courts in Dublin.

All in all, it was a court case that sent a shiver through the heart of what passes for Irish high society.

*   *   *

Once a year Tony Ryan held a barn dance in the courtyard of his Tipperary mansion, Kilboy House, and that's where it all started. Once a massive three-storey pile built by Lord Dunally, Kilboy was where Tony Ryan kept his prize herd of Charolais cattle and from where he managed his global aviation empire. Kilboy had been burned in the Civil War in 1922 and later partially rebuilt. By the time Ryan, a train driver's son from nearby Boherlahan, bought the estate, the house had fallen into disrepair. All that was left was a 'vaguely Georgian' one-storied house and a basement filled with the rubble of the original building.

Ryan, who had established the airline-leasing business GPA in the tax-free Shannon Airport zone, was one of Ireland's wealthiest and most successful businessmen. But building his business empire had ruined his marriage, left him an insomniac and given him delusions of grandeur which included buying stately homes in Ireland, a townhouse in Eaton Square in London, a stud farm in Kentucky and a villa in Ibiza. These various homes were the repository of his huge collection of art and antiques. His enormous wealth had also instilled in him a ferocious insistence on getting his own way that alienated many people who crossed his path and in the end almost bankrupted him. But all that would come later.

When he first bought Kilboy, he had restored the house, cleaning out the basement and rebuilding the crumbling walls with the ancient rubble of the upper floors. Like most things he did, he paid obsessive attention to detail. When it was all finished, the house was filled with antiques and hung with his collection of Irish art and the pastures grazed by his prize herd of cattle.

Ryan ran GPA like a dictator. All his executives were required to live within 50 miles of Shannon Airport so that they could be dispatched at a moment's notice to the far corners of the globe in search of a deal. Most of the better-paid executives settled in fine homes along the shores of Lough Derg. Those paid less were required to live in the suburbs of Limerick, colourfully described by one of them as 'like living in Saudi . . . with drink' – a slighting reference to the cultural attractions of the city at that time.

If he was hard on his staff, the rewards were great. He was no less hard on his two sons, Cathal and Declan, who followed him into the aviation business. To celebrate his own importance and reward his overworked staff, Tony Ryan invited the beautiful people to the lavish barn dance in the old stable yard of Kilboy every year. Businessmen donned jeans and rugby shirts, planeloads of models and glamorous air hostesses were flown in from Dublin and London; airline executives, politicians and GPA staff had a 'piss-up' that started in the local pub, Matt The Thrasher in Birdhill, which he also owned. The party continued in the grounds of his home until well after dawn had brightened up the rolling hills in the background.

And it was here in September 1988, five months after she had acted as compére at the Eurovision Song Contest before millions of viewers around Europe, that Michelle Rocca and Tony Ryan's eldest son Cathal first met. It was the beginning of a long and stormy relationship that would eventually lead to the Four Courts where the details of their private lives would be carved out in a blaze of unwanted publicity.

Cathal Ryan, a pilot by profession, began his career working in Sri Lanka flying one of 'Daddy's' planes which had been 'wet' leased to the local airline. In May 1982 he married Tess de Kretzer, a Sri Lankan, who was pregnant with the first of their two children at the time. Cillian was born that year and their daughter Danielle the year afterwards. The marriage quickly fell apart and the couple divorced in 1985.

After protracted court proceedings in Dublin, Cathal was awarded custody of both children by the Irish High Court. He came back to Ireland in 1986 and became deputy managing director of Ryanair. This was the airline his father had established for himself and his brothers Declan and Shane with the millions he was raking in from his main business, Guinness Peat Aviation (GPA). But Tony Ryan didn't want to be directly associated with the new airline himself, so although it was his money, the family directors of Ryanair were his three sons, Cathal, Declan and Shane.

Cathal was the 'playboy' of the family. Like many sons of wealthy businessmen he lacked the confidence of his father and covered up for it by a constant round of social occasions, a fondness for drink and fast cars and an ever-changing procession of beautiful female companions. But for all that he kept himself out of the limelight and the social diary. He was well-paid and he was still working as a pilot in Ryanair. The airline was then in a state of almost permanent flux because it was operating at a huge loss. It was always in danger of being closed down by Tony Ryan or taken over by the Irish national airline, Aer Lingus.

Michelle Rocca came from a well-known Irish/Italian family. Her grandfather, Egidio 'Nano' Rocca, arrived in Ireland in the aftermath of the Irish Civil War when great public buildings such as the Customs House and the Four Courts were being repaired after the ravages of the years of conflict. A hard worker could do well for himself, and Nano, a qualified stonemason, found plenty of work and made enough money to live a comfortable life and establish his own dynasty.

He liked Ireland and settled down and had a family. But he and his sons also kept in touch with their roots, frequently visiting Italy and importing stone and tiles. The firm of P Rocca & Co was founded in 1957 largely as a tile-importing business, which eventually became Rocca Tiles. Nano's grandchildren were good-looking and ambitious. Michelle's younger brother, Patrick, was the third generation to go into the tiling and property business. (Sadly in 2009 he became the tragic 'emblem' of the end of the Celtic Tiger when he shot himself in the back garden of the family home while his wife Annette brought their children to school.) The other family members, Laura, Bernard, Carl and Seamus, all did well. But it was Michelle who attracted most of the attention, at least up until the tragedy that engulfed the family in 2009.

She had become Miss Ireland at the age of 18 in 1980. Like a character from *Footballers' Wives,* she married a glamorous and promising Irish international soccer player, John Devine, the following year. They had two daughters, Danielle and Natasha. Living in London, where he played for Arsenal Football Club, while his wife continued to live in Dublin was hardly conducive to a healthy marriage. Bedevilled by injury, Devine eventually lost his place on the international team. Gradually, as he faded from the public eye, his marriage to Michelle went in the same direction and they separated in 1987.

Meanwhile Michelle had to find a way to fund her lifestyle and what better way than via the glamorous world of television. Her big moment came when she presented the Eurovision Song Contest with RTÉ's posterboy, Pat Kenny, in Dublin in 1988. But surprisingly there was not a big job at the end of it. In recession-hit Dublin she was back looking for a job. After undertaking a course in journalism she began writing and ended up with a job at the Dublin public relations company, Wilson Hartnell, then run by Mary Finan, a well-known figure on the Dublin social scene for several decades. Finan was a formidable woman who represented important clients, among them Michael Smurfit and Tony Ryan.

During the party at Kilboy in September 1988, Cathal asked Michelle out and their relationship started in earnest around October/November of that year. At the time Michelle was living at home with her parents and her two young children in Castleknock. Cathal Ryan was based in Bedfordshire in England, flying home at weekends to be with his two children. It was a whirlwind romance and Ryan was certainly smitten with his beauty-queen girlfriend. In January 1989 they took off for a romantic weekend in the Lake District of northern England and there Cathal proposed to her and she accepted.

But later when the 'engagement' became the subject of some dispute, like most other things in their relationship, the exact status of his proposal became the subject of some heated debate.

'There was no specific date, it was always like that with Cathal,' Michelle would later recall when she was asked about their wedding plans.

According to Cathal the proposal was 'spontaneous – I didn't buy her an engagement ring and there were no wedding plans'.

At the time their family circumstances were complicated, with both of them going through the courts in Dublin trying to sort out their tangled affairs with estranged partners and custody arrangements for their children.

Because Cathal was married abroad he was able to get divorced. But Michelle had married John Devine in 'no divorce' Ireland and at the time she was involved in a prolonged separation and custody case. They were basically conducting a long-distance relationship, mostly paying flying visits to see each other in Ireland or England or taking short holidays together.

Then in mid-1989, fed up with commuting and lacking a firm commitment for work from RTÉ, Michelle moved to Cathal's home in Bedfordshire, bringing her two children with her. She hoped to start a career in television in England and moving in with Cathal was 'killing two birds with one stone'.

In July of that year they set off for a four-day break in Madeira together. Once again Ryan was in a romantic mood and on the spur of the moment he bought her a cheap aquamarine ring in a jewellery shop they were passing. Michelle Rocca took one look at this 'token of love' and went ballistic.

'I intended to buy her a proper ring later on and I was trying to tell her this, but I don't think I ever got the line "temporary" out,' he later recalled. Michelle didn't 'do' temporary engagement rings. She was used to real 'rocks' and she was furious at the insult from her wealthy fiancé. The holiday was ruined.

But the final straw in the relationship came one night in the house in Clifton, an idyllic English village in Bedfordshire with its own duck pond and cricket matches on the green in the summer. They lived there, rather than London, because it was close to Luton Airport, then the British headquarters of Ryanair.

That evening Cathal was tired and went to bed early. Michelle, dressed in a red jumpsuit, was pacing around the bedroom. Efforts by her agent to land parts at the West End and in television in London had not worked out, but she had made a breakthrough with RTÉ. That night she was rehearsing her script for the upcoming Sunday night game show *Play the Game*. She asked Cathal to help her out and he got out of bed and according to him 'we were having a bit of fun and drinking wine' as they rehearsed. But then Michelle got anxious that he wasn't taking her big moment seriously enough. They began to bicker about it and he got back into bed.

'You don't give a shit about my career,' she said to him, sitting on the bed. He ignored her and tried to go to sleep. Then, according to him, she told him to wake up and began slapping him on the face. He told her to go back to bed in her own room and he claimed that she lashed out at him, scratching him on the face so badly that he had to wear a plaster for several days.

According to Michelle an argument had developed about her sister-in-law and Cathal became abusive and 'went for me'.

'At that time I realised he was different in drink,' she said later. She claimed he was very drunk that night and tried to drag her up the stairs and ripped the red suit off her.

'It was embarrassing as he made a big deal about wearing a plaster on his face the next day,' she recalled. She said it was the first sign of violence she had seen in him, but 'there were many occasions like that' later. The volatile nature of their relationship surfaced again in 1990 during a holiday in Rome, which started with a huge fight on the aircraft on the way out. When they got to Rome she was 'so irate' that she stormed off through the airport terminal and he eventually found her at a taxi rank.

She began returning to Dublin on a frequent basis for her television show, which was now a very successful Sunday night entertainment show. Cathal later claimed he 'got the impression' that the relationship was off. But that changed dramatically that August when she rang him and asked could they meet – she had important news to tell him. They met in the King Sitric, an upmarket restaurant in the fishing village of Howth. Over a pleasant dinner and a good bottle of wine, Cathal realised with a shock that his relationship with Michelle was far from over, whether he wanted it to be or not.

'She told me she was pregnant . . . it was initially a surprise because we had not been together, so to speak, for quite a while,' he said later.

According to Cathal she then told him they would have to get married. But he demurred. He said marriage would be rushing things. That's what he had done with his first marriage to Tess and that was one of the reasons it hadn't worked out.

'It is not necessarily the best formula for a long sustained marriage – it wasn't a reason to get married,' he maintained. But Michelle had a very different and more romantic recollection of how the 'news' was broken to the millionaire pilot. She remembered him coming to her home, climbing up on the balcony and knocking on the door and asking if she was pregnant.

They talked on the balcony 'until late' but she had no memory of marriage being mentioned at that stage.

Now that Michelle was pregnant, Cathal decided their relationship was 'worth another try' and he moved back to Ireland in late August of that year and rented a house in Brighton Hall, a small upmarket development on Brighton Road, Foxrock in south County Dublin. They moved in together – he with his two children, she with her two.

But once they settled in there was 'picture but no sound' for much of the relationship. They argued constantly. She felt it was 'an affront' to her dignity among the matrons of the leafy avenues of Foxrock that he would not marry her. Things were so bad that when he was doing his captaincy exams and needed some peace and quiet, he had to move out of the house and into the Airport Hotel to get some seclusion.

She believed that he was unhappy that she was pregnant. She was working in the busy world of public relations and had a house to run, a pilot for a husband and four young children to look after. Their life was a constant headlong rush and they didn't see all that much of each other. And when they were together there were constant rows about the marriage – or lack of it. He didn't want to get married until after the baby was born but she felt, for the sake of the child, it would be better if they were married before the event.

Then in mid-December they spent the weekend at a house party in his father's mansion, Kilboy. They got up early on the Monday morning and drove to Foxrock where there was chaos as they tried to get the four children ready for school.

'Go and brush your teeth,' Cathal told his son Cillian.

When the boy went to the bathroom Michelle was there and told him to get out.

'Daddy told me to brush my teeth,' he told her.

'Michelle lost it, grabbed him by the neck, pushed him out the door and scraped the back of his neck,' claimed Cathal later.

Michelle's version of events was that she was having a shower and when the boy came into the bathroom she shouted at him to get out.

'I reprimanded him because he was being naughty, I did not assault him,' she said.

Although it was just another small episode for the warring couple, it was a step too far for Cathal and later that day he decided it was 'the straw that broke the camel's back'.

Even though it was the week before Christmas he'd had enough. He went home, packed his things, dismissed the nanny and rang the estate agent to say they were handing back the keys of the house and to terminate the electricity and gas. Later that day he moved with his two children to his mother's apartment in Sandymount, Dublin 4.

'It was not doing the children any good and could not have been good for Michelle's unborn child,' he said about their volatile relationship. Michelle was left in 'a distressed condition' by the latest turn of events, especially as it was Christmas week. She was pregnant, had two young children and a demanding job in public relations. Now she didn't have a home.

She rang Tony Ryan and told him she was pregnant and his son had just walked out on her. After some discussion he agreed to pay the rent on the house and she survived, as you do, in Foxrock on what she was earning from her other activities, the television and the public relations work.

Although he believed their differences were 'irreconcilable', when he got a call at 3 a.m. in April 1991 to go to Mount Carmel, the upmarket nursing home in south County Dublin, to be present at the birth of their daughter Claudia, he had no hesitation and was present for the occasion. In July of that year they all went to stay at his father's palatial villa in Ibiza for a summer holiday.

'She gave birth to our daughter, it was reasonable for her to have a holiday, so I invited her,' he said. But he denied that this gesture had somehow 'rekindled' their relationship. He insisted that there was no relationship between them after December 1990 although they had met on occasions.

They had gone out socially once with a friend of Michelle's, Marian Gale, who owned a well-known clothes shop on Grafton Street at this time. On two other occasions, he said, she had turned up drunk and uninvited at his mother's Sandymount apartment and they had chatted, but he had not slept with her.

When their daughter was christened there was a lavish party at which the

Rocca and the Ryan families joined together to celebrate the occasion. After that he would see his daughter Claudia often and sometimes encounter her mother.

'How can I relate to you the compassion I felt for someone who has had my daughter?' Cathal later told a court.

According to Michelle they were still engaged to be married.

'I was his fiancée, the fact that he did not live with me was my choice. I did not intend living with him unless we got married,' she maintained. When the lease on Brighton Hall ended, Michelle rented another house in Booterstown, County Dublin. Cathal paid the rent for a while but when she moved to another house nearby she paid for it herself.

After that Michelle and Cathal met only when he came to see Claudia, or when they went to his father's house in Tipperary, because Tony Ryan liked to host his grandchildren's birthday parties there. As far as he was concerned their relationship was over, he said. But as far as Michelle was concerned they were still dating and 'trying to get the relationship back on track'.

Then after that fateful dinner in Tulfarris House in 1992, Cathal Ryan slept with her again. Once again, Michelle Rocca thought it was a marvellous night for a moondance and her dreams of marriage were about to be answered.

* * *

As the party at Blackhall Stud got into full swing, Sara Linton began to feel tired. She had been up late the night before at a dinner party hosted by Dr Tony Ryan in his Tipperary mansion not far from where she worked as a personal assistant to a leading horse trainer.

She had stayed the night in Kilboy and then she and her boyfriend, Cathal Ryan, set off for the party in Blackhall in separate cars, because they intended to split up and go in different directions on the Sunday. Cathal Ryan remembered the night he met the tall blonde Sara very well.

It was 2 February 1992 and he had attended a private family birthday dinner for his father that night. Afterwards they all went to the Cashel Palace Hotel where there was a 'surprise' party thrown by his father's then partner,

Lucinda Batt. June Moloney was at the party and had introduced him to Sara Linton.

'I was very grateful for that, we had the opportunity to go on a quasi-blind date and the romance flourished,' he said later. He had not been in a relationship since he broke up with Michelle and this, he said, was a 'very very special time'. Now several weeks later on their way to June's birthday party, Cathal and Sara stopped in Nenagh and bought an antique birdcage for the birthday girl. Sara then followed Cathal's car to the gates of Blackhall Stud and up the driveway to the imposing house, arriving at about 8.30 p.m.

She knew Michelle had been invited to the party and she knew also that Michelle was the mother of one of Cathal's children. But she was totally unaware that her boyfriend had slept in the same bed with Michelle just 48 hours before. She was under the impression that the relationship had ended about a year earlier.

She knew Michelle by her photographs and saw her come into the room, but she made no move to introduce herself and continued talking to her friends. She spoke to Cathal, as couples do, over the course of the evening, but she did not see him making any contact with Michelle.

There was quite a lot of drinking going on and one guest later recalled that the food was very late arriving.

As the night wore on Sara began to feel tired and asked June if there was some place she could lie down for an hour. June brought her to a large upstairs bedroom with two beds – they weren't double beds but they were bigger than single beds. She went to the far bed, took off her shoes and her earrings and fell asleep. After a few gin and tonics and a couple of bottles of beer, Cathal noticed that his girlfriend was missing and asked June where she was. She told him Sara had gone up to one of the bedrooms. He went upstairs and found her in the bed nearest the window, asleep. It was about 11.30 p.m. She was lying on top of the covers, but subsequently she got into the bed properly.

'Are you ok?' he asked.

She said she was, but wanted to sleep. He took off his jacket and shoes and lay down beside her in the bed. He fell asleep with Sara beside him against the wall and both of them facing the window.

As they lay sleeping, David Marshall, the well-known Dublin hairdresser, came into the bedroom. It was about midnight. He had left his things in the room earlier as he was staying the night in Blackhall. He intended to be up early the following morning for a round of golf with June's husband, Brian. Mr Marshall was not in a party mood that night. He was tired after a long day in the salon. Besides the guests were mostly from the horse-racing set and he had no interest in the sport of kings. He knew Cathal and spoke to him briefly at the party but he did not know Michelle at all.

On entering the room he noticed that there was somebody else on the other bed. He did not look closely, but he was aware that there could have been more than one person in the bed. He undressed quietly and got under the covers of the other bed and began to doze.

But the quiet of the room was shattered shortly afterwards when what Cathal described as akin to 'waking from a nightmare' erupted in the room.

'You fucking bitch,' said Michelle, as she stormed across the bedroom to where Sara and Cathal were lying.

'Somebody was hurting me, hitting me in the face and head, pulling my hair and screaming obscene language at me,' remembered Sara . . . 'Miss Rocca was the person hurting me.

'She was hurting me and hitting me. Cathal was lying between us and she was reaching over him to hurt me. I got out of the other side of the bed. I stood up and I was crying. Ms Rocca started to caress Cathal to try to wake him up. She pulled him out of the bed.'

Lying on the other bed, David Marshall opened one eye as he heard a commotion and then he saw a shaft of light from the corridor outside fall on Michelle Rocca, who he described as entering the room in a 'determined and aggressive manner'. He heard her shouting as she approached the other bed.

'I saw Sara Linton being pulled by the hair, I heard the sound of slaps, but it all happened fairly quickly, some in the bed and some off it on the floor,' he remembered.

'I was totally shocked, I was frozen to the bed,' he said.

After the initial outburst, Michelle made a second lunge at Sara as Cathal came out of his slumber. 'She got me by the hair and hauled me around the bedroom. She was very frenzied and she got hold of my hair and I wasn't able to do anything. She wouldn't let go, she was hurting me. She flung me against the table and the lamp.

'I was extremely petrified. I was terribly, terribly upset. I have never in my life experienced such violence. I wasn't able to defend myself. It happened so fast. She was holding me by the hair. I was trying to stop her from pulling my hair. I was trying to get my hair away from where she held me. I was trying to relieve the pain by getting hold of her arm and I landed on the table and lamp.'

The table smashed as Sara hit the floor.

David Marshall remembered a fair amount of 'pushing and pulling' as Cathal finally woke and got between the two women.

There was, said Sara, 'a struggle' as Ryan bundled Michelle out of the room. 'I wasn't watching. I was so upset. I didn't see very clearly,' said Sara.

David Marshall lying on the other bed said he heard what sounded like fists hitting skin and face. He was absolutely stunned.

'When I saw Cathal had gone to the rescue, something inside me just said stay out of this,' he remembered, so he lay back in the bed and pretended to sleep. Later he put his head out the door 'to see if I was safe'.

According to Cathal Ryan, Sara was dragged from the bed and was 'lying pretty much defenceless and being slapped and kicked'. He pushed Michelle Rocca away and 'she hit the far wall and slid down' but she got up and made a second 'charge' across the room.

'I slapped Michelle at that stage. I slapped her across the face,' he said. Then he held her around the back and pushed her out the door and onto the landing.

But once again Michelle came 'rushing' into the room where Sara was standing 'rigid with fear'. At this stage Cathal 'slapped her in the face again' and things seemed to subside.

By now the other guests were streaming up the staircase to see what the commotion was all about. Cathal took Michelle to the bathroom. Her nose was bleeding and she was crying and wailing. He sat her down on the toilet seat, wet a piece of toilet paper and tried to mop the blood from her face. Michelle's little black cocktail dress was ripped.

In the other room Sara could hear Cathal 'consoling' the mother of his child in whispered voices from behind a door. Another of the guests saw

Sara's distress and got his wife who took her into another bedroom and put her arms around her and tried to calm her down.

According to June, Cathal and Sara were 'very distressed' when she first saw them.

'And then I saw Michelle. She was in a bad state, her nose was bleeding, she was hysterical and kept saying the father of her child had beaten her.' A 'few of the girls' ran a bath for Michelle and later she went to bed in Blackhall. She was very worried about the condition of her face; she was shivering and felt sore all over. Her face and mouth were bleeding, she said.

Meanwhile Cathal walked out of the bathroom, past the gaping guests and met June who brought him to a side door of the house where Sara was waiting, petrified with fear and mortified at what had happened. They got into his car and she cried all the way back to his father's house in Tipperary, leaving June's 30th birthday party in tatters.

*   *   *

The following day, Sunday, Michelle arrived home to her house in Hampton Court in Booterstown, in south County Dublin. She was battered and bruised with a black eye and a broken nose. Her sisters had arrived in the house and she received a phone call from Dr Tony Ryan, Cathal's father, who apologised for what had happened the previous night at the party in Blackhall.

Dr Stephen Murphy of The Park Clinic in Cabinteely, Dublin, played tennis at the fashionable Riverview Club in nearby Clonskeagh and was familiar with some of the better known members there. He knew Michelle and Cathal and the Marshall family. David Marshall, his former wife Jackie Rafter and their children were also patients of his. Indeed Dr Murphy was so well thought of that Michelle had once asked him to 'broker' reconciliation between herself and Cathal when their relationship was on the rocks at the end of 1991.

This had led to a meeting in his clinic and he and Cathal had agreed to meet again informally 'for a pint' to discuss his troubled relationship with Michelle. But due to a mix-up he went to The Druid's Chair pub in Killiney, while Cathal sat in The Punchbowl pub in Booterstown near where Michelle lived at the time. However they did eventually meet up that summer in the Royal St George Yacht Club, Dun Laoghaire, because, according to Doctor Murphy, Cathal told him he would be more comfortable in an 'informal' setting.

On Sunday, 22 March 1992, Dr Murphy was called to Michelle's house in Hampton Court where he arrived at about 7.30 p.m. It was the day after the party and he found the beauty queen turned game-show host 'distressed and crying'. She told him she had been assaulted by Cathal at a party the previous evening. She said she had been punched, kicked and dragged around the room by the hair.

When he examined her he found bruising on the right side of her head and on her right eye. Her left eye was black and she had bruising and lacerations on her nose. He also found bruising and abrasions on her elbow and her upper arms and right leg above and below the knees. Her upper lip was cut and still bleeding and she had a small cut to the tongue, a bruise on the left side of her chest and neck and a bruise on her bottom. She was in pain and distressed and he gave her painkillers and sedatives. He wanted her to go to the nearby Blackrock Clinic the following day. He even suggested that she have photographs taken and consult with a solicitor.

When he saw her two days later at his clinic the injuries were going through the 'normal' process. She now had two black eyes and he had to assure her that there was no permanent damage to her features, which given her occupation, would be a very important matter. But the doctor felt that while the injuries would heal within a matter of weeks the trauma would last considerably longer.

A couple of weeks later he was in Riverview and after a game of tennis he bumped into David Marshall. The subject of the row at the party, which was now being widely discussed in Dublin social circles, arose.

'He (Marshall) told me he was woken up by a lot of noise and shouting and he opened one eye and saw a fight going on. Mr Ryan was removing Ms Rocca towards the door and Mr Marshall told me he closed his eye and pretended to be asleep,' explained Dr Murphy later in court.

Two days after the party one of Michelle's two nannies took photographs of her injuries. The 'session' took place in the kitchen of her house, said Norah Griffin and she was helped by Michelle's sister Laura. They got the photographs developed at a booth in the Ilac Centre in central Dublin.

'Ms Rocca was very quiet within herself, she didn't talk about the situation. She had some bad days, on a low and all that,' the nanny said, describing the atmosphere in the house at the time. In the days after the party Michelle had been urged to go to the police by some members of her family, but she didn't think that was the right thing to do because it would attract the media, and she didn't want that.

She rang Tony Ryan, Cathal's father, and he asked her not to contact the gardaí. She had already made her mind up that she wouldn't do that. A few days later Tony Ryan's chauffeur-driven black Mercedes pulled up in Hampton Court where she lived. The aviation billionaire got out carrying a large bunch of flowers which he gave to Michelle as he went into the house.

She made tea and after he apologised again, she told him that Cathal wasn't going to see Claudia, their daughter, again. He was 'taken aback' at the vehemence she displayed. Tony Ryan was a very proud grandfather. He had missed much of his own children's upbringing because he was frequently in America at the time. Now that he was older and had more time, he particularly cherished all his children's children as his own. He asked that some arrangement be arrived at so that Claudia would not be cut off from the Ryan family to which she belonged.

'I always wanted Claudia to be a Ryan,' he told her. They didn't find a resolution, but a few days later, Ryanair's chief executive, Michael O'Leary, arrived at her house with another bunch of flowers. The two of them sat down and discussed both her financial situation and allowing Claudia access to her father and the Ryan family. The discussion went fairly well. O'Leary was a very persuasive person and said he would be back. On 12 April 1992, Michael O'Leary arrived back at her house in Hampton Court yet again.

He had a 'document' in his hand which he wanted her to read. In return for allowing access to her child, to be supervised by a nanny, she was to be given a sum of IR£5,000 and a further IR£1,000 a month maintenance. The document also stipulated that she would make no more claims against Cathal.

'I just hated that guy from Ryanair standing there talking about my child,' she said later.

Michelle signed the document, later saying, 'I knew I was a beaten woman and I was trying to regain some dignity. I didn't want any more shit in my life.' When the lease on her house was up in August of that year she rang Tony Ryan 'because I thought he might be able to help with a deposit,' she said, intimating that she intended to buy a house of her own. He suggested that when she had looked at a few houses she should contact Michael O'Leary again. But the negotiations about the house 'broke down'. Around the same time Cathal started 'getting bolshie', demanding to have access to his daughter alone and without a nanny being present at all times.

He had never apologised to her or admitted assaulting her and by now the festering wound of what had happened at the party in Blackhall Stud was getting to her. She decided to take the advice of her friends. She went to see the celebrity solicitor Gerald Keane, a Bentley-driving lawyer who wore loud pinstriped suits, smoked fat cigars, hung around with Premiership footballers and had a flamboyant lifestyle. He would later experience even more widespread prominence when he broke up with his own wife, Clodagh, and formed a relationship with Michael Flatley's ex-girlfriend Lisa Murphy.

Throughout 1993 a number of attempts were made to settle the dispute between Rocca and Ryan.

Although faint murmurs of what was going on reached the media, there was a veil of silence until March 1994 when a defence was finally lodged by Cathal in reply to allegations made in legal letters by Michelle. The defence denied that there had been an assault by Cathal Ryan on Michelle Rocca and said any injuries she received that night were the result of him acting in self-defence and in defence of his date for the night, Sara Linton.

As the storm clouds gathered, Dr Stephen Murphy met David Marshall in Riverview fitness club and once again the fateful party came up for discussion.

'Michelle has no case,' Marshall told Dr Murphy.

That bold statement was about to be tested in court.

* * *

'This case will not fall within the realms of a Vicarage tea-party,' the cricket-playing Judge Michael Moriarty told the jury of five men and seven women arranged across from him in the wood-panelled surroundings of the High Court in Dublin on Wednesday, 5 February 1997.

The Rocca v Ryan case had finally found its way to the august portals of the Round Hall of Dublin's famous Four Courts almost five years after the now infamous 30th birthday party at Blackhall Stud. For years there had been rumours around Dublin of these sensational events but the witnesses had either stayed silent or the media had backed off for fear of the Ryan's high-priced lawyers.

Nobody had ever expected the one-time beauty queen Michelle Rocca and the millionaire pilot and son of one of the most famous businessmen in Ireland to square up to each other in public. The chattering classes were agog. With all their money, beauty and fame, with all their famous friends, their private jets and their palatial homes, that they should face up to each other in open court was almost beyond belief.

But through the big oak doors they came that morning, accompanied by squads of lawyers with friends fluttering in their wake and journalists with their pens poised for a story that had all the ingredients of a soap opera and a reality television show rolled into one thrilling event.

The participants and the evidence that would spill out from the witness box in the days that followed did not disappoint. Michelle Rocca had swapped the 'little cocktail number' for a white blouse and a sober black suit, her dark hair blowing behind her in the cold winter breeze. She was accompanied by her solicitor Gerald Keane in a fawn overcoat and a pinstriped suit which had a muted pattern compared with his usual attire. On Rocca's other side, after alighting from her pink Jaguar, was Keane's then wife Clodagh, her blonde hair swept back behind her ears and her arms filled with legal folders and transcripts. Rocca's barristers, the flamboyant Nicholas 'Nicky' Kearns SC and Liam Reidy SC, completed her legal team.

Cathal Ryan, dressed in a sober black suit, arrived alone each day. The 15-stone pilot whose address was given as De Vesci Terrace, Monkstown, County Dublin, looked grim and serious. His barrister was the formidable Garrett Cooney SC – a member of a well-known Fine Gael legal family. Cooney, best known for his work as a barrister specialising in libel actions against newspapers, was aggressive, articulate and a formidable opponent who would show Michelle no mercy.

Also dressed in black, June Moloney, in whose home the drama had unfolded, stubbed out a cigarette on the steps of the court and, flashing gold jewellery, tore herself from her mobile phone as she entered the courtroom. On hand to see the sensational case unfold was the rock singer Van Morrison. He and Michelle met at a dinner party in Leixlip Castle, the home of the Hon Desmond Guinness, in 1993 and had fallen in love. By now they were in a long-term relationship which would defy the sceptics and lead to another family who desperately wanted to stay out of the limelight. Among the black-clad glamorous women were Michelle's sisters and her friend Marian Gale. The ranks were swelled with more well-heeled onlookers who wanted a ringside seat at what would give many people a first-hand glimpse into how the other half lived, loved and litigated.

Nicky Kearns SC drew first blood – comparing Cathal to convicted wife-beater, Paul Gascoigne, the notoriously unstable English footballer.

'He hadn't even the courage to apologise to her after the incident in Blackhall Stud, instead he sent daddy with flowers,' he said.

As lawyers for Cathal got up to protest at these comparisons, Judge Moriarty said that it was a feature of cases such as this, involving the rich and famous, that lawyers for both sides got overexcited by the celebrity drama and 'a measure of sparks is going to fly'.

And fly they did.

When Mr Cooney complained that Ms Rocca was using every question to 'blacken' the good name of his client, Nicholas Kearns SC replied 'these are not the sort of remarks that a responsible senior counsel should be making'.

Michelle did nothing to tone down the controversy when she went into the witness box on the first day and said that she felt like 'a Belsen victim' after she was punched, kicked and dragged around the bedroom of Blackhall Stud at the birthday party. The one-time beauty queen denied that she was drunk, saying she had three dry Martinis at the party.

'I was very wary, because I knew Cathal was drinking,' she said. She said that when she went upstairs to look for Cathal after she noticed he was missing, it was not premeditated. She went to the ladies' toilet and wondered where he was and thought maybe he had gone home. She said that she knew what Cathal was like when he was drinking. 'He often collapsed and I had to bring him home.'

She went upstairs to try to find him and looked in a bedroom – and saw the two figures on the bed.

'What's happening?' she said, loudly.

The girl, Sara Linton, 'shot up' in surprise.

'Was she clothed or unclothed?' asked her counsel, Mr Kearns.

'She did not look naked,' answered Michelle.

She conceded that she called Ryan 'a bastard or a bollocks, or something like that,' adding flippantly, 'I didn't have a one-to-one conversation' with Sara Linton, the girl in the bed who she had addressed as 'a fucking bitch' among other epithets.

She then described how Ryan had pushed her across the room. As she tried to get up he hit her with a 'haymaker' between the eyes, breaking her nose. He dragged her across the room by the hair, she claimed, punching her again and again in the face and chest and kicking her on the bottom, arms and legs.

'Every time I have to look at my daughter I have to realise that her father is a woman-beater,' she told the court. When she went back to work she pretended that she had been in a car accident.

'For a while I felt like a victim. I thought I deserved it,' she said.

She told Judge Moriarty that the case was not about the money, but she never believed that they would end up in court.

'I never thought it would go that far,' she said.

She said she had signed the agreement with Michael O'Leary because she wanted her daughter to be looked after. The money was to pay off credit card debts and an overdraft, but it was not a settlement of her action for assault she said.

'I would probably put a higher price on myself.'

When Garrett Cooney SC for Cathal Ryan said that David Marshall, an independent witness, would say that she attacked Sara Linton and Cathal only acted in self-defence, Michelle said that was untrue.

'He was drunk and passed out on the bed – how would he know?' she countered.

However when she was asked about this again, she said she was sorry about this reference to Mr Marshall.

'It was strange that he never moved to defend a woman if he was just asleep, maybe he was taking something so that he slept through everything that happened.'

She also said that Cathal was 'slumped' on the bed and he was 'the worse for drink'.

'Are you saying that because he was your fiancé you were entitled to track him down at this party?' asked Garrett Cooney.

'I was not entitled to track him down, but as his fiancée I was entitled to be angry if I found him in bed with another woman,' she answered.

Told that he would say he had woken to the 'nightmare' of seeing his girlfriend dragged across the bedroom floor by the hair she retorted 'bullshit'. She said that Cathal was 'different in drink' and that he was very drunk that night.

Then they came to the question of her relationship with the singer Van Morrison, who was sitting with her sisters in the courtroom.

'When did you become engaged to Mr Morrison?' he asked.

'Do I have to answer that question?' she asked the judge.

'You do, but I will only permit a limited number of questions,' answered the judge.

'Yes, I am engaged to Van Morrison, the singer. I got engaged to him about March or April two years ago (1995).'

'Can you tell me how long you were going out with Mr Morrison before you got engaged?'

'We were good friends and it developed into a relationship.'

'I object to this line of questioning,' said Mr Nicholas Kearns, representing Michelle.

'This case is not to turn into open season on all aspects of Ms Rocca's private life, but the defence is entitled to establish how she coped in the aftermath of the alleged assault,' said the judge.

'She has portrayed herself as a person struggling to look after three children, including Claudia,' replied Mr Cooney.

'She is painting a picture that she and the children were abandoned by Mr Ryan – he's had to sit here in court and hear a tirade of evidence, four hours of personal abuse being heaped upon him – I am entitled to put his case. It has all been one-way traffic up to this.'

Mr Cooney then asked her again about her relationship with Van Morrison. She said she first met him, she thought, in November 1993 when she was working for Wilson Hartnell as a public relations consultant and she had been working with him on interviews. She said she leased a mews house in Clyde Road, Ballsbridge, next door to a house owned by Morrison. Since they had become engaged he had let her have the house. She said her three children were looked after by the nanny, paid for by Cathal, who gave her IR£1,000 a month.

When Van Morrison did concerts she sometimes accompanied him 'but he does not tour'. She could bring the children to London or if they were going to America they would leave the nanny in charge. She said she travelled with him 10 or 15 times a year, but he also had a home in Bath in England and they sometimes stayed there.

'Even when I am travelling you can have trauma. Trauma is about emotions and how you feel inside,' she said.

Questioned about her life since the incident in Blackhall Stud, she said it had been 'four years of hell'. She also said that she did not say Cathal had a drink problem because she wanted to get an advantage over him.

'I am not here to blacken him. I mention that because it is the truth,' she said.

In reply to questions she told the court that she herself had been a patient at the Rutland Centre in Dublin in 1996, but it was for stress and not for alcohol problems.

Cathal, wearing a sober dark suit, sat for four days taking notes and handing them to his legal team. He did not speak and unlike others in the courtroom made no facial gestures as he listened to the evidence which portrayed him as a wife-beater and a man who drank a great deal.

'I want to make it clear that I have never struck a woman before that time in Clane,' he said, when his turn came to give evidence.

'Do you have an apology to make to Michelle?' he was asked by her counsel, Nicholas Kearns.

'I apologise to all concerned for any hurt,' he said.

'I slapped Michelle, I slapped her across the face,' he admitted.

He said he had also carried out a 'smothering tackle' to stop the 'frenzied' attack on his girlfriend, Sara Linton.

He said he had profound 'regrets' about what had happened, but he had used minimum force.

'Do you think 18 separate injuries and a broken nose are the minimum force?' asked Nicholas Kearns.

'Michelle can be unbelievably strong when she's like that,' he answered.

'Strong enough to match your 15.5 stone – do you fully understand the concept of a "smothering" tackle?'

But if the case was painful for Ryan it was also painful for Michelle. Her solicitor Gerald Keane had been very busy. He phoned David Marshall's estranged wife, Jackie Rafter, to try to find out what she thought of her former husband's behaviour at the party. Jackie Rafter immediately contacted Cathal's lawyers, who complained about the matter.

He also tracked down Tess de Kretzer, Cathal's former wife in Colombo, Sri Lanka, to find out more about him. But she had already given a sworn statement to Cathal saying that she had never encountered any violence in her marriage to the pilot.

But it was June Moloney, the host of the 30th birthday party, who was most annoyed about the case and the wall-to-wall publicity it attracted. Called as a witness for the prosecution – Michelle Rocca's side – she said she just did not want to be there.

'I am angry and annoyed that this whole episode has been brought to court and splashed all over the papers – it is an invasion of my privacy. This should have been settled out of court, it should never have come this far,' she insisted.

She said she was appalled at the 'inaccuracies' which she had heard in the first few days of the case although she was not asked to spell out what these were.

Another unwilling participant was Sara Linton, who reluctantly came from Italy, where she was then living, to give evidence on behalf of Cathal. She was not aware of the case until her solicitor, Mr John Power, had contacted her a week before it was due to be heard and informed her that she might be required as a witness.

'I was very reluctant to get involved and to relive the whole horrible scene again,' said Sara, now living in Tuscany and working as a nanny.

'She was the real victim – she has the emotional scars remaining with her for the rest of her life,' said Mr Garrett Cooney SC summing up the case for the defendant, before going into a flight of fancy about the fragrant Sara Linton.

'Wasn't she a lady? Wasn't she wholesome? Wasn't she restrained in her evidence?' Then he finally declared: 'She told it as it was.'

Speaking on behalf of Michelle Rocca, Mr Nicholas Kearns SC was less theatrical.

'What was undeniable was that at some stage a 15-stone man got off the bed and decided to deal with Ms Rocca. The word slap had been used and there had been references to Ms Rocca being thrown against the wall and that she had become more and more frenzied. This was being used as some sort of spurious justification for what came afterwards,' he said, as if Ms Rocca was 'some sort of female Tarzan and a woman of virtual superhuman strength'.

Summing up the case after six days in Court No 4 of the Round Hall at the Four Courts, Judge Michael Moriarty said they [all parties involved in the court case] may have partied in famous stud farms, stayed in charming hotels and dined in fancy restaurants but he cautioned the jury against believing that: 'Because these are big people, you should award big damages.'

He also cautioned them against the poisonous tone that had crept into the case – the reference to Michelle Rocca's 'cocktailish' dress and repeated remarks about Cathal Ryan's excessive taste for alcohol.

After less than 2 hours the 11 jurors (one got sick and retired) came back with a verdict.

The first question was: Was Michelle Rocca assaulted by Cathal Ryan at Blackhall Stud? The answer was 'Yes'.

If so, did he use more than necessary force. They answered 'Yes'.

If they answered 'Yes' to those questions, the jury was instructed that it would have to apportion damages – compensatory or aggravated.

The jury decided not to award aggravated damages to Michelle Rocca but to award her a sum of IR£7,500 in compensation. It was not a derisory sum, but in a case that took six days in the High Court at a cost of at least IR£300,000 it was a very small award.

It was an anti-climax to a fascinating court case which had enlightened the general public better than any glossy magazine as to what went on in 'high society'.

'Ms Rocca herself looked more shell-shocked than delighted,' said the report in *The Irish Times* the following day. Her solicitor Gerald Keane went about kissing the defendant and members of her family. Her sister Laura said she was 'delighted' at the verdict and Michelle herself 'performed like an Oscar winner', thanking her legal team, her family, her fiancé Van Morrison and the media.

Later that month, February 1997, the matter of costs was once again discussed in the High Court. Technically because the award was so low, Cathal Ryan could have insisted that Michelle Rocca pay the difference in costs between a Circuit Court and a High Court case, which would have been significant. But in a magnanimous gesture he waived his right to this. Mr Ryan had carefully considered such an application, said Mr Garrett Cooney SC on his behalf.

'He is most conscious of the need to lessen the unnecessary bitterness generated by the case and to allow the parties some measure of dignity. This is most important in relation to the children and in particular to his daughter, Claudia,' said Mr Cooney.

The judge concluded the costs hearing saying that both parties appeared to show magnanimity 'that seems to reflect some anxiety to put the situation behind them' and that it seemed to him that both parties were totally devoted to their joint child and the other children.

And then it was all over and they all went back to doing what they do in the privacy of their ordinary lives.

Tony Ryan died of pancreatic cancer in 2007. At his lavish funeral in Lyons Demesne, the stately home built by Lord Cloncurry near Celbridge, County Kildare and which he had restored at a cost of €100 million, one of the mourners remarked to Cathal that he wasn't looking so good himself.

Sadly, just seven weeks later, in December 2007, Cathal himself died of cancer at the age of just 47.

It is clear from his Will, which was drawn up in his home at Stacumny House, Celbridge, County Kildare, just two days before he died on 18 December, that the events of the party for June Moloney still haunted Cathal Ryan. Although their relationship did not survive the bloody episode in

Blackhall Stud, he was determined that willowy blonde Sara Linton, who had been so traumatised by the events of that night, would not be forgotten.

'To my Trustees the sum of €2,000,000 free of all taxes whatsoever arising to be held in trust for Sara Linton for her own absolute use and benefit', he dictated in the 18-page document.

No further explanation for this generous bequest is offered in the document.

He left Swordlestown Stud at Naas, County Kildare and a house in Pelham Crescent, London to his eldest son Cillian. He left Stacumny House in Celbridge to his daughter Danielle and he left the contents of the house to be divided between these two children with his first wife Tess de Kretzer. Although he was divorced from Tess, he left her €3 million, provided that she did not contest the Will.

He left €2 million to his daughter Claudia, his daughter with Michelle Rocca, to be held in Trust until she reaches the age of 24.

He left his villa in Lake Como, Italy to his four children, Cillian, Danielle, Claudia and the youngest, Cameron, to be held in equal shares until Cameron, who was born as a result of Cathal's relationship with a schoolteacher in a well-known Dublin private school, reached the age of 18 years.

Cathal Ryan also showed a caring side that might not have been obvious to the curiosity seekers who thronged the Four Courts for the humiliating trial when he stood accused of assaulting Michelle Rocca. He most generously left €10 million to Irish charities for children in need and a further €25 million to other charitable purposes in Ireland or abroad. How the money is distributed is left to his Trustees, his brothers Declan and Shane, his solicitor Patrick Ryan and Ann Mulchay and George Gill.

In all, his estate came to a total value of €249.6 million, the bulk of it to be held in a Family Partnership and a Discretionary Trust for the use of his children and his grandchildren and heirs. He left his share in the estate of his father Tony Ryan to be held in a Family Partnership for his four children in equal shares.

He also established a Discretionary Trust which would make a series of staged payments to each of his four children, €25,000 on their 25th birthday, €1 million on their 30th birthday, €1 million on their 35th birthday and

€5 million on reaching the age of 45.

There is something poignant about his final signature, an illegible but firm scrawl. The document was counter-signed by two solicitors, Patrick Ryan of Leeson Street, Dublin and Richard Burke of Ballina, County Mayo.

'He was a wonderful father to Claudia; he and I had a very good relationship over the past number of years and he will be greatly missed by all of us,' Michelle Rocca said in a fitting tribute that put an end to the passionate love affair and bitter split that had characterised their relationship.

After a broken engagement Van Morrison and Michelle Rocca reunited in 1996 and later married. Their daughter Ailbhe was born in January 2006 in Mount Carmel. Their second child, a son called Fionn Ivan Patrick Morrison, was born in August 2007 in the Coombe Hospital. Michelle and Van's children are younger than her first grandchild Alannah who was born in 2002 to her eldest daughter Danielle. The couple, who both describe their occupations as 'writer', now live on Sorrento Road, Dalkey, County Dublin.

Like her husband Michelle now shuns publicity and the celebrity circuit.

But she was to find that the ending of the court case against Cathal and her new life with Van Morrison did not bring the peace she craved. When her 42-year-old brother Patrick shot himself in January 2009 the whole family was once more engulfed in publicity. The Roccas were not destined to live quiet lives it seemed.

Patrick had run the family tile business with his sister Laura. But in 1998 they sold the business and he embarked on the Irish dream – buying and selling property. But it wasn't just any old property. The deals went into hundreds of millions, as he accumulated shopping centres and warehouse units in Britain and other properties in Ireland and as far away as Russia.

He and his beautiful young wife Annette became a 'poster' couple for the Celtic Tiger era in Ireland. He had his own helicopter, which he lent to Bill Clinton during one of his Irish visits, and he drove a sports Bentley when he brought his two young boys to their football matches in the north Dublin league. They had a home in Marbella where they hung out with the rest of the 'Irish' set, drinking in Victor's beach bar and enjoying the life that seemed on the surface to be an idyll.

But in the end his life came to a sudden halt. When the property boom ended he seemed to lose something. Maybe it was the excitement that kept his demons at bay. His wife and family said he had no money worries. Yet on a cold January Monday morning he went out and put his legally-held shotgun in his mouth and pulled the trigger. The Ryan-Rocca case was a footnote in his tragic story. Michelle found the limelight and then fled from it with her new love. But her brother Patrick couldn't take the dark side and died rather than live in the shadows of the new Ireland.

Chapter 2
Twink and the Fink

Dapper Elio Malocco looked around the gleaming chrome and black marble surfaces of Giordani's, his trendy new café on Grafton Street, roared at the staff about some imagined imperfection, then smiled self-indulgently at his own importance. He sauntered out into the balmy Dublin summer's night well satisfied with life.

The grandson of a poor Italian emigrant had arrived. He had money. He had status. But most importantly of all he had the ear of important men in his adopted town.

As he walked up Grafton Street he got a kiss and a hug from his great friend and client Adele King, the entertainer known as Twink, who was on her way to a show in the nearby Gaiety Theatre.

'Darling,' she swooned, begging him to come along to the show. But he resisted. He had important business elsewhere. He was a busy man. With a promise of a cappuccino in the morning at his new emporium, he disengaged himself. His white scarf fluttered in the evening breeze as he got into his Porche, a distinctive red 928, and drove as far as the Shelbourne Hotel. He gave a ten-pound note and the car keys to the concierge and went into the Horseshoe Bar to see who was around. This was Dublin in the early 1980s, long before the so-called 'Celtic Tiger'. Young Elio was always ahead of the game when it came to spotting new trends.

Elio Malocco was one of the more colourful characters of his generation. His flashy café at No 81 Grafton Street was a mere plaything, a symbol of how far he had come from his 'chipper' Italian roots. More importantly he was a man about town and fast becoming one of the city's most flamboyant lawyers. His law firm Malocco & Killeen had signed up a string of high-profile clients.

But even that was part of the show – the work was largely carried out by his one-time college friend and associate, Conor Killeen. Elio was the deal-maker. He had the contacts, the eye for an opportunity and the strong smell of money in his nostrils.

He also had a fair dollop of charm at his disposal. And he had married into the establishment; not just at the ground floor, but right at the very top. His wife, Jane, was a de Valera, one of two daughters of the last surviving son of the founder of Fianna Fáil, Éamon de Valera. His sister-in-law was Síle de Valera, sometime Fianna Fáil TD for County Clare, MEP and Minister for Arts and Culture. Elio's father-in-law Terry de Valera, apart from being the son of 'The Chief', was Master of the High Court and the owner of Charton, one of the grandest houses on the stylish Kerrymount Avenue in Foxrock, the leafy south Dublin suburb where Ireland's 'old money' resided behind high walls and tall trees.

Such airs and graces were not lost on his son-in-law, who called his first company Charton Investments after that house and its eminent connections. But as he expanded his empire, Elio, who lived with his wife and their son David in a house called Wincanton in nearby Westminster Road, renamed his company 'Eliocorp' to reflect the growing status of his diverse business empire.

In keeping with his love of horses he named his newly-acquired properties after famous British racecourses. There was Ascot on the Bray Road and Haydock on Westminster Road. He also had property in central Dublin, in Nutley Lane in Dublin 4 and some commercial property scattered around the city.

His real plan was to expand his business empire so that he would not be a mere solicitor but a well-known and respected business magnate in the mould of Tony O'Reilly or Michael Smurfit. With his boyish good looks and his white suits he might even have imagined himself as he was described in one newspaper profile of the time: The Last Tycoon.

The reality was that Elio Malocco was never really part of the establishment. He would always remain the son of an Italian immigrant who opened a chipshop and worked all his life to give his son and the rest of his family the kind of status he'd never had himself.

Like a Jay Gatsby of Dundalk, Elio was an outsider and a dreamer who had used his charm and talent to infiltrate a family that was never really his. Among his misfortunes was that in plundering the business of his adopted family, the de Valeras, he also robbed his client and good friend, Adele King, or Twink as she is known to generations of Irish theatre and television audiences. In so doing, he would forever after be known in the endless publicity that surrounds the Diva of Rathfarnham as 'the solicitor who trampled on Twink'.

Elio Malocco was born in Dundalk, County Louth on 23 February 1956, although neither his first name nor his surname were the names he was born with.

His father, Pietro Magliocco, was an Italian who had come to Ireland as a child. He started work in a Wimpy Bar in O'Connell Street and married an Irish woman. As he began to get some money together he did what most of his compatriots did – he moved on and up, opening his own chipshop and restaurant in Dundalk, County Louth.

He was a well-known personality in Dundalk – a border town sometimes dubbed El Paso in the 1970s because of the number of IRA gunmen who were operating from it.

Magliocco was a colourful character and his restaurant, Quaglino's, was one of the best patronised in the town. His son, Elio, would add another vivid layer to the family's colourful history.

Although he was christened Antonio his father called him Elio for short. When he was a teenager he changed his last name from Magliocco to Malocco because it retained some of his Italian origins but tripped more easily off the Irish tongue.

Intelligent and ambitious, he did not want to go into the family firm and was sent away to boarding school in St Patrick's College, Cavan where he was a good scholar and got an excellent Leaving Certificate. From there he progressed to University College Dublin (UCD) where he did his Law Degree. Like other solicitors who would later fall foul of the law, he was in a great hurry to make his mark. By 1977, at the age of 21, he set up his own legal practice.

This was the era of Charlie Haughey and the young men in mohair suits. Opportunity was in the air for those who wanted to grasp it and there was a general feeling around that if you wanted something badly enough you could get it, even if that meant cutting a few corners, calling in favours from rich and powerful connections and having the guts to bluff anyone who got in your way.

Soon tiring of the constant grind of running a single legal practice, Elio teamed up with an old college friend, Conor Killeen, to found Malocco & Killeen. By then he was already married to Jane de Valera, whom he met in UCD, and impatient to make a success of his profession and lots of money in his other business venture. He began advertising the firm on the side of buses but he also began to push all the contacts he had to bring in legal business.

'To become a lawyer you're trained to lie and cheat, to find out what the rules are and bend them. It's not a nice way to live your life. When I look back on it, I got some really dodgy people off who should have gone to prison. I wouldn't want to do that job again,' he later recalled.

But back then he had no such qualms in his headlong rush for success and fortune.

Elio moved along – investing in property, taking on a raft of high-profile clients in his solicitor's business and sorting out the highly-profitable legal affairs of the Italian community in Ireland.

It was hard work, but it gave him the money to buy the good things in life. He had two Porches and a Mercedes for his wife Jane. He lived in a fashionable home and he diversified into property, with plans to expand into the world of big business.

'He had a fatal character flaw – a touch of the Walter Mitty that caused him to over-reach himself,' said a friend from that era.

But for a time Elio Malocco had the appearance of the 'coming man'. That was why he was one of the hundreds of guests who mingled at the lavish 'society wedding' in 1983 of his good friend Twink as she married a young oboe player in the RTÉ Concert Orchestra, David Agnew.

In an interview Twink revealed that her memories of her 'big day' were marred by John Feeney's (the controversial *Evening Herald* columnist) graphic account of the wedding in the next day's newspaper.

'I remember coming down the stairs to cut the cake and seeing him (John Feeney) on the phone and I shouted to him, "you're not working today, let your hair down" . . . I didn't realise he was phoning the *Indo* to give them all this shit. My beloved dog Jane had just been diagnosed with cancer and I had her there with a big bow around her neck, because I love my dogs, and there was all this crap about "her dog being handfed morsels from the top table while guests queued for food", making it out to be like a cheap

Hollywood wedding.

'Oh, oh, oh, I was affronted. I had always played fair with them, and I just thought: How dare they. The next day David and I were in London on our way to Rome when I got a call from Elio Malocco and he read the piece to me. So we never got a honeymoon. I came straight home to fight the case.'

Well, it probably didn't happen in quite that timeframe, because libel actions take a long time from the solicitor's letters, which Elio Malocco duly dispatched to Independent Newspapers, to the actual hearing of the legal action. But the case did eventually come to court, and Elio Malocco milked it for everything he could. Twink walked out of the Four Courts in Dublin with a hefty sum of money, leaving John Feeney very irate and vowing never to mention her in his column again.

Tragically he was killed in an air crash the following year, 1984. But the case was to be the high point of Twink and Elio's professional relationship – it was all downhill after that.

In the meantime Elio had notions of opening a café bar in Grafton Street. As usual he was ahead of his time, but he had not done his research very well. At that time in the early 1980s the publican's lobby virtually controlled the Fianna Fáil government and opening a public house was one of the most restrictive practices operating in the country. To open a bar in Grafton Street you had to 'extinguish' two pub licences in that Ward of the city. While Elio managed to get his hands on one bar licence, he couldn't get a second – because the people who owned the nearby pubs made sure no one would sell him one. So instead of the café bar he had dreamed about, he had to settle for a fancy coffee shop and restaurant.

With high rents and huge investment it might have been successful ten years later – but at the time Ireland wasn't yet ready to embrace the 'coffee society'.

'These guys, they spend their time in school. They think this is a simple business but that's not the way it is,' said an old Italian businessman, who ran The Ritz Café and Grill in Middle Abbey Street and had watched the Giordani's disaster unfold.

Eventually Elio had to bring in Pietro Magliocco and Tom Forte, two wealthy businessmen from the Italian community in Ireland, to try and salvage the business. But while there was a lot of money in fish and chips, there was little enough in coffee and cakes, and anyway Bewleys had that market sewn up on Grafton Street. Elio simply couldn't compete and the company went into liquidation in 1983 with debts of IR£230,000 (€292,000), which was an enormous sum at the time. He looked to his father-in-law, Terry de Valera, to restart his career. De Valera, who styled himself 'Master de Valera' in the telephone book, was a rather remote figure who had a deep interest in books and music. He was the youngest and last remaining son of Éamon and Sinéad de Valera after his brother, Major Vivion de Valera, the TD and Managing Director of the Irish Press Limited, died.

The running of the Irish Press newspaper group then passed on to Major Vivion's son, Éamon de Valera, known in the pubs around the newspaper office in Burgh Quay as 'Major Minor'. Terry de Valera retained a large and influential shareholding in the business. As his nephew Éamon prepared to bring in an American investor, Ralph Ingersoll, to shore up the ailing newspaper group, he needed those shares. Terry de Valera had no sons himself. His eldest daughter Síle was a Fianna Fáil TD while his second daughter Jane was married to Elio.

At around the same time two highly-respected Dublin businessmen, Donal Flinn and Seán McHale, who had been brought in to modernise the frumpy image of the Irish Press newspaper group, resigned in sheer frustration at the old-fashioned plodding pace of change in Burgh Quay.

So Terry de Valera did a deal with his nephew Éamon. He sold him most of his stake in The Irish Press group – with the proviso that Elio Malocco would be given the newspaper's legal work and appointed to the tight-knit board of directors of the company. Elio was to be Terry de Valera's 'representative' on the board and would also retain a small shareholding.

'He is a solicitor by profession, a restauranteur by tradition and a newspaper director through marriage,' stated one newspaper profile, as he started to make a name for himself around town. Elio didn't like the profile – and promptly dispatched a solicitor's letter to its author, claiming damages and disputing facts and opinions. Nothing came of the matter, but it was a pattern that Elio was to become quite familiar with in the years that followed.

It was an exciting time to be a director of the Irish Press group. The newspaper company, hit by declining sales and advertising, was trying to modernise and was about to bring in the American investor Ralph Ingersoll to transform its fortunes and help it compete against the growing power of Independent Newspapers across the River Liffey in Middle Abbey Street.

The Irish Press group was to prove both the foundation of Elio's fortune and the ruination of his reputation. It was a business account that would eventually lead him through the lonely gateway of Mountjoy Prison in Dublin, one of the first 'white collar' criminal solicitors ever to 'do time' in the history of the Irish state which his wife's grandfather had done so much to bring into existence.

But in between he had much fun with his good friend Twink, his client Father Paddy Ryan – who sucessfully fought extradition from Belgium to Britain for possession of explosives – and enemies like Dermot Morgan, the well-known comedian from *Scrap Saturday* and *Father Ted* whom he tried to intimidate with writs and threats. Morgan had lampooned the solicitor and some of his high-profile clients. Also numbered among his enemies was Unionist MP Ken Magennis who had denounced him in the House of Commons because of his choice of clients.

Elio was to take over the Irish Press group's legal work from an old-fashioned Dublin Fianna Fáil solicitor Tommy O'Connor, who was principally known as the brother of the more famous Pat O'Connor. Pat represented Charlie Haughey and was later to become known as 'Pat O'Connor O'Connor' because he was caught voting twice for 'The Boss' at a polling station in Kinsealy.

Apart from becoming a director of the Irish Press newspaper group and handling their growing litigation department, Elio Malocco also had a penchant for picking up high-profile clients who were seldom out of the news. Among them was, as mentioned, the priest Fr Paddy Ryan who a judge ruled wouldn't get a fair trial in England on charges of possessing detonators which were destined for the IRA. His other 'newsworthy' client was Kevin McDonald, an official at the Irish Embassy in London, who was trying to do the opposite to Paddy Ryan. He was an employee of the Irish Embassy in London who had been accused of selling forged Irish passports and was resisting extradition back to Ireland to stand trial. It was a hurly-burly life for Elio, lived in the public eye.

As Elio rushed to defend the Irish Press group from libel actions he was also issuing enough gagging writs against RTÉ and newspapers to paper the walls of his office in Wexford Street, Dublin.

A profile of Elio in the *Sunday Independent* ran as follows, 'But if there were financial problems at the restaurant, where he personally lost £17,000, and at the *Irish Press,* Elio Malocco can certainly be described as "upwardly mobile" in Dublin social circles, moving as he has done in the last couple of years from exclusive Glenamuck Road in Carrickmines to a detached home in the ultra-fashionable Westminster Road area of Foxrock. As the Fr Ryan case threatens to turn into a full-blown Anglo-Irish rift and extradition takes on a life of its own, the unlikely sounding Irishman, Elio Malocco, is going to be in the news for some time to come.'

How right they were – but he would be in the news for all the wrong reasons, because it was all a front.

In 1991 things began to unravel. Elio Malocco had been receiving large cheques from the Irish Press group in order to pay other solicitors' firms who had won libel settlements against the newspaper. But instead of passing the cheques on to the solicitors for the other side, he had been quietly pocketing the money himself to stay solvent. How he expected to get away with it probably illustrated what a fantasist he really was. The Irish legal system was so old-fashioned and slow-moving that for a time nobody noticed. Malocco was desperately playing for time, hoping to get in a big cheque himself with which he could 'make everything all right'.

His private life, too, appeared to be in tatters. The well-known private detective Billy Flynn, who carried out work for Malocco and was on 'friendly' terms with the solicitor, got a bizarre telephone call from him one Sunday afternoon. Malocco told Flynn that he was being threatened and his life was in danger and arranged to meet him for a clandestine briefing in the car park of the Lamb Doyle's public house in the Dublin mountains.

Malocco told Flynn to bring a gun if he had one.

'Malocco normally drove a flashy Mercedes, but he arrived at our moonlit rendezvous in the relative anonymity of a Volkswagen Golf. He was taking this seriously. He dashed from the car and ran over to me. Then his story gushed out. Malocco was in love. He had fallen for another woman and her husband was threatening him. It was ludicrous. I pointed out my disgust at his behaviour, but he was moonstruck, his eyes blinded by passion. By passion and fear,' said Flynn in his account of their meeting.

According to Flynn 'our noble lawyer' believed that the cuckolded husband had put a 'contract' out on him and he believed that Flynn could get it lifted. The private eye thought the whole episode 'too silly for words'.

But he continued: 'A client is a client, and as far as I was concerned, Malocco – at this time – was still precisely that. I telephoned his mistress's husband from my car phone. I explained about the "misunderstanding" and told him to lay off Malocco, that the man was in my protection now. (I never know why people take this sort of claim seriously, but it invariably works . . .) Malocco was ecstatic. He couldn't thank me enough. He owed me his life. I just wanted to get away, back home to the real world of sensible people.'

It was a good insight into the bizarre private world of Elio Malocco at that time. As things got increasingly crazier he tried to raise IR£1.3 million (€1.65m) to take over a Dublin football club, Shelbourne, in the hope that he could get his hands on the club's cash and its valuable grounds which he intended to sell at a huge profit to a property developer.

It was just another one of his schemes that was about a decade too early – in the later Celtic Tiger era it could very well have worked. But time was running out.

'It was a frame of mind at the time,' he told one interviewer later. 'More money was going out of the law firm than was coming in. It's a situation people from different walks of life find themselves in, like a builder who gets a deposit to start one job and uses it to finish another.

'Borrowing money from Peter to pay Paul was something people did in Ireland in the 1980s. I wish it had never happened – but I also wish I had never been a lawyer. I wish I had started making films instead of studying law.'

If borrowing from Peter to pay Paul was the norm in the building trade, it was certainly not approved of in the august surroundings of Blackhall Place, the rather grand Georgian building in Dublin from where the Law Society of Ireland policed its members. Of course there had been scandals among the solicitors' fraternity before, but in a closed society they were mostly kept 'hush hush'. Sanctions may have been taken, but it was done 'in lodge' as the legal fraternity liked to say and there was no washing their dirty linen in public.

But Elio Malocco was different. He was a brash outsider in a business that was generally handed down in the family for generations. He was not going to be shown any mercy.

Sometime in 1991 at a dinner in the King's Inns a barrister who had won a case against the Irish Press group complained loudly after a few large glasses of claret that he had never been paid his fees for the successful libel action. Another lawyer who was present was quite surprised – he knew the money had been given to Malocco & Killeen to pay the clients their damages and the legal team their costs. He also knew that Malocco was related through marriage to Major Éamon de Valera who was running the Irish Press group.

He made discreet inquires and these resulted in some disturbing discoveries.

At the time the Irish Press group was being jointly run by Éamon de Valera and his new American shareholder Ralph Ingersoll. The board was bitterly divided. A re-launch of the once-profitable *Evening Press* had been a disaster and the staff were badly demoralised. All the paper now needed was to become embroiled in a major scandal in its own boardroom.

That was exactly what was about to engulf them. Elio Malocco heard that a complaint was about to be made against him to the Incorporated Law Society by Éamon de Valera, who was then acting as chief executive of the newspaper group and who was horrified at the turn of events.

Having established that money had been siphoned illegally out of the company by Elio Malocco and bank documents had been forged, Éamon de Valera made an official complaint to the Law Society on 25 September 1991. When the Compensation Committee (a subcommittee of the Law Society which deals with complaints) met on Thursday 26 September 1991 it was so concerned about the workings of the firm of Malocco & Killeen that it directed that Mr Tim Bolger, a chartered accountant, be employed to investigate the firm and that the Society's solicitors go to the High Court the following day, Friday, to seek an order freezing the assets of the firm.

So far they managed to keep the story out of the newspapers.

On the Saturday night Elio, in what was described as 'an agitated state', phoned the deputy chief executive of the Irish Press group, Vincent Jennings, and admitted taking the money from legal settlements intended for other solicitors and using it for his own purposes. But to use his enemy Dermot Morgan's famous phrase from *Father Ted,* he claimed the money was 'resting in his account' and it would be paid back with no loss to the newspaper group.

He pleaded for a face-to-face meeting. Jennings refused 'on legal advice' at which point Malocco became 'agitated' and said that he and his partner Conor Killeen might be sent to jail.

Events followed swiftly.

On Monday morning, 30 September 1991, the High Court directed that the solicitors' bank accounts be frozen and it suspended the practicing certificates of the two solicitors, Elio Malocco and Conor Killeen. The story was splashed all over the newspapers. The high-flying solicitor who had effectively gagged RTÉ and the Irish newspapers was now 'the disgraced solicitor Elio Malocco'. As well as an investigation by the Law Society, the Garda Fraud Squad had also been called in and further proceedings were promised.

'I am satisfied beyond doubt that the defendants in these proceedings have utilised the funds of Irish Press Newspapers in a manner inconsistent with the instructions given to them when the funds were put into their power and in a manner which had no honest explanation,' said Vincent Jennings, a former editor of *The Sunday Press* in an affidavit.

The following Wednesday, Elio Malocco consented to orders restraining him from withdrawing any funds from bank accounts in Dublin and Spain and in late September or early October 1991 he 'fled the jurisdiction'.

Ironically Elio was not short of money. On 8 June 1992, two bank accounts in his name were opened in the Allied Irish Bank in Dame Street, Dublin and over IR£55,000 (€70,000) was deposited in them. Where the money came from has never been properly explained – some of it was undoubtedly from the sale of property he still owned around the city.

But when Adele King began to scream, 'I've been robbed', it certainly echoed around the chambers of the Law Library in Dublin. In the end it would emerge that Elio Malocco had taken millions from a variety of clients, but it was Twink's little piece of real estate that would make most of the headlines for years to come and join their names together in a thousand newspaper stories.

Adele King has been a fixture on the Irish entertainment scene for so long that the somewhat younger Samantha Mumba rather cuttingly nicknamed her 'Barbie's Granny'. But for all the headlines and all the shows, she lived in a rather plain semi-detached house on Anne Devlin Avenue in Rathfarnham. However, she'd always had her heart set on living in Beauford House, described as 'an imposing detached house' in nearby Butterfield Avenue. It was, she said, her 'dream home' where one of her childhood friends had lived and where she had been a guest at children's parties.

As often happens coincidence took over. She was out shopping with her young daughter Chloe sometime in 1990 when a storm broke and she took shelter under the tall trees surrounding Beauford House. The owners saw her sheltering in the garden and kindly invited her in. They got chatting and the old couple revealed that they were selling the house. She idolised the place but was too polite to ask 'how much' because she thought the price would be too steep for her purse.

It went to auction and was withdrawn at IR£186,000 (€237,000).

When Twink saw the price she thought, 'God, I wouldn't mind buying it myself,' and she rang Elio Malocco, her solicitor and friend, to ask his advice.

Price was never a problem for Elio, and he immediately took over negotiations. He 'advised and counselled' and the price dropped when another interested party withdrew from negotiations. Twink and David Agnew got the house for IR£180,000.

'The day Elio said, "I've got your house", I couldn't believe it,' she said. 'Now there was still the question of selling the Anne Devlin Avenue house, but we were on a year's bridging finance, so the whole thing started on a very shaky footing.'

How 'shaky' the entertainer wasn't to know. When she bought her first house, No 25 Anne Devlin Avenue, Templeogue in 1984, Twink did so with a IR£25,000 mortgage with the Irish Permanent Building Society. When she sold it, with Elio Malocco acting as her solicitor, the mortgage was never redeemed and the building society later began legal action against her which dragged on for a number of years and totted up to IR£11,000 for mortgage arrears and interest.

She then took out a IR£117,000 mortgage with the First National Building Society to buy the new house. They too began legal proceedings against her for repossession of her dream house when she fell into arrears on her repayments. There was IR£13,500 owed to the building society.

Twink was not long in blaming Elio Malocco for her financial woes.

'He has taken every brass farthing we have,' she said.

'People keep asking me how I could trust a solicitor like that. I did. I trusted him because he was my friend and why wouldn't you trust a friend. For God's sake our children played together,' she said, tragically.

But Judge Cyril Kelly, who was trying to sort out her tangled financial affairs, was not having any of it. He directed that Twink and her husband should disclose their income and said he had been 'misled' on their financial affairs.

Twink told the court that part of her financial difficulty stemmed from the fact that she had paid a penalty of IR£11,000 for breaking her contract to appear in a Gaiety pantomime so that she could perform with the American star Perry Como on a duet in The Point Depot [now the O2 Arena].

But the judge granted the application to the First National Building Society to repossess her house, putting a 'stay' on it, which meant that the order was delayed to give her time to negotiate with the building society to decide how to make her repayments. Eventually the Law Society of Ireland, which was picking up the tab for Elio Malocco's adventures in the business world, paid off what was now a IR£30,000 debt to the Irish Permanent Building Society. Then Twink successfully negotiated a deal to pay off the arrears she owed on her new house by presenting a cheque for the entire amount – something which puzzled Judge Cyril Kelly, who said that he had been told Twink and her husband 'had no means'.

The proceedings were finally struck out at the end of May 1994. But not very long after she was hit with another bill, this time of IR£19,000, for not paying her taxes. The Collector General got a writ against her, publishing the details in *Stubbs Gazette*.

'It's like a big oil spill,' she explained in order to illustrate how easy it was to get into a financial mess. 'We've cleaned up the initial mess, but the deep-down damage, financial and emotional, will always be there. I'm not sure we'll ever recover.'

Certainly the emotional damage would later surface when Twink's husband, David Agnew, ran off with a much younger woman, Ruth Hickey, who bore him a child and then had to endure a series of 'toxic texts' from the woman who is known and loved by the tabloids as 'The Panto Queen'.

Even before Agnew left her for good the marriage was going through a torrid time, as she told Barry Egan in an interview for the *Sunday Independent.*

One of her husband's lovers she described as 'a slapper' and another as a 'gold-digger digging in a place that has no gold'. But she was highly offended when these remarks appeared in print.

When Agnew eventually left her for public relations consultant Ruth Hickey, who was 30 years younger than Twink, the 'Panto Queen' used some colourful language in a series of voicemails left on her former husband's phone. How these got into the public domain is unknown, but the 'Toxic Texts' as they became known were eventually broadcast on the internet site YouTube.

One of her choice sentences, 'Put your mickey back in your trousers... zip up your mickey . . . if I was near you I'd slap the fucking face off you,' became a byword for vulgar abuse around Dublin.

'I had to keep my chin up in public, I'm not a whinger,' she later told Barry Egan. 'I don't think it's fair when you are in the public eye to whinge, because everybody has their own problems. I think you just need to shut up and whinge at home.'

She also lashed out at Ruth Hickey, who went on to have two children with Twink's former husband David Agnew.

'I texted her and told her in no uncertain terms what I thought of her and her behaviour – I called her a slut, a bitch and a tramp . . . I think those were the terms of endearment I remember using,' she later told Gerry Ryan. She talked about it further to Gerry Ryan for a chat show he was doing. But when a 'trailer' promoting the programme was aired, Ruth Hickey sent a solicitor's letter to RTÉ and the interview was never broadcast.

But for all the 'vulgar abuse' she became known for, Twink actually showed a great deal of character and compassion when it came to Elio Malocco and the financial difficulties he left her with. She never bitched about Elio himself and she didn't kick him when he was down. In fact the opposite is the case. She couldn't pass him by and pretend not to have been friends with him like many others did – she just wasn't that kind of person.

But she wasn't the only one to rue her association with Elio Malocco. Among those who soon also found themselves in financial trouble was his wife Jane de Valera, who had a mortgage with the ACC bank only to find out after her husband fled to America that he had never paid off the old mortgage on their family home either. She was now faced with ruinous bills.

Also facing a criminal prosecution for 'aiding and abetting' the solicitor's nefarious practices was his partner Conor Killeen. Meanwhile 'the bould' Elio, as the fugitive solicitor was now known, had re-invented himself as David Elio Malocco and enrolled in film school in New York where, according to reports, he was hanging out with some leading actors and was about to become a famous Hollywood film director, which in his mind was rather better than being an infamous Dublin solicitor.

'I've now found something that I love doing,' he told *The Irish Times* film critic Michael Dwyer. His adventures in film school lasted until 1993 when he decided to come back to Ireland before extradition proceedings started against him in the United States.

His trial was eventually narrowed down to a series of 'sample' charges rather than a hearing of all the accusations against him. During the trial the court was told that the Irish Press group's libel department, which Elio was in charge of, was in a complete mess. A sitting judge, Maura Roche, had successfully sued the newspaper and when Elio Malocco was asked about it he claimed to have settled the case for a certain sum of money and produced a 'Notice of Discontinuance' to an executive of the Irish Press group. The document, if real, certified that the case had been settled. But it turned out to be a forged document. Elio later told a Detective Garda that he did so because he did 'not want to get into trouble'.

He was also questioned about a cheque for IR£43,200 which was sent to a firm of solicitors in Cavan called O'Donovan Mackey to settle a case handled by Malocco & Killeen. He was asked if this was part of a IR£50,000 cheque given to him by the Irish Press group.

'Not deliberately, I wouldn't tell you a lie. I would not have written a cheque to O'Donovan Mackey if I thought it was Irish Press money.'

The specific charges were that he forged receipts and other documents with intent to defraud, converting IR£15,000 for his own use and obtaining IR£53,242 by a series of false pretences. The 11 charges involved more than IR£121,000.

He denied them vehemently.

But after an 11-day trial the jury at the Circuit Criminal Court in Dublin did not believe his protestations that it was all a big mistake. He was found guilty of fraud and forgery and sentenced to five years in prison. By the time the Law Society of Ireland had cleaned up the mess left behind by Elio Malocco, it had paid out over €2.3 million in compensation, interest and fees as a result of this major case of fraud by a practicing solicitor.

'I served two years and six months and then they started letting me out as a kind of part-time prisoner. It was the turning point in my life because that's when I started writing seriously. And while I was in prison I got a first-class honours degree – I did a Bachelor of Science in cognitive psychology and child development with the Open University – I loved that.

'I spent five years in boarding school and that would equip you for anything in life. I knew I was going to be in prison for some time and I asked myself what would I do to make the time fly, so I decided to do the degree and to learn all about computers and start writing. It was great. It was like taking two-and-a-half years off, getting your life together, learning new skills and getting focused on what you want to do.'

The following year, 1994, his partner Conor Killeen, who admitted helping Elio defraud the Irish Press newspaper group, was sentenced to 12 months in prison for his part in abetting his partner in the fraud. Passing sentence, Judge Patrick Smith said that as a solicitor Killeen was an officer of the court. Although he knew documents produced by Malocco were forged, he (Killeen) went along with his partner's deception and deserved a custodial sentence.

He was also 'struck off' as a solicitor not only because he acted 'dishonestly' towards a client of his firm, the Irish Press group, but also because he permitted a deficit of IR£1.25 million in the firm's client account. Killeen, of Tudor Lane, Foxrock, County Dublin was sentenced on 2 July, just as the courts were closing down for the six-week legal holiday. But with a speed rarely seen in the Irish legal system an appeal against the severity of the sentence was held before Judge Hugh O'Flaherty in the High Court 'vacation sitting' on 28 August, the only case of its kind heard so far that summer. There were no reporters present in court and *The Irish Times* quoted 'legal sources' saying they were surprised the appeal had been heard so quickly.

Giving his judgement Judge O'Flaherty said the court considered the sentence against Conor Killeen too severe, taking into consideration that Malocco had pleaded guilty and paid IR£40,000 in restitution. He gave the solicitor a reprieve and ordered him to be released from prison. Conor Killeen served just 12 weeks of the 12-month sentence. Questioned about his handling of the case Judge O'Flaherty told *The Irish Times* that there was 'no mystery' about the events. He said the appeal would have been heard in July, before the courts broke up for the 'long vacation' but court transcripts of the original trial were not available.

'It is desirable in the public's interest and in his own interest to dispose of the case expeditiously,' said Judge Flaherty.

Later the early release of a drunk driver called Philip Sheedy, who had killed a young mother, would lead to the resignation of both Judge Hugh O'Flaherty and Judge Cyril Kelly – but that's another story altogether.

As for Elio Malocco, his two-and-a-half year prison 'break' had given him time to get educated a bit more, to think and to plan.

His marriage had not withstood the strains of prison and the betrayal his wife Jane felt he had inflicted on her personally and more generally on her family. Styling himself David Elio Malocco he set up Earl Street Films and set about pursuing his dream of becoming a film-maker. In the meantime he earned a crust shooting wedding videos and commemorating Holy Communion days through the firm 'Executive Video Services'. His first and only feature film was called *Virgin Cowboys* which went around the 'festival' circuit and indeed got some backing from the Irish Film Board.

'People ask me if it's about my own life . . . I have no intention of making a film about my own life, because it's too boring,' he said in one promotional interview. He never resumed his 'man about town' status, but he did turn up in The Oval bar, a newspaper hangout in Abbey Street, at the time, and had a couple of pints with journalists he had previously threatened to sue and issued with lengthy gagging writs. He did it with a smile. He was jovial and charming but beneath it all he had a serious aim – he was desperately trying to peddle the 'new' Elio, the artistic film-maker with a big future.

He told one journalist that he intended to make a feature film called *Dancing At the Crossroads* – a phrase made famous by his wife's grandfather, the former President Éamon de Valera, who used it to paint a picture of an idyllic Ireland before radio and television and delusions of grandeur took hold in the countryside.

He even met up with Twink – and while it didn't lead to any reconciliation, it didn't lead to fireworks either.

'I will never say a bad word about Elio,' she said afterwards. 'Alright, a lot of shit went down, money had been misappropriated, the old mortgage had never been discharged and we were engaged in a tangle between two building societies. But hey, what doesn't kill you makes you stronger. It was only money. It wasn't my children or my health or my life and I don't have a bad bone in my body. Holding a grudge gives you cancer because you're internalising all that anger and I don't have an ounce of malice towards anyone.

'I gave him a big hug when I met him in town a while ago. I feel he was very harshly punished. He was young and adventurous and he was the most engaging company, funny and debonair and charming and good-looking, and I wish him new beginnings. But we did go down big and we're not in the millionaire league. That's an awful lot of singing and dancing.'

Elio too was no longer consumed with mere material things, but he still wanted the fame. After his spell in jail he was quite happy without the trappings of a business magnate, the things that put him in jail, the social life, the fast cars and the business ventures.

'It proves you don't have to have a Porche and a huge house to be happy – those things are irrelevant,' he said.

But when the film 'business' didn't embrace him, a rather disappointed Elio decided that maybe there was room for him in the media. He knew a lot about it from his dealings with journalists over the years, and with his legal and film background a smart men's magazine was just what Dublin was waiting for in those hedonistic days of the late 1990s.

Patrick was born – or rather strangled at birth. Modelled on John Kennedy Jr's magazine *George,* it aimed to become a must-read for the young, influential and monied classes, with a mixture of serious business and outrageous gossip. But as Elio Malocco would soon discover, the creation of serious gossip is a heart-breaking business. Not only has it to be true, but you have to be able to prove it's true. Most of the gossip heard around the bars and the late-night dinner parties in Dublin just isn't true. They're usually good yarns all right, but 'standing them up', as journalists call it, is never easy.

To get his new creation off the ground, Elio began by recycling a few old stories. He decided to do a feature on the controversial de Valera money, which had originally been raised to set up a 'Republican newspaper' but which had led to the Irish Press newspapers becoming a de Valera family enterprise and had greatly enriched the sons and grandchildren of the founder. But while he was on safe enough ground with the de Valera story, another of his 'targets' was John Reynolds, a nephew of the former Taoiseach Albert Reynolds, owner of the trendy Pod nightclub in Dublin and a partner with showbusiness veteran Louis Walsh in the successful boyband Boyzone.

Reynolds heard about the story and went to the High Court to seek an injunction against Elio to stop the first edition being printed. He claimed that an article alleging drugs were sold openly in his club was defamatory and asked for it to be stopped.

Although Elio argued that the article was true and production of the magazine should not be halted, he ran into a major problem almost straight away in that he had to admit that the authors of the article, Declan Murray and Frank White, did not exist and were actually pseudonyms for himself and a 'relative' named in court documents as Luciano Magliocco. There was also little or no information about the publisher of the magazine, a man called Peter Laur, or Fanville, the publishing company.

The article headed 'Operation Night-Cap Causes John Reynolds Sleepless Nights as Cops Raid Night club' was, complained John Reynolds, by its 'ordinary meaning' or by 'innuendo' alleging he had been charged with permitting the sale of drugs in his nightclub.

According to *The Irish Times* report of the case on 11 December 1998 before Judge Peter Kelly, 'Mr Reynolds said the words meant that he was turning a blind eye to the sale of drugs on his premises; and that he was a homosexual'. The report went on: 'Dealing with the drug-dealing allegations, Mr Justice Kelly said he noted that Mr Reynolds accepted that he, together with 19 night-club operators, had received notification from police concerning drug activity and conduct relating to drugs on his club premises. Mr Justice Kelly said he had concluded that, in parts of the article, there was an innuendo to the effect contended for by Mr Reynolds.'

Interestingly, a report in the *Irish Independent* written by John Maddock, although quite similar, had an additional paragraph.

'He (Judge Kelly) said that in the article Mr Reynolds was referred to on a number of occasions as a "gay bachelor". Mr Reynolds said that in its natural and ordinary meaning, the word gay was nowadays taken as meaning homosexual. The defendants accepted Mr Reynolds was not homosexual but said they never alleged he was.'

Judge Kelly granted an injunction to Reynolds banning publication of the article about him, pending a full hearing of the case. *Patrick* magazine duly appeared with a sticker over the missing story saying 'Banned by the High Court'. But it still didn't sell many copies and *Patrick* died a quick death.

Afterwards Elio seemed to disappear from public view. He was fleetingly mentioned, but usually in connection with someone else's doings or in connection with the entertainer Twink.

He popped up again in connection with the trial in Belfast of Cork-born Finbarr Ross who was acquitted of 42 charges of fraud in connection with the losses suffered by clients of his firm International Investments, which folded owing depositors £7 million. It was revealed that the Gibraltar-based liquidator of International Investments, James Galliano, sold a site owned by the company in Aungier Street, Dublin to Elio, who 'flipped' it on the very same day for three times the price he had paid for it.

Then in March 2008 it was revealed that the will of Terence de Valera, one-time father-in-law of Elio and owner of Charton, a substantial house in Westminster Road, Foxrock, contained a clause that the €2 million willed to his daughter Jane be left to her on condition that she would receive an income from her share for life and that afterwards her children would inherit the capital and income. In other words, Elio could not get any of the money willed to Jane. The 'Taxing Master' as he was known, also left a small portrait of himself and a pair of cufflinks to his grandson David Malocco.

Elio Malocco's name cropped up with almost perfect symmetry in connection with another high-flying solicitor, Michael Lynn, who basically left every previous crooked solicitor in the ha'penny place when he fled Ireland leaving debts of about €80-€120 million related to taking out multiple mortgages on extensive properties he owned in Ireland, Britain, Portugal and Bulgaria. The collapse of his empire became a symbol for the collapse of the Irish 'boom' and was quickly followed by the virtual collapse of the economy. But the smiling Michael Lynn, despite promises to return and unravel his complex web of deceit, has never come back to Ireland. Eventually a bench warrant was issued by an impatient judge saying that if he ever set foot in Ireland again he was to be arrested and brought before the High Court to explain his contempt.

In a bizarre twist Lynn agreed to give video evidence in an Irish court case from the offices in London of a solicitors' firm called Merriman White. The practice manager of Merriman White, it was revealed, was none other that Elio Malocco. Nobody knows if Elio Malocco and Michael Lynn were buddies or had ever met each other, but what a film their story would make if ever Elio got around to writing the script.

Chapter 3
The Battle for the Rock

When the thoroughbred racehorse Mull of Kintyre came storming down the straight at York to win the prestigious six-furlong Gimcrack Stakes on 18 August 1999, none of the famous friends connected to the stallion could have foreseen that within a few years this victory would destroy friendships and lead to a bitter feud that would threaten the very future of the most famous football club in the world, Manchester United.

The Gimcrack, named after a well-known racehorse from the early days of the sport, has been run at York since 1846. The victory of Mull of Kintyre, trained by the famous Aidan O'Brien, was the high point of that horse's career until it retired to stud at the famous 6,000-acre Coolmore farm in Tipperary in 2002.

The two friends who would later fall out as a result of Mull of Kintyre's victory were the owner of Coolmore, the fabulously wealthy 'stallion master' John Magnier, a man of Joycean silence, exile and cunning, and Sir Alex Ferguson, manager of Manchester United and one of the most successful and ruthless men in that cauldron of international football where winning means everything.

In a way it is unfair to blame Mull of Kintyre for the rift that destroyed the friendship between these two powerful men, led to the intimidation of their families and threatened to disrupt both soccer and racing in England – such were the passions that it unleashed. But the horse, in a strange way, was the catalyst for a series of events that led to this bitter dispute.

The reality is that a minor squabble spiralled out of control mainly because of the characters of the two main players: Magnier, intensely private yet unswerving in the certainty of his own cause, and Ferguson, whose will to win overwhelmed his better judgement and led him into an arena where sportsmanship takes second place to money.

It was the threat of a high-profile court case in Dublin that seemed to set the drama alight and led to private investigators ransacking the rubbish bins of the Manchester United manager and questioning the ethics and propriety of his club's business relationship with Jason Ferguson, the manager's football-agent son.

Ironically the counter-attack on behalf of Alex Ferguson came from his Dublin-based legal and public relations team, whose highly-secret offensive against Magnier, horse-racing's most powerful figure, was code-named 'Project Rathgar' after the Dublin suburb where the blueprint was drawn up.

* * *

At the time Mull of Kintyre won the Gimcrack Stakes, Alex Ferguson, as he then was, and John Magnier were casual friends. They admired each other's domination of their chosen sport and they met occasionally and enjoyed each other's company. Magnier had no interest in football. Indeed he appears to have little interest in anything outside horses, his family and making money.

He had never seen United play, but his long-time friend and business partner JP McManus was a fanatical Manchester United fan. McManus would frequently fly by private jet from his opulent home in Geneva or his mock-Palladian mansion outside Limerick to watch his favourite soccer team play in England and Europe. McManus, as one of the world's top gamblers and racehorse owners, was on first-name terms with Ferguson. So it is possible that he introduced the two men and imparted to Magnier some of the passion he felt for the game.

For his part Ferguson, who grew up in Govan in the shadow of Glasgow's Clyde shipyard and remembered his father having a 'tanner Yankee' (a six-pence accumulator bet) on the horses every Saturday, had little interest in anything outside football. Like McManus, his love of racing was reserved for the 'poor relation' of the sport – the National Hunt over jumps rather than the flat-racing 'sport of kings' favoured by Magnier and his millionaire partners.

But Ferguson certainly caught the horse-racing bug when he became one of the highest-paid figures in world soccer as manager of the internationally successful Manchester United, one of the biggest brands in the world. This allowed him to dabble in horse racing and helped occasionally to take his mind off the game he had come to dominate.

One of his horses, Queensland Star, won a maiden race and afterwards he kept a few horses in training, running in his favoured colours, the scarlet and white of the 'Red Devils', Manchester United football club.

Around 1997, another colourful sporting man who knew most of the big players in sport, the affable Mike Dillon, a public relations specialist for the Ladbrokes bookies chain, introduced Ferguson to the flat-racing side of the sport. Ferguson bought his first yearling in 1997 and his first runner was the Ed Dunlop-trained Candleriggs, who raced as a two-year-old in 1998.

'One of the reasons I like racing is that, largely, people leave me alone. And when they do talk to me it is likely to be about what is going to win the 3.30 rather than football,' said Alex Ferguson later.

But that was not going to last. What neither Magnier nor Ferguson could have foreseen was that Mull of Kintyre's victory in the Gimrack Stakes at York would unleash a series of events which would pit the two men against each other and turn what was a friendship into a deadly rivalry. When Sir Alex Ferguson, as he had become, issued proceedings for damages against Magnier and his famous Coolmore Stud in the High Court in Dublin, he enraged the reclusive 'stallion master' and boss of Coolmore. He was effectively calling into question the word of one of the wealthiest men in Ireland, an intolerable position for a man like Magnier, who lived by the dictat that a 'man's word is his bond' and who often sealed multi-million Euro deals with the shake of the hand or the nod of his head.

* * *

York, like other provincial centres, has what could be termed an inferiority complex. It regards itself as the civilised centre of northern England. With its great Cathedral and its famous racecourse, York also needs an annual social event to allow others to recognise its importance. The annual racing festival at the Knavesmire is just that – a celebration of the new blood annually coming into racing. It is where the breeders, the owners, the trainers and the racing public can see the cream of the crop of two-year-old horses beginning their racing careers. It is the opportunity to watch the stars of the future in action.

So a tradition has grown up that the owner of the winning horse in the Gimcrack Stakes at York should address the annual Gimcrack Dinner which is held in the city just before Christmas each year. It is a major social event in York. In the enclosed world of horse racing it was the daunting prospect of having to speak at this event that faced John Magnier after Mull of Kintyre won the Gimcrack Stakes in 1999.

As the Rolls Royce, Bentley Sedans and sleek black limousines decanted their blue-blooded passengers outside the door of York Racecourse on the night of 12 December 1999, there was an expectation from some of the arriving guests that they would hear pearls of wisdom from one of the greatest racing men of his generation. After all, John Magnier, who had to leave school at the prestigious Glenstal Abbey in Murroe, County Limerick at the age of 16 to take over the family stud farm when his father died, had built probably the biggest bloodstock empire in the world.

But more of that later.

That frosty night at York the guests' expectations were to be disappointed. It's safe to say Magnier was not given to public speaking and therefore was not going to be present at the dinner. (In fact he had been honoured with a seat in the Irish Senate by his friend, Taoiseach Charles Haughey and managed to get through the term with just one brief speech on a piece of horse-racing legislation in what is known as 'the upper chamber' of the Irish parliament.)

However he had endeavoured to provide that night's guests in York with a top-class replacement and that's where the problem arose. When the invitations were first issued he informed the organisers of the Gimcrack Dinner that he would not be speaking but had nominated a replacement, probably one of the best-known sportsmen of his generation. Just as Sheikh Mohammed had been represented by his racing manager Michael Osborne in 1997, John Magnier proposed that his 'stand-in' for the night should be the manager of Manchester United, Alex Ferguson.

He assumed that the men who ran racing at York would be delighted to have such an honoured guest. It was here that a certain element of snobbishness came into play.

The titled gentlemen of York whose fortunes were founded mostly on coal and other business activities, found Ferguson, the dour Scot who was raised in the shadow of the Glasgow shipyards, unacceptable as a stand-in. It may have been his origins, it may have been a snobbish belief that footballers were 'naff', with their flamboyant wealth, their gaudy wives and girlfriends and their thirst for alcohol, or it may simply have been York looking down on Manchester. Or it may have been that they regarded Ferguson as a relative newcomer who had a few horses in training but was not a serious player in the sport and not to be compared in any way with their own activities as the aristocrats of the turf.

They rejected Magnier's suggestion. Instead that night, after the sumptuous Gimcrack Dinner, the guests were treated to a few words from Bob Lanigan representing Coolmore. If his speech was memorable the event is not recorded. But he then followed his few words in true Irish tradition by singing a ballad commemorating Mull of Kintyre and other great horses from the Ballydoyle Stables. It wasn't a great ballad either, although a friend and neighbour of Magnier's in Tipperary, the world-famous composer Sir Andrew Lloyd Webber, had lent a helping hand composing the ditty.

What is known, however, is that John Magnier was seriously annoyed about what he regarded as a 'snub' to his friend Alex Ferguson. And John Magnier was never a man to accept that things could not be done his way. When he wanted his child christened, he asked some friends in the church to have a word with Pope John Paul II, and so his child was duly christened in St Peter's Basilica in Rome by the pontiff just as he wished. When he wanted the rock singer Rod Stewart to play a 'gig' at his daughter Katie's wedding, it was organised and Rod topped the bill at the lavish affair in Tipperary.

He was not a man who liked to be thwarted in anything, whether it was a deal over a horse or a matter of friendship. He was one of those racing people who valued ability over blood lines, in both horses and people. The night of the Gimcrack Dinner in York, John Magnier resolved that his friend Alex Ferguson would make the Gimcrack speech in his own right whether those who ran York's social life wanted him or not. Whether Alex Ferguson was even aware of Magnier's plans is not known, but once John Magnier decided he wanted something, he usually got it.

* * *

John Magnier was a 16-year-old schoolboy attending the prestigious Catholic boys' school of Glenstal Abbey run by Benedictine monks in the village of Murroe in east Limerick when his father died in 1964. He got the call to return to the family's Grange Stud near Fermoy, County Cork.

It was a mixed dairy farm with a horse-breeding enterprise on the side. Magnier's father Michael had bred Cottage, a horse that would sire Cottage Rake which brought a young trainer called Vincent O'Brien to national prominence when it won three consecutive Cheltenham Gold Cups. It was a connection that had cemented the relationship between the two families.

O'Brien had also started out in National Hunt racing but after dominating Cheltenham he went on to become the world's best known flat-racing trainer. His Tipperary stud 'Ballydoyle' was a byword in the business for professionalism, prestige and, most of all, winners.

The young John Magnier not only relied on family friend Vincent O'Brien for sound advice on how to survive in the intricate world of Irish racing, he also fell in love with Susan O'Brien, the beautiful young daughter of Vincent and his Australian-born wife Jacqueline. O'Brien's success on the racetrack had already made him a wealthy man, but when most of his top stallions, like the legendary Nijinsky, retired from racing they were sent back to America to stand at stud. Of course O'Brien was paid well but nothing like the sums he could have earned if he kept his Derby winners in Ireland.

That was the plan devised by Magnier.

In 1975 the 27-year-old 'stallion master' John Magnier became the third partner in an enterprise that would change racing forever. He brought his expertise in horse breeding to join his father-in-law Vincent O'Brien's unrivalled knowledge of horse racing. The third secret of their success stemmed from the seemingly bottomless wealth of Vernon Pools multi-millionaire Robert Sangster.

Together the three men set out to revolutionise the sport of kings. To do this they had to outbid everyone else in the world and this they did. Magnier had devised a simple but highly-effective plan for domination of the racing classics. He identified the progeny of the American sire Northern Dancer as the stars of the future. Using Sangster's money and a war chest of more than $50 million they bought up all the best foals at the Keenland Sales in

Kentucky and other sales in Ireland and Britain.

O'Brien then turned the yearlings into a string of top Group 1 winners at his famous Ballydoyle stables. But not only were they looking at dominating the 'blue riband' of the turf, the Epsom Derby, the trio had plans well beyond that. Simultaneously they established Coolmore Stud on a 400-acre farm they bought near Fethard in County Tippeary which had been the property of another partner of O'Brien's called Tim Vigors.

After excelling on the racetrack, horses like Danehill, Galileo, Montjeu and Giants Causeway left Ballydoyle and travelled a short distance to stud at Coolmore where they commanded huge prices each time they covered a mare. But the star of the enterprise was undoubtedly the 'incomparable' Saddlers Wells (retired in 2008) who is said to have earned Coolmore at least €20 million during his illustrious stallion career. Year after year they raided the biggest sales in America and Europe – some, like Stormbird and The Green Monkey, turned out to be duds on the track but successful sires. Others like George Washington were successful on the track but duds at stud. But whatever way it worked Coolmore reigned supreme. And Alex Ferguson, who was to join the illustrious roll of owners at Ballydoyle, should probably have known when he joined 'the Irishmen', as they were known, that it was John Magnier who made the rules and nobody else.

Behind the shrewdness of Magnier, the brilliance of O'Brien and the wealth of Sangster and his various successors (most notably the London barrow-boy turned bookie Michael Tabor), there was an underlying advantage bestowed on Coolmore. That advantage was conferred by the controversial Charles J Haughey in 1969 when as Minister for Finance, he inserted a clause in the Finance Act/Budget of that year which made fees earned from stallions in Ireland exempt from any form of tax. It was a controversial but brilliant piece of legislation from the point of view of Coolmore.

This tax concession has conferred countless millions on Magnier and his associates and made him one of the wealthiest men in Europe. It also made Ireland a world 'centre of excellence' for horse-breeding and racing. And to be fair to John Magnier, this tax advantage was open to everybody – he was the one who exploited it best, because his knowledge of horse-breeding and his instincts for great sires gave him an advantage that not even the wealth and enthusiasm of the great Arab owners could match.

How well Haughey and Magnier knew each other in the early 1970s is not clear but it is quite likely that they had socialised together as both had an interest in racing and horse-breeding. Haughey, it is said, modelled himself on the Earl of Harrington who lived near Patrickswell, County Limerick and was a well-known figure in Irish hunting and racing circles. Haughey would later come to own Abbeville, near Malahide in County Dublin – a Gandon mansion set in several hundred acres where he bred horses and aspired to the life of a country squire while telling the downtrodden taxpayers that they were 'living beyond their means'.

Whatever the connection between the two men, Haughey also took the unusual step of appointing Magnier to the Irish Senate, an honour rarely conferred on people outside the political world and one which the shy and retiring Magnier did not refuse. The tax exemption created untold wealth for John Magnier and his Coolmore associates in the 39 years of the exemption's existence. In one year alone, 2008, the exemption was worth €91 million to Irish breeders and with Coolmore dominating the stallion business in Ireland it is likely to have got the lion's share of the benefits. It was a windfall that put Magnier in a position to take on virtually anybody he chose – and after his feud with Ferguson finally came to an end, he followed it with a feud with Sheikh Mohammed, the fabulously wealthy ruler of Dubai, a man not many would care to tangle with, let alone trounce. (Part of the feud with Sheikh Mohammad was due to the fact that the two empires – Coolmore and the Sheikh's Godolphin – were pitted against each other in the sales ring for the top yearling foals. The Sheikh felt that while he was buying Coolmore foals, the Irishman was not reciprocating by buying from his stud farms. But in the end it was the Sheikh who suffered most – by refusing to buy from Magnier, he lost ground on the racecourses as the Coolmore colts trained by Vincent O'Brien's successor, Aidan O'Brien, swept the glittering prizes of international racing.)

The 400-acre farm near Fethard, County Tipperary where Coolmore originated is now a 6,000-acre pristine holding, hogging the limestone-rich lands of the Golden Vale. The tax-free millions were used to turn it into a billion-euro enterprise with associated stud farms in Kentucky and Australia. And when the old master Vincent O'Brien retired to the anonymity of the K-Club outside Dublin, it was not his son Charles who succeeded him, but a young pretender called Aidan O'Brien who is no relation but has proved just as single-minded and effective at turning out winners from the high-priced yearlings that Magnier has provided.

Leading horse-breeding figures will say that 'many would-be stallions are a disaster at stud – nine out of ten fail'. Magnier more than anyone else knows that. Several of his most expensive buys have never raced or were found to be infertile when they were sent to stud.

'He's always been a big man who thought on the grand scale,' Stan Cosgrove of Moyglare Stud told Alastair Down – for a profile of Magnier in the *Racing Post* in 2001. 'Even when he wasn't going that well he would think big. You never saw John Magnier in a small car.'

Cosgrave, who was vet to the famous Shergar and was a central figure in the drama that followed the IRA kidnapping of the Aga Khan's wonder horse, noticed something else early on about Magnier. 'He has a terrific team and they are mainly horsemen, not academics, and he looks after them. He has a natural touch with people and I can think of loads of folk he has done good turns for down the years. You always got a fair deal; if a foal died or was born crooked, he would always do something for you. People remember that sort of thing.

'He is not a showman, never one to boast. And the outstanding thing about him is the number of people who have worked for him who became millionaires – he was always encouraging his people to take shares and make a few bob. A lesser man would resent his employees doing that because he'd think they were trying to get level with him. Not Magnier. Nobody ever gets headhunted out of Coolmore, because nobody else would look after them so well.'

But above all, Magnier and his associates have an amazing determination to win – whether it is in the sales ring, the racetrack or the world of high finance. Using his wealth from Coolmore, he has branched out into financial partnership with the legendary Limerick gambler JP McManus, who started life driving a JCB before becoming a bookie in Limerick and a feared gambler on the racetrack, and Dermot Desmond, a billionaire financier known as 'The Kaiser' who worked for the World Bank in Afghanistan before coming back to Ireland to establish NCB stockbrokers. The three men are secretive to the point of paranoia. McManus is supposed to operate from Geneva and Limerick and Desmond from Monaco and Dublin. But with mobile phones, private jets and unlimited funds they are international businessmen who hunt for ventures instead of foxes and have a multi-million credit line which they use to trade on the international currency and commodity markets. Although each has different ventures, they also operate in consort in some business activities. And it was through these that they came to British football.

Desmond, a long-time friend, ally and advisor to the late Irish Taoiseach Charlie Haughey, has a nationalist streak that led to a large and profitable investment in Glasgow Celtic football club. Whether the three men discussed this venture on the golf course or in the boardroom, Magnier and JP McManus soon followed suit, buying up a stake in another club which has a large following in Ireland, Manchester United.

While they were already on friendly terms with Alex Ferguson, it is unlikely that they either consulted him or informed him that Cubic Expression, a company formed specifically to hold their Manchester United stake, was investing millions in the club where he was the legendary manager. But their friendship with him did give the story another layer of intrigue for the analysts and bankers who watch large financial transactions taking place.

The £50 million stake they bought belonged to Martin Edwards, whose family had been long-term owners of United. But the gossip was that Edwards didn't get on with Alex Ferguson, although the manager was paid £5 million that year for his services to the club.

'That they (Magnier and McManus) are both friends of Sir Alex Ferguson, the United manager, sharpens the tabloids' teeth,' wrote journalist Alan Ruddock of the Irish businessmen's foray into the club.

'Ferguson has been at war with his board and particularly his chairman, Martin Edwards, over the past few years. Entering the final straight of his career, he appears to have won the major battles by getting enough money to buy big name players like Van Nistleroy and Veron, as well as getting a £5 million pay package for himself last year.'

It seems bizarre now to think that in 2002 most observers thought Ferguson was coming to the end of his career – when, from today's vantage point, it seems he was only at the beginning of it. But that's another story altogether.

What is obvious is that Magnier's business model in horse racing was exactly the same as Ferguson's in football – have the money to buy up all the best players/horses and you're sure to win most of the prizes. That's the theory anyway.

While he was eyeing up the prospects of Manchester United in the year 2001, John Magnier had not forgotten the promise he made to himself back in 1999 in York, that one day his friend Alex Ferguson would make the Gimcrack speech. Socially, Alex Ferguson was now close to the 'Coolmore Mafia' as they are sometimes called, not because of any criminal tendency, but because of the code they lived by: stick together and take on the rest of the world without fear or favour.

Ferguson was happy to fly over to Ireland to tour around Ballydoyle and he was also happy to be picked up by private jet to attend a charity dinner hosted by JP McManus at Adare Manor. There he played golf and mingled comfortably with the 'set' – John Magnier and Dermot Desmond, JP and his friends, including the legendary Tiger Woods.

*   *   *

Heritage Hall, Zentov Street and Juniper, three Coolmore-bred horses trained by the taciturn young Aidan O'Brien, had already raced in Alex Ferguson's distinctive red and white silks. He had been listed as a co-owner of all three. But according to writer Martin Hannan, in the case of Juniper in particular, there was a 'bewildering pattern' of ownership with Ferguson being registered and de-registered as owner for different races. It seems clear, according to Hannan, that Coolmore was deliberately listing Ferguson for what they believed were their best Gimcrack prospects – but at that stage they just weren't sure which horse would run in the race.

Although registered as joint 'owner', Ferguson hadn't paid training fees – which were as high as £600 a week at the time – or borne any of the considerable expense involved in getting any of these horses ready for the big races in Ireland or England. Then, in the summer of 2001, John Magnier and Aidan O'Brien began to notice something special about their promising two-year-old Rock of Gibraltar as they put him through his paces at Ballydoyle. A son of Danehill by Offshore Boom, he had been bred by Anne-Marie O'Brien, Aidan O'Brien's wife and her father Joe Crowley. But while the two-year-old performed well on the gallops at Ballydoyle, he was by no means considered a stable 'star' when he ran in the dark blue colours of 'Mrs John Magnier' in a 5-furlong Maiden at the Curragh on 21 April 2001. He went on to win as the '11/10 on' favourite.

But his next outing in the prestigious Group 3 Coventry Stakes at Ascot in mid June did not bode so well when he came home sixth out of 20 runners. Yet on 1 July he had regained his form, winning the six-furlong Railway Stakes at the Curragh. It was after watching this performance that John Magnier realised he had something special. When Alex Ferguson phoned him in early August, Magnier told him about the horse and his plans for it – it was a phone call that would later become of vital importance to both men, but the exact details of what was said that day still remain shrouded in mystery.

The end result was that on 17 August 2001, Alex Ferguson was registered with Horse Racing Ireland as a 50 per cent owner of Rock of Gibraltar with the other half vested in Mrs John Magnier – the same day as the horse was 'declared' to run in the Gimcrack, five days later on 22 August.

Although the trainer, jockey and registered 'owners' would remain the same for the remainder of Rock of Gibraltar's career, from then on the horse ran in the red and white colours of Alex Ferguson. In 2002 Ferguson told *The Observer* newspaper in England, 'My first real memory of Rock of Gibraltar was at the Gimcrack Stakes at York in August. I had bought him a couple of months earlier and he had already won once.'

What did that one word 'bought' mean? Alex Ferguson hadn't actually paid any money for his 'share' in the horse. Nor had he contributed to its expensive upkeep. He hadn't 'bought' the horse months before, as he said – he had been registered as half-owner just five days before the biggest race of the horse's career to date.

On the other side he was listed as 'joint owner' with Susan Magnier. But it appears he had never established what exactly that meant. As far as John Magnier was concerned it was just a formality to give Ferguson a thrill that many wealthy and powerful people crave: having a top-class horse win prestigious races in their name and pick up a share of the lucrative prize money involved.

But there can be little doubt that in Ferguson's own mind he believed, or was coming to believe, that he really was the true owner of a blueblood of the turf. However the Turf Club 'registration' with Horse Racing Ireland did not have any legal standing. According to Martin Hannan in his book *Rock of Gibraltar,* things were further complicated. In the Stud Book which is kept by Weatherbys and is the bible of horse breeding in England and Ireland, the horse's owners were listed as 'Rock of Gibraltar syndicate' and not Alex Ferguson and Mrs John Magnier.

The Manchester United boss could not make the racetrack at York to see Rock of Gibraltar reach the first milestone in his astonishing career when he ran in the Gimcrack Stakes. But he did delay the team bus leaving for an evening fixture against Blackburn Rovers so that he could see 'his' horse scythe through the nine-strong field to claim victory in the prestigious race. It was a win that also set him up to make the speech at what one journalist described as 'the frightfully grand' Gimcrack dinner in York later in 2001, an honour that had been denied him just a few years previously.

Basking in the first flushes of racing success, Alex Ferguson, the sometimes dour Scot from the wrong side of the Glasgow tracks, certainly gave his listeners value for money when he stood up to speak at the dinner in York Racecourse just before Christmas.

'My deepest gratitude is, however, due to two friends who are not here, Sue and John Magnier,' said Alex Ferguson. 'I have been given the privilege of teaming up with them, and standing up before you this evening. Nobody could be blessed with better friends than them.'

They were prophetic words that would soon come back to haunt him.

After finishing second in his next race, the Champagne Stakes at Doncaster, Rock of Gibraltar began to stamp his mark on horse-racing history in a carefully planned campaign from October 2001 to his retirement exactly a year later.

As a three-year-old he won seven Group 1 races in succession, starting with the Grand Criterium at Longchamp, followed by the Dewhurst Stakes at Newmarket, the 2000 Guineas at Newmarket, the Irish 2000 Guineas at the Curragh, the St James's Palace Stakes at Ascot, the Sussex Stakes at Goodwood and the Prix du Moulin de Longchamp at Longchamp on 8 September 2002.

He was, said trainer Aidan O'Brien, known for his habit of under-statement, 'a serious horse' – the highest accolade he could pay to one of his charges.

'You always have to be surprised when something like this happens,' said John Magnier in a rare RTÉ interview about Rock of Gibraltar. 'He is a tough, durable, versatile horse. No doubt about that. And Alex (Ferguson) is lucky.'

The Rock, as he was now known among racing fans where he had gained celebrity status, started as favourite in his final race, the Breeder's Cup Mile in Arlington Park on 26 October 2002 and was unfortunate to be narrowly beaten into second place. He was then promptly retired to stud at Coolmore on his return to Ireland. It was the end of a glittering career for Rock of Gibraltar and the beginning of a bitter feud over the future of one of the most thrilling and exciting horses to grace the turf in a generation.

Alex Ferguson had always been ruthless in his pursuit of success, whether it was on the football field or the racetrack. Friendship was one thing, but business was business. That was why he had sold Eric Cantona who, it is argued, had 'made' the modern Manchester United and his 'son' David Beckham. The 'father/son relationship' with Irish footballer Roy Keane also came to a bitter end when expediency dictated that Keane was no longer part of his plans.

Ferguson's single-minded goal of success meant that friendship, in the professional sense, was a means to an end. When that end was served it was time to move on. Ruthlessly unsentimental in his professional life, Ferguson now looked at the value of Rock of Gibraltar in terms of money rather than racing prestige – after all he was registered as half-owner of the most talked-about thoroughbred in the world. An article in *The Daily Telegraph* in November 2002 speculated that the stud value of Rock of Gibraltar could be as high as £50 million and that a half share would mean a colossal windfall profit for Alex Ferguson that would dwarf the millions he was getting from running the most valuable football club in the world.

But racing is very different from football. The leading players like

Magnier operate on a nod and a handshake to seal a million-euro deal. It is a world where 'a man's word is his bond' and fortunes are won and lost on trust. Even the registration form on which Alex Ferguson was named as 'half owner' of the horse had no legal standing. It was just a piece of paper. What exactly was the meaning of a 50 per cent share in Rock of Gibraltar? John Magnier and Alex Ferguson had very different ideas of exactly what it meant.

To Alex Ferguson it meant what it said, that he owned half the horse and would now be eligible for half the horse's projected earnings at stud. But Ferguson had not paid out anything to acquire a half share, nor had he contributed anything to the training fees and expenses that had been incurred by Coolmore in the horse's international campaign for stardom.

Of course he had been 'registered' as half owner, had led the horse into the parade ring after several of his successes and he had been presented with expensive silver replicas of some of the most prestigious trophies the horse had won. But did that entitle him to half the stud value of Rock of Gibraltar?

What had Alex Ferguson contributed for his half share? Of course there had been a publicity spin-off for Coolmore. Magnier, the reluctant 'celebrity', had allowed Alex Ferguson to take the glory, and indeed Ferguson had been used in Coolmore's promotional videos to 'sell' the famous global horse-breeding enterprise. But how much was that worth? Hardly half the estimated value that was now being put on the head of Rock of Gibraltar.

There are also many other considerations when it comes to the exact ownership of a top racehorse when it is put out to stud. Its breeder, in this case Anne-Marie O'Brien and her father, could have reserved at least a number of 'nominations' a year when they sold the horse to Coolmore. In other words, they would be entitled to have the stallion cover one of their mares for free or take the cash equivalent each year. The jockey Michael Kinnane, who was part of Rock of Gibraltar's success and rode him in almost all of his races, may also have been rewarded with a yearly nomination, depending on his agreements. Aidan O'Brien too, as trainer, may have had some entitlement to nomination fees. A seasoned horseman like John Magnier would be well aware that it would be most unwise to dilute the value of a prize asset by handing over a massive 50 per cent to one individual with no strings attached. But that's what Ferguson asserted in a letter to Magnier in early 2003.

Tensions had already been rising between the two sides. Even before Rock of Gibraltar's racing career was over there was an obscure but 'telling' paragraph in the Peterborough column of *The Daily Telegraph,* speculating that a dispute over the ownership of the horse was looming. When Alex Ferguson and John Magnier finally sat down to thrash out the exact ownership of Rock of Gibraltar, it was clear that there was more than just a cultural difference in their approach to the problem.

Magnier was clear – the ownership was a nominal honour that would entitle Alex Ferguson to 50 per cent of Rock of Gibraltar's earnings of £1,164,804 or one stud nomination a year in Ireland and one in Australia where the horse would 'stand' in the winter. The probable value of these was over €150,000 a year for an expected 10 years.

But Ferguson wasn't having any of it. In his mind 50 per cent was 50 per cent.

By the summer of 2003 the Stallion Master of Coolmore and the Manager of Manchester United were haggling over money on one level, but over supremacy on another. Their friendship was already badly dented. What made Magnier even more uncomfortable was the media spotlight that was beginning to settle on him and the dispute over Rock of Gibraltar.

He then went so far as to offer Ferguson four stud nominations per year – two in Ireland and a further two in Australia. And with the horse already earning about €10 million a year in stud fees it was a tempting offer. But the tough Scot, now appraised that others also had claims to 'nominations', held out for between 15 to 20 per cent of the stud value of Rock of Gibraltar.

It was then that things began to get personal. Magnier felt that his honour, the honour of his word as a gentleman, was being impugned by Ferguson's behaviour. As stories about the dispute began to filter out, Magnier became more incensed. Firstly because he loathed any mention of his private business affairs in the media, and secondly because he now believed something he had stood by all his life, his word, was being questioned.

* * *

As the row between the two men began to escalate, it became far more serious than simply a dispute over the value of a horse. In a way it became a battle for the future of Manchester United. For Alex Ferguson it became a family agony that would eventually lead to pleas from his wife Norma for him to withdraw from the affray with the powerful Irishman he had once counted among his friends and who was now making family life a nightmare.

When the row between Magnier and Ferguson first arose, Magnier and his long-time business associate JP McManus held 6.7 per cent of Manchester United, which they bought for about £50 million. The two Irishmen were variously described as 'good friends' of Alex Ferguson who were motivated by their love of sport. Some sources believe that when the conflict between Magnier and Ferguson finally came out into the open, JP McManus and Ladbroke's Mike Dillon found themselves in a deeply embarrassing position, caught between their loyalty to Magnier and their friendship with Ferguson. Both men appear to have accepted that Magnier was right and Ferguson was wrong, but they didn't want to get directly involved in the row. What followed wasn't pretty, but it was typical of the ruthless attitude of the Irishmen towards business and pleasure.

In late 2003 the row over who owned Rock of Gibraltar finally found its way into the Irish courts when Sir Alex Ferguson began formal legal proceedings in the High Court in Dublin against John Magnier and Coolmore Ltd. What enraged Magnier was that this was not only a slur on his word as a gentleman but it also threatened to open up the ultra-secret world of Coolmore to public gaze. The Irish Revenue Commissioners had never bothered to estimate the value of the 'stallion tax break' that had made him a multi-millionaire. But the case was now adding to pressure for them to do just that. The tax break was already under scrutiny by the European Union competition authorities and had long been a focus for grumbling and discontent from those who wished for taxes to be levied on the ultra-rich, rather than showering them with tax shelters that made them even wealthier.

The 'Statement of Claim' lodged on behalf of Ferguson with Coolmore and in the Dublin courts stated that Alex Ferguson's name had contributed to the massive stud fees now earned by the horse; that he was a half-owner of Rock of Gibraltar and that he was entitled to half of its earnings which could be in the region of €50-€70 million over the following 10 years.

Magnier was not only incredulous at these claims, but he was incensed that they had been made at all. His public relations advisors in Dublin, Murray Consultants, went into overdrive to protect Magnier's good name and to try to convince the general public that Coolmore, the best-known stud farm in the world, was an asset that Ireland should be proud of and that the 'stallion tax' concession was what had made the country the centre of world excellence.

On another front, a New York private detective agency, Kroll, was employed with a brief to 'find out everything about Ferguson'. If this entailed going through his rubbish bins and those of his sons, trawling through his financial records and his dealings in some of Manchester United's high-profile transfers and signings of footballers, then so be it.

But even more serious for Ferguson was what was happening to his club. On 7 October 2003 it was disclosed that the company Cubic Expression, the Magnier/McManus 'vehicle', had spent £62 million acquiring another 10 per cent stake in Manchester United held by BSkyB, the British broadcasting arm of media magnate Rupert Murdoch. Events were beginning to move almost as fast as the first-class thoroughbred they were fighting about. Just over a month later it was all coming out into the open.

'Coolmore Stud has today been advised that legal proceedings have been initiated against Mr John Magnier by Sir Alex Ferguson, alleging certain ownership rights to the stallion Rock of Gibraltar. Coolmore Stud and John Magnier consider the action to be without merit and it will be vigorously defended,' said a statement from Murray Consultants on behalf of John Magnier, issued on 17 November 2003.

As the legal manoeuvres continued, another figure had entered the Manchester United boardroom battle in the shape of American sporting tycoon Malcolm Glazer who began to build up a stake in the club. On a personal level the Irish shareholders, Magnier and McManus, opened up a number of inquiries directly related to Alex Ferguson's position as manager of Manchester United. A series of questions were put by Cubic Expression to the board of Manchester United. They were clearly directed at Sir Alex Ferguson's stewardship of the famous club. What business arrangements, they asked, existed between United, with Ferguson as manager, and the Elite Sporting Agency, run by Ferguson's son Jason who received significant commission from United on the transfer of players, notably Japp Stamm. They also put a series of questions to the Manchester United board and its solicitors relating to payments to players, the financial organisation of transfer deals and payments to Ferguson himself. These had the effect of delaying negotiations between Manchester United and Sir Alex Ferguson about signing a new contract. The result was that the most famous football manager in the world was put on a rolling yearly contract rather than signing the normal five-year deal that would have been expected.

Cubic Expression's first share purchases in the famed British football club, which had seemed to be a friendly gesture just 18 months before, now began to take on a more sinister turn as their stake in the football club began to approach the limit for a takeover bid. By February 2004 Cubic Expression owned 28.39 per cent of Manchester United and there were strong indications that Magnier and McManus might take over the club. In the meantime they were asking questions about the governance of Manchester United which were getting uncomfortably close to Sir Alex Ferguson himself.

Another racing 'associate' of the Irishmen, mining multi-millionaire Harry Dobson, spent £21 million acquiring a 5.6 per cent stake in Manchester United. Dobson, a bluff Yorkshire man, had 40 horses in training in Ireland but no interest in football. Yet like his pals, Dermot Desmond, John Magnier and JP McManus he was always searching for another deal that would add to his already considerable wealth.

Dobson, who had invested heavily in property around Dublin, which he was unable to develop due to re-zoning issues but which was soaring in value because of escalating land prices, had diversified into Manchester United shares because he thought they were a bargain at the time. Dobson declared that he was acting alone – but his intervention can only have seemed menacing to Ferguson, because of Dobson's friendship and previous business dealings with 'the Irishmen'.

Cleverly, as Ferguson came under more and more pressure from the Magnier/Cubic Expression questions, it was to a group of Irish advisors that he turned. Led by the well-known Dublin barrister Colm Allen SC, he assembled a team of advisors who operated in secret what was known as Project Rathgar – aimed at advising Ferguson on the legal, financial and public relations aspects of the battle for the Rock of Gibraltar.

Among those who were asked for advice was Tony Blair's former advisor Alastair Campbell, a long-time admirer of Ferguson. One of those involved said it was like a 'covert operation' with specially encrypted e-mails and scrambled phones to thwart surveillance of any sort. They also began to defend their client Ferguson from what they believed was a 'dirty tricks' campaign which included a rumour that he had charged a fee to attend a charity dinner in Dublin for an injured jockey.

Whether the covert aspect of the operation was rampant paranoia or whether it was justified by the tactics being used against them is immaterial. There was a real fear in the air in both Manchester and Dublin as events moved inexorably towards a court case in the famous Round Hall of Dublin's Four Courts.

'Ferguson was reported by friends to be at an all-time low, and seriously worried that his family were now "in play",' said Martin Hannan in his book on Rock of Gibraltar. 'But help for the beleaguered manager was at hand in the form of United's fans.'

A group called United4Action began to take the war to Magnier and McManus's own turf – the racecourse. A series of protests were planned which would culminate at a rally in favour of Ferguson at the famous Cheltenham Festival. Magnier would not be in attendance, but JP McManus was an annual visitor and his horses – trained in Ireland, England and France – were out to plunder the big races.

That anyone should threaten this Holy Grail of racing, and the possibility of injuries or otherwise, led to a further hardening of attitudes. The message was made clear to Sir Alex Ferguson that as the figurehead of the club he could be held responsible for any disturbances that might take place and that if things got out of hand he might find his own position at the club untenable. Added to that was the agony of his wife Norma who was now begging him to back away from the dreadful pressure that the Ferguson family was under: from the media, from the prospect of a high-profile court case and from the forensic examination of her husband and son's business relationships.

Finally Sir Alex Ferguson stood on the steps of Manchester United and read out a statement which effectively ended the Rock of Gibraltar affair.

'The reputation of Manchester United is paramount to my thinking. The private dispute I have is just that and I don't want to exacerbate the whole thing. Cheltenham is such a great festival and I don't want it marred in any way. There is a lot of concern about what could happen and I would ask supporters to refrain from any form of protest. I am strongly opposed to any violent, unlawful or disruptive behaviour which may reflect badly on the club and its supporters in general,' he said.

The statement was a clear signal that Ferguson no longer had any stomach for the impending legal battle in Dublin. His reputation was battered, his job was at considerable risk and his family was finding the pressure intolerable. On the other side of the feud there was also a clear will to get this 'over and done with' as one of the participants admitted.

There had been a suspected arson attack on a stud farm associated with the Magnier family in Cork and they too wanted the nightmare to end.

Whatever about Magnier, a mysterious figure who seems to shimmy between Coolmore, his opulent home on the seafront at Marbella or the Sandy Lane resort in Barbados which he owns, the last thing JP McManus wanted was some sort of outrage at Cheltenham. While some sources claim that McManus had been pitted against Ferguson, Martin Hannan asserts that in fact McManus had never really taken sides in the dispute. Although he remained loyal to his long-time business partner Magnier, his involvement in Cubic Expression and the purchase of 75.7 million shares in Manchester United was, for him, purely an investment.

McManus has always been a legendary figure at Cheltenham. Indeed the publicity surrounding his betting coups at the track was one of the reasons the Cheltenham Festival became the huge event it is today. Back in 1981 I remember standing in the winners' enclosure with McManus and the Queen Mother as he was about to be presented with a trophy sponsored by the British Tote. I knew of his reputation but thought that some of it was exaggerated, especially in the writings of the wonderful Raymond Smith, a journalist with the *Sunday Independent* in Dublin, a friend of McManus and a man who loved to dramatise a good story. Slightly sceptical about the whole thing I was standing next to McManus when the cigar-smoking Woodrow Wyatt, the quintessential British establishment figure and personal friend and advisor to the British Prime Minister Margaret Thatcher, walked up to us.

'I'm delighted you won the race. Nobody I know has put more money into British racecourses than you have, JP,' he said. My scepticism about the man known as 'The Sundance Kid' evaporated on hearing those words.

McManus, who worships National Hunt racing and is now one of its biggest supporters, valued the annual festival too much as an owner and a gambler to allow anything to happen. Added to that, Magnier and McManus, notoriously shy of the limelight were becoming alarmed at the increasing intrusion into their private lives. One particular photograph showed Magnier in shorts walking along the beach in Sandy Lane accompanied by a very large minder – it wasn't something he was used to.

The Irish duo had also become the subject of unseemly chants at Manchester United's hallowed ground, Old Trafford, and they were finding it difficult to concentrate on their enjoyment of racing, punting and buying and selling horses due to the voracious appetite of the British and Irish press for stories about the feud. Although determined to fight the case and convinced that they would win, neither was looking forward to the prolonged legal nightmare that a lengthy court battle would constitute for all concerned.

They now took Ferguson's conciliatory words as a sign of goodwill that needed to be met, if not half-way, at least some part of the distance. It was the sign that all sides needed and the catalyst for Dermot 'The Kaiser' Desmond to enter the ring. The major shareholder in Celtic, a shareholder in United and a long-time business associate of McManus and Magnier, he approached Ferguson with a deal that needed to be almost as carefully choreographed as the Good Friday Agreement.

The basic settlement was that Alex Ferguson would be paid a lump sum of £2.5 million, he would renounce all claims to Rock of Gibraltar, discontinue the contentious legal action instituted in the Dublin courts and remain silent forever on the 'Rock of Gibraltar' saga.

The deal was signed.

But the Irishmen had one more deal to pull off before the saga was complete – they sold their holding in Manchester United.

Malcolm Glazer, the 76-year-old Florida-based owner of the Tampa Bay Buccaneers American football team, had been quietly stalking United all through the Rock of Gibraltar drama. Magnier and McManus had 28.39 per cent of the club – once they pushed it to 29 per cent they would have to bid for the entire business. That wasn't part of their gameplan. Outside of racing they were business investors not business owners. Glazer had 28.2 per cent, but with his track record in the sports business and his television contacts he was keen to own Manchester United 'lock stock and barrel'. He was given a 10-day window to 'put up or shut up' in his quest. Glazer swung into action.

On Wednesday 11 May 2005, John Magnier and JP McManus took a conference call from the American. It is not known where they were at the time or what transpired in the telephone call between the three men. But the following morning an estimated £230 million dropped into the bank accounts of Cubic Expression, netting Magnier and McManus an estimated profit of £80 million on their Manchester United adventure.

Their pal Dermot Desmond made about £12 million when he threw in his stake, and a couple of days later another associate, Harry Dobson, sold his 6.5 per cent. Glazer's bid valued Manchester United at £800 million, most of which was borrowed in the United States and Britain from banks specialising in high-risk investments.

'We feel completely betrayed by John Magnier and JP McManus,' Oliver Houston, a fan and member of 'Shareholders United' which represented small shareholders, told *The Independent* newspaper. 'They said they were long-term investors, but they have taken the 30 pieces of silver offered by Malcolm Glazer.'

But who could really blame them?

Ironically John Magnier was at York, the scene of his triumphs with Mull of Kintyre and Rock of Gibraltar, watching his latest crop of two-year-olds flash past the winning post when the news broke that he had sold out and cut the last link with his one-time friend Sir Alex Ferguson and his famous club Manchester United.

'I really don't have anything to add,' said Magnier when asked about the deal by reporters. 'Let's talk about horses now.'

John Magnier then retreated into silence, exile and cunning and his horses continued to plunder the great prizes of the turf in Britain and Ireland. Wearing a top hat and with the trademark gold half-glasses sitting at the end of his nose, he was relaxed and good-humoured as his horse Yeats, trained by Aidan O'Brien, won the Ascot Gold Cup for a record fourth time in June 2009.

Sir Alex Ferguson too went back to doing what he does best, winning matches and running the most famous football club in the world. The 'Rock' saga is now long behind him and far from retiring or being fired as manager of United, he continued to line the trophy room with silver, winning two European cups and the elusive double in 2008. He led his team to another Premier League victory in 2009 and starts off a new football season as determined as ever.

Manchester United is not so much a vocation as an obsession – it's his life and he very nearly lost his club over a short, and what turned out to be an unhappy, love affair with a wonder horse.

Chapter 4
The Sex of Bono's Baby

The reason why a libel action by John Waters (*The Irish Times* journalist and father of Sinéad O'Connor's child) against *The Sunday Times* columnist Terry Keane turned into a controversy about the sex of Bono's baby is not as mysterious as it might at first glance appear.

Keane first come to national attention when she wrote a social column called 'The Keane Edge' on the back page of the *Sunday Independent.* Her decision to publicly reveal her affair with then Taoiseach Charlie Haughey led to an offer from rival newspaper *The Sunday Times* to write a social column for them which she duly accepted. Her columns with *The Sunday Times* were never as talked about as her earlier columns with the *Sunday Independent.* In any case, Garrett Cooney SC, Waters' barrister, was determined to steer the libel case in the direction of her time writing the famous *Sunday Independent* columns a few years earlier rather than her less controversial contributions to the *The Sunday Times,* where the libel had been committed.

'Had you squeezed through the barristers and other luminaries packing Court No 3 in the Four Courts, Dublin, last Friday morning 19 April 2002 to see Garrett Cooney SC cross-examine Terry Keane, you might have assumed that you had made a mistake and that you were at the wrong trial,' wrote one court observer.

'From 11 a.m. until 12.45 p.m. approximately, Mr Cooney was on his feet, questioning Mrs Keane about her 12 years at the *Sunday Independent* where she wrote "The Keane Edge".

'A transcript of Mr Cooney's cross-examination of Mrs Keane reveals that over half of it was about Terry Keane's column in the *Sunday Independent,* rather than the piece in *The Sunday Times* about which she is being sued.'

In the course of this cross-examination Terry Keane agreed that she now believed her column in the *Sunday Independent* was 'poisonous and pernicious' and that she had not in fact written some of the stories that appeared under her name, something she said she now deeply regretted.

And that is how the sex of Bono's baby became the central issue in what would otherwise have been a dull if rather cantankerous clash between herself and Cooney. The matter arose when Cooney questioned Terry Keane about a column which appeared in 'The Keane Edge' in the *Sunday Independent* on 16 June 1991 under the heading 'Ali's Little Secret'. The story went like this:

'Ali Hewson has six weeks to go before the birth of her second child. But the big event holds no mystery for the pop king and his wife. They have already ascertained the sex of their child. It will be a daughter, their second little girl. Despite speculation that they were both longing for a son the pair are thrilled with the news – the result of a recent scan. 1991 is going to be a year for girls. The Inchiquin's are celebrating the recent birth of their second daughter (the only reasons they hoped for a son was to have an heir.) And I'm betting that Caroline and Sam Stephenson who got married yesterday will also be rag 'n' rolling the nursery a chic shade of Schiaparelli for their arrival in September. Proud dad-to-be Mark Kavanagh is also thrilled that his American bride Kathleen is expecting a baby in November. And the odds are 2 to 1 – on past performance - that they'll have a girl to join Keelin, Michael and Serena from his first marriage. It goes like that. One year's all boys, another all girls. Something in the soup, I always say.'

Although the story would seem witty and informative to most people, especially the one million readers of the *Sunday Independent,* that is not how it was portrayed in the tense atmosphere of a libel trial.

After deliberately fiddling with his papers Mr Cooney folded his arms in his black barrister's cloak and asked Terry Keane why she had written such a 'vile story' revealing the gender of the baby due to be born to Bono and his beautiful wife, Ali Hewson, and implying that this announcement in the gossip column of Ireland's biggest selling and most controversial newspaper, was the first they knew of it themselves.

Sitting in the witness box with the poise and confidence of a woman who had been married to the man who was now the Chief Justice and had long been the mistress of the former Taoiseach Charles J Haughey, she answered in the Dublin 4 drawl of a Ranelagh Matron. But instead of defending the story she claimed she hadn't even written it.

'I was deeply shocked by the story,' she replied, falling into the trap.

'Paul McGuinness rang me up and said, I know Terry, you had nothing to do with this because you would not have anything to do with anything as disgusting as that,' she continued.

That took the wind out of Garrett Cooney's sails for a moment, although he did manage to characterise it as a 'Nuremburg Defence' – a defence used by Nazi war criminals to excuse their actions by claiming that they were only following orders. But it was far from the end of the matter. Because 48 hours later the evidence was finished but before the jury had given a verdict, Mr Cooney was back on his feet – this time brandishing a letter from Paul McGuinness, manager of the famous Dublin rock band U2 and long regarded as the 'fifth' member of the group. Mr Cooney wanted to call McGuinness to give his version of the saga of the sex of Bono's second baby.

'In fact Mr McGuinness informs us that after he saw this article he wrote to Mrs Keane and he has a copy of the letter, My Lord, in which he asked her whether she or whoever wrote the article would apologise to Bono. He will give evidence My Lord, that she telephoned him . . . [and] in the course of that conversation, she first of all did not deny that she was the author of that particular piece.'

'Secondly My Lord, the more important aspect is that she refused to apologise for the article, either personally to Mr McGuinness or to write a letter of apology to Bono and Ali, My Lord. This is contrary to what she swore to, My Lord.'

The Hewsons, it seemed, were the nearest thing you could get to Irish royalty. Although Judge Nicholas Kearns declined to recall Terry Keane to be questioned about this conflict of evidence, the two letters connected to the matter were later made public. The first was a copy of a letter Paul McGuinness sent to Terry Keane after the story had appeared in 'The Keane Edge' in the *Sunday Independent.*

'Should you wish to apologise to Bono and Ali for this offensive and vulgar intrusion, I will be happy to pass on in confidence anything you may wish to say to them,' he wrote.

Obviously Terry Keane, whether she wrote the story, as was generally assumed, or not, as she later implied, decided that she had nothing to say to Bono and Ali and she was going to stand over the story at that time. The second letter, also from Mr McGuinness, was written to Bono and Ali Hewson.

'Terry Keane called me and when I returned her call she stood over the story saying: "It's not as if we paid five grand to a scanlab technician . . . Bono and Ali were telling all their friends about the fact that it was a girl. That is where we got the story."'

McGuinness added his own addendum: 'I said that was absolutely untrue'.

As it transpired, that story, however 'The Keane Edge' acquired it, was not only witty, but it was factually correct.

As surprised as anyone about the controversy about the sex of Bono's baby that suddenly erupted in 2002, over a decade after the original story was published, was the editor of the *Sunday Independent,* Aengus Fanning.

'*The Sunday Independent* – whatever about Terry Keane personally – never received a complaint about an item revealing the gender of Bono and Ali Hewson's unborn baby 11 years ago. Not a letter, not a phone call, no representations whatsoever from any agent of Bono's or his wife, Ali. The item itself was inoffensive – and Bono had, in fact, revealed the gender of Gabriel Byrne's unborn baby to a crowded concert some time earlier.'

Mr Fanning, writing in his own newspaper, said that there was a 'touch of Irish madness' about the legal proceedings involving John Waters and Terry Keane.

'Even though "The Keane Edge" had not been published for three years, and then in the *Sunday Independent,* not *The Sunday Times,* it remained a strangely obsessive focus for much of Mr Cooney's conduct of the case,' he said.

Indeed it is difficult to know where to start the story, because it certainly doesn't start with the sex of Bono's baby.

In fact it started out in the Abbey Theatre on the night of Tuesday 13 June 2000, before a performance of the ancient Greek tragedy *Medea,* a

2,500-year-old play in which the woman of the title kills her husband and then murders her two children.

John Waters had been asked by the director to give a talk about the play and its significance in the modern world.

The journalist and author, whose columns had lately concentrated on how the Irish court system disregarded the rights of fathers when family relationships broke down, proceeded to give a talk to the audience about the play and his own view of the world we live in. The ending went as follows:

> 'So when it comes to actions like these at the core of this play, or even the passions that provoke them, I'm afraid I don't believe in love and I don't believe in personal disorder. I don't believe in negative childhood experience. I don't believe in female biochemistry. I don't believe in postnatal depression. I don't believe in hormones; I don't believe in mood swings. I don't believe in self-pity. I don't believe in victimhood. I don't believe in heroines. I don't believe in universal motherhood. I don't believe in strong women. I don't believe in grand passions. I don't believe in Yoko. I just believe in right and wrong. Good and evil. Either we think it is ok to kill children or we don't. If Medea was a man, we wouldn't tolerate this play, unless it involved throwing away the key for good.'

Sitting in the audience that night was the broadcaster and journalist June Levine, her husband, the tin-whistle-playing psychiatrist Ivor Browne, and their friend Tony Boland, a former producer in RTÉ. So struck were they by the talk that after it ended Tony Boland went up to the stage and asked John Waters if he could have a copy of his script, which John Waters obligingly gave him.

That night after the play the three of them went back to Ivor Browne and June Levine's house in Ranelagh where they discussed the play and John Waters' contribution in detail. The following morning June Levine went over to Terry Keane's imposing Victorian home nearby for coffee and they talked at length about it again. The John Waters' script mysteriously vanished that day and was never seen again, but the following Sunday, Terry Keane got a full column from the affair. And boy did she seem to enjoy it.

Dublin is a small town and that's why 'The Keane Edge' in the *Sunday Independent* became the most talked-about newspaper column of the decade. Edited by the paper's deputy editor, Anne Harris, it operated along very simple lines – the column should be fun to read, it should chronicle the lives of well-known people and it should tell the readers, the ordinary people of Ireland, the things that the rich and famous did not want them to know.

'The gossip column was not considered a dishonourable trade – after all, it was treading in the footsteps of Daniel Defoe, of William Thackeray and of Malcolm Muggeridge, who said, before he got religion, that human beings are far more interested in who a man sleeps with and what he earns, than in the dreary discourses of politics,' wrote one of the paper's contributors during the controversy. It also followed the direction of the great newspaper magnate Lord Beaverbrook who told his minions, 'Always remember - names make news'.

That's why the story of Ali's little secret in 'The Keane Edge' in 1991 was a textbook case of how a great gossip column should be written and edited. The story itself wasn't even the lead story – that concerned the break-up of the relationship of airline magnate Tony Ryan and the love of his life, Lady Miranda Iveagh. Other 'diary people' dotted around the page were Mick Jagger's one-time lover Marianne Faithful, then living in the Shell House on the Carton estate near Maynooth, the actress Alison Doody and a story about Colonel Sean O'Driscoll who was Charles Lindbergh's special aide and was living at Castle Matrix in County Limerick.

But the 'Bono's Baby' story was special because it told people something exclusive that the very rich and very powerful, presumably Bono and certainly Paul McGuinness, did not want them to know. Despite this it was kindly written for a column that could at times be bitchy. It is difficult now to see how Paul McGuinness or Garrett Cooney could use the adjectives 'disgusting' and 'vile' to describe it. The story also included such luminaries as Lord and Lady Inchiquin, the well-known architect Sam Stephenson and his new wife Caroline and wealthy businessman Mark Kavanagh and *his* new wife Kathleen.

In newspaper terms, at least, it had everything. But what may also have upset Paul McGuinness was that other 'diary people' of those weeks in early 1991 were U2 guitarist The Edge and his first wife Aishling, who were splitting up at the time, a break-up that was chronicled in 'The Keane Edge'.

But the weekly column also had something else that was special. Terry Keane, who was separated from her husband, the former High Court Judge and later Chief Justice Ronan Keane, had conducted a long-running affair with the then Taoiseach, Charles J Haughey. It started when he was Minister for Health and continued through his years in the wilderness and his eventual ascension to power. It was a full-blooded affair and they were a familiar sight to the chattering classes at 'First Friday' dinners in the home of a well-known Dublin hostess, at country house parties where discretion could be guaranteed and occasionally on dangerous liaisons on his international travels. And so Charles Haughey, under the pseudonym 'Sweetie', became a familiar character in the weekly diary.

It was a masterful device because it was letting people in on a secret without actually revealing who he was. But to those in the know, 'Sweetie's' doings in 'The Keane Edge' were of far more interest than Charles Haughey's doings as Taoiseach. It is even believed that he quite liked the semi-anonymous notoriety it conferred upon him.

Terry Keane had worked as a fashion writer for the *Sunday Press* before crossing over to the *Sunday Independent* where she was given a staff job and the rather pleasant task of taking someone important to lunch each week and writing what was essentially a cross between an interview and a restaurant critique. But it was her deep connection to the heart of Irish social life, from Charlie Haughey to other wealthy lovers and the 'movers and shakers' of society that led to the column, which Terry Keane herself later claimed she was reluctant to write.

And so 'The Keane Edge' was born. Terry Keane would later describe how she came into the office of the *Sunday Independent* and literally didn't know what to do. Deputy Editor Anne Harris turned up to see how she was getting on and asked her if a bit of gossip about a politician having an affair was true. Terry said she didn't know, but she picked up the phone and with just one call and in a matter of minutes they had a story that none of the other reporters had been able to crack.

After that it quickly became the most talked-about column in the Irish newspapers.

Not only did she reveal the sex of Bono's baby, but a whole string of other scandalous gossip appeared each Sunday, well-written, informative and great fun for the readers. Businessman Michael Smurfit's 'snub' to Charles Haughey, when he refused to share his Chateau Petrus at the official opening of the K-Club, came straight from 'the horse's mouth'. Smurfit would later explain that he always drank from his own bottle, because in that way he was able to measure his intake. But Haughey, who was given an equally good vintage to drink, was incensed because he believed that it was an insult to him that his host would not share the same bottle of wine. Sunday after Sunday the stories poured forth, people were enraged and engaged and for many readers it was a case of straight to the back page after a glance at the front-page headlines. Eamon Dunphy, who was also a columnist with the *Sunday Independent* during much of the same period, would later say of 'The Keane Edge': 'It's pernicious, it's evil, it hurts people'.

But Fintan O'Toole, the Ayatollah of *The Irish Times'* intellectual wing and sometime friend of Dunphy on the Dublin social circuit, described it as 'a delightful satire of Irish social life'.

'Anne Harris has always acknowledged – many times in print – that she was the editor of the diary. She has always acknowledged that the writing was "a collective effort", with a team of writers led by herself and including Terry Keane. Its purpose was social observation and self-satire – something desperately needed in the newly-affluent Ireland. And some of the best writers contributed,' wrote Aengus Fanning in 2002.

But by 1997 Terry Keane had effectively stopped writing the column, although she continued to draw a salary from it. A number of people contributed or wrote pieces including journalists such as Michael Sheridan and John Ryan. Eventually Terry Keane defected to *The Sunday Times* and sensationally revealed her long-term relationship with Charles Haughey on Gay Byrne's last day hosting *The Late Late Show* on RTÉ. It was a devastating blow for Haughey, who was already under pressure from the Moriarty Tribunal which was investigating his once lavish lifestyle. Subsequently Terry Keane started to write a column for the Irish edition of *The Sunday Times*. Occasionally she had a good story but her writing would never come close to the style and sheer exuberance of 'The Keane Edge'.

In the fishbowl of Dublin journalism John Waters was also something to behold. Born in Castlerea, County Roscommon, he had been a clerical worker in CIE before taking over his father's job as a postman. He began sending articles to the music magazine *Hot Press* and they were so well received that in 1984 the editor Niall Stokes gave him a full-time job as a writer and journalist. He later worked as a columnist and editor with *Magill* magazine.

But by now he was the sage of *The Irish Times,* out of step with the trendy, liberal, green-thinking, wine-loving, human rights activists who controlled the paper's news agenda. He had an old-style rural Fianna Fáil ethos, although he managed to articulate it from the safety of south Dublin. John Waters is a good writer and generally regarded as 'a decent fellah'.

But his short-lived relationship with the singer Sinéad O'Connor, with whom he had a child, Roisín, would also greatly influence his writing. His own personal experience of their turbulent relationship and the relentless intrusion of the media caused him to begin a crusade on behalf of the rights of single fathers and would raise the ire of what he called 'femanazis', a number of whom were then working in *The Irish Times.*

John Waters met Sinéad O'Connor in 1995 and they had what was described as 'a brief romance' during which Sinéad became pregnant with her second child. The relationship lasted two months after this event and the couple had even contemplated marriage. The break-up was acrimonious, mainly due to the pressure of publicity.

O'Connor, always a controversial singer, had become world famous after her hit song 'Nothing Compares to U', and controversy turned to notoriety when she pulled a number of publicity stunts, including tearing up a portrait of Pope John Paul II on TV.

Sinéad was living in London and John Waters in Dublin. He did attend Roisín's birth in London on 10 March 1996. The day she was born he wandered out of the hospital and passing a church he went in on impulse. Sitting in a pew he vowed that he would always love and protect his newborn daughter. He also vowed to be an integral part of her upbringing and he would visit her at least once a week if he could make the trip.

During the first three years of her life he made more than a hundred round trips from Dublin to London to be part of her life.

Initially he and Sinéad had a 'reasonably' good relationship and would share custody of their daughter. But then there was a serious breakdown in communications between them. Lawyers were called in on both sides. There were so many newspaper headlines that Waters had to get court orders to prevent further stories about their private family affairs being aired in the press.

In the course of this litigation Waters consulted Dr Ivor Browne in his professional capacity as one of the best-known psychiatrists in Ireland. Indeed Browne had been asked to go to London to give evidence to the family law courts there, but in the end he wasn't needed and had not appeared as a witness. In May 2000 the family case was transferred from London to Dublin and Roisín's future was sorted out. With the consent of Sinéad, she lived with John Waters.

Gradually the long-running saga of their squabble began to fade away, although John Waters continued to voice his concerns on behalf of single fathers in his columns in *The Irish Times*. But then along came Terry Keane in the wake of the *Medea* play in the Abbey Theatre with her column in *The Sunday Times* on 18 June 2000. Not only did she decide to write a column on John Waters' 'Uncredo' as he had called it, but unwisely she decided to draw his still very young daughter Roisín into the squabble.

Under the heading 'Allow Me the Last Word on John Waters' World' the column read:

> Last Tuesday Ireland's foremost masculinist, John Waters, gave a pre-performance talk on *Medea,* which is being staged nightly at the Abbey Theatre to rave reviews. Mr Waters used this opportunity for a gender-based assault. He told us: In the end Medea goes unpunished. Having lost her husband and murdered her own babies, we are to suppose she lived happily ever after?
>
> According to Waters' World: 'I'm afraid I don't believe in love; I don't believe in personality disorder; I don't believe in negative childhood experience; I don't believe in female biochemistry; I don't believe in postnatal depression; I don't believe in hormones; I don't believe in mood swing; I don't believe in self-pity; I don't believe in victimhood; I don't believe in heroines; I don't believe in universal motherhood; I don't believe in strong women; I don't believe in grand passion; I just believe in right and wrong, good and evil.'

His un-credo makes me cringe and my sympathy goes to his toddler, Roisín. When she becomes a teenager and I hope, believes in love, should she suffer from mood swings or any affliction of womanhood, she will be truly goosed. And better not ask dad for tea or sympathy . . . or help.

He also left the stage quickly, thus depriving his audience of any right of reply. But I suppose we can hardly expect him let a woman have the last word.

John Waters said that his reaction on reading this article was one of 'absolute horror' because she had dragged his daughter Roisín into the article. There was, he claimed, a clear implication that he was a bad father, an unsympathetic person, particularly in relation to his daughter and her needs, and that he was an unhelpful or unsupportive father who would not provide assistance when she needed it.

To make matters worse, he said, when he declined to write what is called in newspaper terms 'A Right of Reply', the paper published a clarification without his agreement.

Terry Keane wrote that John Waters had expressed concerns about the tone and content of her article and said that there was a suggestion that he was an unfit father.

'That is not what I said or meant to say. While I disagree strongly with his views on women and their place in society, I have no doubt that John is fit and capable of bringing up his daughter.'

But John Waters found this 'clarification' even more offensive.

'The difficulty is that this would have involved me in a squabble with Ms Keane in *The Sunday Times* about my private capacity as a father (and people) would believe I protest too much. I would have been dragged into it in the context of a debate . . . my fatherhood is an intimate private matter. Why should I have to debate with her if I am a good father . . . I will debate, but not my children's relationship with me. I am a father of a little girl, a single father. Under no circumstances would I engage in any kind of discussion of the private intimate relationship between me and my daughter.'

John Waters sued for libel and the various efforts to settle the matter came to nothing. So on Wednesday 17 April 2002, the case was called for Court No 3 of the Four Courts in Dublin. Waters was accompanied each day by an old friend, the colourful showband singer Derek Dean, and he was represented by two of the best-known barristers in the country, Garrett Cooney SC and Gerry Danaher SC.

Terry Keane came to court accompanied by her friend June Levine and then editor of *The Sunday Times,* Fiona McHugh. It was combative from the very start.

'That Roisín should be metaphorically dragged from her bed and put into the debate left me weak and dizzy with nausea and that any human being would do that to me and to Roisín took my breath away,' said John Waters.

Terry Keane had trawled through the speech looking for something she might 'mangle' to suit her own purposes, he said. What she had done was to misuse his words and what appeared in *The Sunday Times* was the opposite of the truth, which he said was that he loved his daughter above anything else in this world or in his life. He also said that by leaving out the first sentence, which read, 'So, when it comes to actions like these at the core of the play, or even the passions that provoke them, I'm afraid I don't believe...' she had completely distorted the content of his talk at the Abbey.

He also claimed that the article was 'an assault' on his journalistic integrity, in that it implied he would use a talk at the Abbey to engage in 'a rant against women'. He also maintained that by claiming he left the stage hurriedly, there was an implication that he was a coward, which was not true. He had been asked to give a 30-minute talk and he had done so. As someone who 'relished controversy' he would have been able to defend his views if there had been time. But there was not, because the play itself was about to begin.

John Waters said he had written about the family law system in Ireland and how it discriminated against fathers. He said his quarrel with 'feminism' was that it had no interest in putting men back into family life. For 30 years there had been a 'one-sided' debate on gender issues. Although his writings were 'pretty strong stuff', he stood over his views. He disagreed that his views were in any way 'misogynistic' or indeed that he was in some way elitist.

Cathal Ryan, playboy and pilot, died in 2009, 17 years after his scuffle with Michelle Rocca at a birthday party led to the infamous court case in Dublin's High Court.

Michelle Rocca, pictured here (right) during her campaign to win Miss World in 1980, exposed the hedonistic lifestyle of the rich in Ireland during the sensational court battle in 1997 between herself and Cathal Ryan.

Sara Linton, girlfriend of Cathal Ryan at the time of June Moloney's birthday party, was not happy at having to return to Ireland from her new home in Italy in order to testify in the court case.

David Marshall, celebrity hairdresser, witnessed the fight between Michelle and Cathal in the guest bedroom of June Moloney's house on the night of June's 30th birthday.

Even the Ryanair boss got in on the action! Michael O'Leary turned up at Michelle Rocca's house offering a cheque and flowers to try to bring an end to the dispute between Michelle and Cathal.

The relationship between Michelle Rocca and Van Morrison also came under scrutiny during the 1997 court case. The couple later married and had two children.

Adele King, better known as Twink, was caught up in Elio Malocco's web of fraud. However, despite being left in a financial mess by the solicitor, Twink has since forgiven and forgotten.

Elio Malocco, solicitor-to-the-stars, newspaper director, café owner and most famously – guilty of embezzlement.

← One of the richest and most successful businessmen in Ireland, John Magnier worked hard to build up Coolmore Stud and his reputation – and he had no intention of letting Manchester United manager Sir Alex Ferguson ruin either.

← Colourful Dublin barrister Colm Allen was employed by Manchester United manager Alex Ferguson to take his case against John Magnier for a half share in Rock of Gibraltar to the Irish courts.

↑ Man United manager Sir Alex Ferguson (far right) was cosy with Magnier until money got involved – but he picked the wrong Irishman to tangle with this time.

← Magnier's pal JP McManus (left, carrying a newspaper) is also a successful businessman. McManus may have been a Man United fan but when it came to business, he sided with Magnier over Ferguson. He is pictured here with Dermot Desmond.

↑ Magnier's wife, Susan (centre), is also deeply involved in the horse-racing world. In fact Alex Ferguson's horse, Rock of Gibraltar, raced several times wearing her colours.

Writer and *The Irish Times* journalist John Waters took great exception to Terry Keane's comments on a speech he gave on the opening night of a play, *Medea*. The dispute ended up in court where Keane demonstrated her resistance to intimidation.

The second daughter of Bono and his wife, Ali Hewson, was the subject of Terry Keane's gossip column, 'The Keane Edge', before she was even born!

Famous barrister Garett Cooney not only represented John Waters in the libel case he took against Terry Keane, he also represented Cathal Ryan in his court case involving Michelle Rocca.

Terry Keane, pictured here with then Taoiseach Charles J Haughey, was part of a team who wrote the entertaining and witty column 'The Keane Edge' in the *Sunday Independent*. Readers enjoyed speculating on the identity of 'Sweetie', the petname Keane gave to her romantic interest. Over time, it became an open secret that 'Sweetie' was in fact Charlie Haughey.

Keane officially named CJ Haughey as her lover on *The Late Late Show*. She came to regret this action in her later years, believing it would have been better to refrain from openly admitting it.

Sinéad O'Connor and John Waters had a brief relationship which led to the birth of their daughter Roisín. After a rocky beginning, the ex-couple now enjoy a very friendly relationship.

Stanley Roche, a member of the reserved and fabulously wealthy Roches Stores family in Cork, was dragged into the public limelight as a result of his affair with Heide Braun. Braun's husband, Werner, famously sued him for 'criminal conversation', i.e. damaging his 'property'.

Werner Braun, Heide's first husband. His decision to take Stanley Roche and his estranged wife, Heide, to court resulted in some sordid details about his own private life being publicly aired.

Heide Braun, kitted out in a smart suit and jaunty striped hat, was the centre of attention during the court case.

Paul Goldin was one of Ireland's most successful entertainers. His hypnotism shows were almost guaranteed to sell out across the country.

Goldin with third wife, Helen Breen (right), and their daughter Katie-Jane (left).

Goldin faced his fair share of legal disputes. However, when it came to domestic disputes, he favoured his 'disappearing act' as a solution!

Goldin, pictured here with Helen Breen, ended up in court numerous times, fighting cases against disgruntled customers who hadn't found a miraculous cure at one of his many clinics.

A promotional flyer for a young Paul Goldin. Promotional materials dating from the start of his career are littered with incorrect birth dates and false claims to university degrees.

← Anne Bullitt, daughter of writer and American ambassador William C Bullitt, fell in love with Ireland, not least because of her interest in horse racing.

↓ The diamond necklace Anne Bullitt treated herself to when she married Roderic More O'Ferrall in Mexico. The necklace was specially made for her by Cartier in Paris.

↑ Palmerstown House, the mansion Anne Bullitt bought in 1956, was snapped up by developer Jim Mansfield in 1997. After a lengthy legal dispute with the Trustees of Anne Bullitt's Estate, he turned it into the PGA National Ireland golf resort.

A photo showing a teenage Anne Bullitt, her father William C Bullitt and their West Highland terrier, Pie-Pie. This photo was taken at the Château de St Firmin, Chantilly when William was the US Ambassador to France.

Property developer Jim Mansfield fought hard to retain the treasures he discovered in Palmerstown House after he bought it from Anne Bullitt. These treasures included a Picasso painting, a Ming vase, love letters from Eugene O'Neill, dresses by Dior and Givency and a pair of duelling pistols handed down by George Washington.

Dallas star Patrick Duffy came to Ireland in the summer of 1986 to find his Irish roots. At the time, *Dallas* was hugely popular with Irish TV audiences.

Irish actor Daragh O'Malley was eager to start a film production business in Dublin but had no idea that his would-be business partner, James 'Danger' Beirne, was a con-man and fraudster of the highest order.

Hylda Queally (right) was Daragh O'Malley's girlfriend at the time of Danger Beirne's plan to ship fish to Nigeria. She soon realised that Dublin was a very small place in which to establish a talent agency. She moved to LA where she has found enormous success as an agent and now represents some of Hollywood's leading ladies, including Kate Winslet (above left), Angelina Jolie and Cate Blanchett.

James 'Danger' Beirne, the Roscommon football star who ended up in the limelight for all the wrong reasons.

PJ Mara, public relations consultant and former adviser to Charles Haughey, was one of the many movers and shakers attending the party at Whites on the Green when Patrick Duffy visited Dublin.

'There are many kinds of journalists. I have a deep respect for most of them. If you are saying I have some form of snobbery with regard to gossip or social columns, you are wrong. If I was the editor of a newspaper, I would have a gossip column,' he said. But it was when Terry Keane was called to the witness stand that the case became more than just an ordinary libel trial. Witty and debonair she had no intention of lying down under the cross-examination of Garrett Cooney SC, then regarded as the pre-eminent libel lawyer in the country.

Cooney, a big man with a head of steel grey hair, described as behaving in the case 'with the fury and zeal of an Old Testament prophet' was opposite in every way to the witness he was about to cross-examine. From an old Fine Gael family in Athlone, his brother Paddy had been Minister of Justice at the height of the IRA terror in the mid 1970s. Patrick Cooney had been known by some Republicans in the midlands as 'Concrete' Cooney because he had ordered the grave of dead IRA hunger striker Frank Stagg to be encased in cement to prevent the IRA from digging him up to give him a military funeral. His brother Garrett had an equal measure of that implacable determination.

The legal strategy adopted by Waters' lawyers, which became clear from early on, was to turn the jury of 12, 7 women and 5 men, against Terry Keane rather than get involved in a debate about feminism, the rights of single fathers or the issues at the heart of the Greek tragedy *Medea*. The way to do this was to steer clear of such issues and concentrate on Terry Keane and, more importantly, her 12 years as the face of 'The Keane Edge' gossip column in the *Sunday Independent.*

During the early part of his evidence Waters even tried to debate the issues.

'My problem with feminism . . . ,' he began.

'Never mind your problem with feminism, we know your problem with feminism,' interrupted his own counsel, Gerry Danaher SC abruptly. He clearly didn't want to go down the road of thrashing out this issue in court. Both Mr Danaher and Mr Cooney were on far more solid ground, they believed, in tackling the reputation of Terry Keane. And so Garrett Cooney persisted in talking not about *The Sunday Times,* where the libel had been committed, but about the *Sunday Independent* where Terry Keane's notoriety as the author of 'The Keane Edge' was still fresh in the minds of the jurors.

Mr Cooney began cross-examining Terry Keane about an interview she gave after she suddenly left the *Sunday Independent* so that she could sell the story of her love affair with Charles Haughey to *The Sunday Times*. In this interview she agreed with the interviewer that the column she had written and contributed to for 12 years was 'poisonous and pernicious' and she intimated that she only lent her name to it because that was what she was paid to do.

'When something is put to you, you say, "I wasn't there, I was only following orders,"' thundered Mr Cooney. 'Are you telling the jury that although you lent your name to these articles ("The Keane Edge"), you had no responsibility for the content one way or another?'

He then brought up two items in 'The Keane Edge' which had mentioned John Waters and tried to join them with the current article in *The Sunday Times*.

'I put it to you – is it part of a vendetta?' he said.

'I am not conscious there was a vendetta in the *Sunday Independent;* he (John Waters) was regarded in the *Sunday Independent* as a man with a blind spot about men's rights,' answered Keane.

'Who said it?'

'I don't know who said it. I would have had that impression. I don't know if anybody had heard of him until he started going out with Sinéad O'Connor.'

Mr Cooney then referred to a story in 'The Keane Edge' which he found 'most offensive' in which the piece had 'sympathised' with Sinéad O'Connor for not divulging the name of the father of her child.

'Maybe sympathy was the wrong word to use,' replied Keane. 'I mean, I was probably so glad that she had shut up for once about being a nun or a priest or a lesbian or whatever. It's just – actually I probably should have said it if I had written it – I also am very relieved that she is not burdening us with any more of her details.'

After he had finished with the substantial issue of Terry Keane's views of Sinéad O'Connor and John Waters, Mr Cooney then moved back again to her columns in the *Sunday Independent,* asking her the meaning of 'Her

Poloness' – a nickname she frequently used for Mary Robinson, the first female President of Ireland.

'She mostly wore polo necks and she was deified by everybody and it was a funny remark – it was a pun on polos and holiness.' She had, she said, worked for 12 years on 'The Keane Edge' as part of a team but she had been either 'very bad or very dim' to allow her name to be used as the author of these columns. She claimed that some of the time she was living in Kerry and when she read the columns she found them 'cringe-making'.

'It started off as funny and entertaining, not malicious and pernicious, but it did become that,' she said. She added that she had been uncomfortable with the column for a number of years and didn't actually write it, although she continued to draw a salary from Independent Newspapers.

'When you have very little money you sometimes have to do the unpleasant job. If I had known, I would have cleaned latrines,' she said, using a military term for toilets. 'We have to regret the past, not change it.'

Then Mr Cooney referred to another piece about John Waters, which she wrote for the *Sunday Independent,* which he claimed was part of the 'vendetta' against his client. The piece accused him of 'populist rubbish' as he had called Independent newspaper journalists 'lackeys' because they referred to the proprietor as Dr A J F O'Reilly (later Sir Anthony O'Reilly) and not 'Tony' as he had been known during his sporting career as an Irish and Lions rugby player. Keane made the point that *The Irish Times* journalists were equally guilty as they did not refer to their then proprietor as 'Tommy' McDowell, they gave him the dubious title of 'Major' Thomas McDowell.

Terry Keane said that she left the *Sunday Independent* suddenly after she was offered IR£65,000 'hello money' by *The Sunday Times* to write the sensational story of her long-running affair with Charles Haughey and a 2-year contract at IR£50,000 to write 48 articles. Pressed by Mr Cooney to reveal the difference between her salaries at both papers she answered, 'I suppose after tax a couple of hundred quid.'

When the case eventually moved on from the *Sunday Independent* and got into the details of what the libel action was actually about, (i.e. the talk that John Waters had given before a performance of the play *Medea* in the Abbey Theatre,) Terry Keane continued to hold her ground in spite of the onslaught from Mr Cooney SC. Although she had not been present on the night she said that after reading the script she found his views, 'at least intemperate and insulting and obsessively cracked'.

'Did you say cracked?' asked Judge Nicholas Kearns.

'Cracked, cracked pot, crackpot . . . in that context,' she answered. 'I think it was an assault on women, he frequently does have these gender assaults on women in his column.'

In relation to her piece she said that if Waters' views were really those expressed on the stage of the Abbey Theatre, he would be unsympathetic to his daughter in the future if she was having boyfriend trouble or PMT. Lots of parents, she said, were unsympathetic if their children came in late. It made them concerned parents. She did not think Waters was a bad father. As a mother of four children herself, she thought children needed 'sympathy'.

'John Waters is eccentric and very sensitive,' she said.

'Only somebody paranoid and oversensitive would have read my piece the way he did,' she added.

Questioned about the writing process, she insisted that she had not seen the original script, indeed she didn't know that June Levine had a copy of it. She said she had taken notes from her friend and later phoned her back to check if they were accurate. She was using June Levine's impressions as a member of the audience on the night that John Waters gave the talk and she had no reason to believe that June Levine had any 'agenda' or was lying about what had happened that night.

What puzzled Gerry Danaher SC, who was also relishing his role acting for the offended Waters, was how the words of his client's 'Uncredo' appeared in *The Sunday Times* in such detail, even if their meaning was distorted. June Levine, who had been given the script on the night, claimed that she had mislaid the original document. Terry Keane said she was never shown the script, yet it had appeared in her column, word perfect, right down to the punctuation.

'You saw how the stenographer had to ask John Waters to slow down,' Mr Danaher told the jury. 'Yet June Levine takes down her notes at the talk and then from them Terry Keane takes down notes and gives them to the typists and they got the punctuation just right, down to the semi-colons. It's funny that chain, that luck, all the way along the line to the article – that they got it right.'

Mr Eoin McCullough SC, who acted for the defence, said that the central issue in the case was whether the words bore the meaning of which John Waters had complained – that he was a bad father. The case, he said, was unusual, in that it was between two well-known and controversial journalists. His columns were 'forceful' while Terry Keane's columns had always been controversial.

It was after the closing speeches that Mr Cooney SC then dramatically stood up and sought to call Paul McGuinness, the manager of U2, to refute Terry Keane's recollection of 'the sex of Bono's baby' saga and to produce letters which were written at the time in which she did not deny she was the author and further refused to apologise to either the singer or his wife Ali.

Garrett Cooney SC wanted to recall Terry Keane to the witness stand.

'The purpose will be simply to relate to Mrs Keane's credibility, because the constant theme throughout her evidence was, yes, she was associated with a gossip column which was pernicious and capricious, which had done a lot of harm to people, but she always regretted it, and at the first opportunity she expressed regret and apology, and she signalled this by referencing this incident. In fact the evidence of Mr McGuinness is to the contrary – she was given an opportunity to apologise personally and she never did it,' he said.

Judge Nicholas Kearns said that while he understood 'the sensitivities' that prompted Paul McGuinness to offer to give evidence, he decided there was no legal basis to re-open the case. As Terry Keane was already out of the country on holidays in Spain she could not be recalled to give further evidence. Judge Kearns concluded that deciding the case, which took three days to hear in the Four Courts, was not 'rocket science'.

'Bring buckets of common sense in making your decision and conduct your deliberations in a calm and dispassionate way,' he told the jury. There were three issues to be decided. Firstly, did the words of Terry Keane mean what John Waters took them to mean, that he was a bad father. The second issue was whether *The Sunday Times* had justified its grounds for using the article. The third issue was the question of damages.

There were only 11 members left on the jury, as one of them had been excused the previous afternoon. After 2 hours and 30 minutes they came back to find that John Waters had not used his speech in the Abbey to mount a 'gender-based attack' on women. They also found that the article written by Terry Keane did imply he was a 'bad father' who would unfairly withhold sympathy from his daughter and that he had acted in a cowardly manner by denying the audience a 'right of reply' by hurriedly leaving the stage.

The jury awarded him €84,000.

The following morning on RTÉ's *Morning Ireland* radio programme, one observer noted that 'Terry Keane was John Waters' best witness'.

Sadly Terry Keane, who had added so much to the 'gaiety of the nation', died at the age of 68 on 31 May 2007.

John Waters continues to write for *The Irish Times* and shrugged off the further ire of his newspaper's intelligensia by writing Ireland's Eurovision Song Contest entry in 2006. He has also collaborated with his former lover, Sinéad O'Connor, on a song called 'Baby, Let Me Buy You a Drink'. Waters acknowledged to the music magazine *Hot Press* that 'eyebrows might be raised' by this – 'particularly' considering their much publicised break-up following the birth of their daughter.

'This is life,' he added. 'Time changes everything. We get on wonderfully these days. We had a very full-on relationship while it lasted. Nothing that happens is separate from who you are. We were very full-on people and, inevitably, when a feeling turns, it goes radically in the other direction for a while.'

'I have great time for Sinéad, quite separately from our relationship as parents. I think Sinéad is a genius – a musical genius. So we get on very well now and we have the most amazing child, who fills us with wonder every day. How could you be looking at that – the creation you've been involved in – and not be reconciled in some profound way, you know? I have a much better relationship with Sinéad than with pretty much any other ex of mine.'

Bono's baby, Memphis Eve, who was born in July 1991, and became the unintended subject of such a turbulent court case, has grown up to become a beautiful teenager.

Chapter 5
The Merchant Prince and the German Chattel

Werner Braun walked through the grand lobby of the Imperial Hotel on the South Mall in Cork, approached the reception desk and casually asked for the key to Room 34. He had phoned earlier and knew that was the room in which she was staying. He asked politely, with the practised air of a regular guest.

The receptionist asked Werner for the name the room was booked under. He told her it was booked in the name of his wife, Heide Braun.

'She's out visiting some friends right now,' he said, his soothing German voice calming whatever suspicions the receptionist might have. She handed him the key.

He turned and walked across the marble hallway of the city's finest hotel. Keeping his calm, he walked up the fine staircase and quickly found the room. It was Valentine's Day, Sunday 14 February 1971 but Werner Braun's thoughts were anything but romantic that afternoon.

He looked around the empty hotel bedroom touching her things, all so familiar yet all so distant now. As he did so he became more agitated and he began to rummage through the bureau and the drawers in the wardrobe.

He scattered her underwear and other personal belongings across the bed as he continued his search. With almost triumphant relish, he found a packet of contraceptives and a pornographic magazine. He hadn't seen her for several weeks and all the time the pain and the hurt of her betrayal had gnawed at him, occupying every minute of his waking hours and even preventing him from sleeping at night. Now it was turning to rage.

He took a breadknife from the bag he was carrying and put it on a table near the window. There was also a bottle of pills in his bag and he began to consume them, one by one, chewing on them for no other reason than because it heightened his emotion. He knew that after years of rancour, after numerous affairs and reconciliations, things were finally coming to a head.

Heide was his and his alone. He knew, of course, that like him she had taken lovers before. But it had never really been serious. They had been living out the Sixties – the sexual revolution. They had been playing. But now she had met a man who was different, a man of power and influence, a man who seemed just as besotted with her as she was with him. Heide was getting away from Werner.

The pills didn't seem to be having much effect. He stopped his restless pacing of the room, pulling at things. He sat on the bed and began to undress. But then he changed his mind. He was slightly confused and instead of putting on his trousers which were thrown on the other side of the bed, he found a pair of her slacks hanging over a chair. He put them on and sat back on the bed to wait. It was about 3.30 in the afternoon and the breadknife still lay menacingly on the table on the other side of the room when she opened the door and walked in.

She got a shock when she saw him sitting half dressed on the edge of the bed, his eyes bulging from the pills and rage, his face seething with anger.

'I won't tolerate it – you behaving like Stanley Roche's whore,' he screamed in German as the door closed behind her with an ominous click.

'I'll do whatever I want, I'm not married to you anymore,' she shouted back. She was accustomed to this kind of scene. She had put up with it all her married life, but she wasn't having any more of it now. Now it was all over, the shouting, the beating, the ill-treatment. She had found someone new, someone who knew how to treat a lady, someone who was not consumed by these jealous rages and fits of uncontrollable anger.

The sound coming from the room was so loud it carried down the elegant hallway and into the foyer of the hotel where guests sipped afternoon tea. Hearing the racket above, the porter left his desk and began to make his way up the staircase, alarmed at the noise and the disturbance it was causing to other guests. From inside the room he could hear what was being said.

'If you don't do this I will kill you,' Werner Braun was shouting at his wife, brandishing a piece of paper which said that she, Heide Braun, was the wife of Werner Braun, and demanding that she sign it.

She told him she would sign nothing. Suddenly he jumped up and rushed across the room and hit her on the head. It was a glancing blow, but she felt it. But her surprise turned to fear when she saw him locking the bedroom door. She knew he was now dangerously out of control. It wasn't the first time that he had hit her. But those other times when she had admitted having affairs, it was like clearing the air, and they would get back together again. Love and hate, hate and love – such close emotions. But this time she knew there was no going back.

He knew it too – and that was why he was so enraged. She couldn't take her eyes off the breadknife lying menacingly on the bedside table. She didn't know whether he intended to carry out his threat to kill her. He was in such a rage that she believed he was capable of anything. But she was a tough woman. She knew this man since she was a teenager. Their life together had been turbulent. They had both had affairs before and yet they had survived the rows and recriminations that followed.

They had come here to Cork to escape their past, but now it looked as if the present was even more dangerous than she had ever imagined. Now the noise and the threats from inside Room 34 roused the hall porter to finally intervene.

'Let me in,' he asked plaintively. But they ignored him, screaming at each other in guttural German and sometimes in Cork-accented English.

'I'll make you pay for this,' said Werner Braun again. 'You'll sign a document that you are my wife,' he roared.

'I'll sign nothing,' Heide screamed back at him.

And it went on and on until the Gardaí arrived, and together with the porter they forced the door open and burst into the room. Heide was dishevelled but unhurt. Her husband Werner cowered in a corner, knowing it was all over now. He was bundled discreetly from the hotel and into a waiting Garda car.

What was going on, hotel guests wondered?

But the affray was covered up. The reputation of Werner and Heide Braun was hardly an issue, although Cork was then a small town where everybody knew everybody. Neither of them had been around long enough to be very well known or cared about.

But already there were whispers in the wind. Heide Braun was having an affair with Stanley Roche, a man who was so well known in that small city that he was regarded as one of the 'merchant princes' of Cork. That was most certainly a very different thing.

Stanley James Roche, the son of William Roche, founder of Roches Stores, a man of wealth and importance, was married to Carrie and had two teenage children. Stanley Roche was a man of substance in the city where substance and status were so very important in such an obvious way. A scene in a well-known hotel, talk of an affair and the scandal that was involved – well, that was very different altogether. Some things could be brushed under the carpet, but as one wealthy sage said, they had a dreadful habit of re-appearing when least expected.

That was something Stanley Roche would find out to be true and it would haunt him for the rest of his long life. The events that took place that Valentine's Day in the Imperial Hotel in Cork were hushed up, but Werner Braun was determined that if his marriage was over he would do his best to destroy the reputation of the man who had made a mistress out of his wife.

Sex, it was claimed, started in Ireland with *The Late Late Show*. But in the steamy atmosphere of the monied classes in Cork there wasn't just sex, there were exotic varieties of it that most Irish people had never contemplated and certainly wouldn't hear publicly aired for at least another generation.

Back in 1972 the sexual revolution of the 1960s had yet to sweep across the Irish Sea. But there was a lot going on in the peace and tranquillity of rural Ireland that the clergy and the middle classes didn't know very much about.

When Ans Doppe described in the High Court in Dublin on Wednesday 21 June 1972, a 'threesome' involving herself and a couple of friends called Werner and Heide Braun, the term was a mystery to most of those who read the tastefully described but lurid details buried on page 13 of *The Irish Times*. Ironically the readers were being treated to the intriguing and scandalous details of a case of Criminal Conversation, or as the lawyers like to call it 'Crim Con' – a legal offence which recognised a wife as a 'chattel' (legal property) of her husband. A husband could sue a man for damaging one of his possessions (i.e., his wife) in the same way that somebody could sue a person who damaged their car, house, antique furniture or livestock. This 'offence' had been abolished in Britain in 1857, but it was still happily on the Irish statute books when this particular case was called before the High Court in Dublin more than a century, 117 years to be precise, later.

After his 'episode' in the Imperial Hotel in Cork, Werner Braun had not been charged with assaulting his wife, causing an affray or any other offence. It was, the authorities believed, an 'unfortunate' episode that was best swept under the carpet. But Werner Braun didn't want his wife's affair with Stanley Roche swept under any carpet. He wanted the world to know about it.

And he knew exactly how to go about it. Just two years earlier a prominent Senator in the Irish parliament had been seriously embarrassed when a case of Criminal Conversation was brought against him in the High Court. Werner Braun was determined to go down the same route – even employing the same barrister, the thunderous Ernest Wood SC, described as 'a tremendous advocate' who relished the job of acting for the small man against powerful and wealthy interests.

And that's why Braun embarked on a case of Criminal Conversation against Stanley Roche in the High Court in Dublin. This was an event that would have to be covered by the newspapers. The court action and the press coverage could only cause maximum embarrassment to Stanley Roche and the highly respected business family he came from – a family that liked to keep very much to themselves.

And that's how Ans Doppe ended up describing to an Irish jury how she was in the home of Werner and Heide Braun in Amsterdam drinking sherry when Werner and Heide went into the bedroom together. A few minutes later she followed, taking her sherry with her. The three undressed and got into bed. She and Werner had sexual intercourse while his wife Heide looked on. It was, she told the rather frigid gathering in Court No 4 of the High Court in Dublin, an 'enjoyable experience' but after this great understatement she did not further elaborate – and with typical Irish distaste in the 1970s for sexual mores, she wasn't asked to.

Heide Braun was also quite matter-of-fact about the encounter. She told the court that her husband had at least five affairs that she knew of – and on this particular occasion she was absolutely sure of her facts because he had sex with another woman while she was present in their marital bed. It all made for a rather exciting court case in dull old Dublin of the early 1970s – a city afflicted by recessions and IRA violence where the most you could expect from an exciting court case was a headline like the one further down the page of *The Irish Times* – 'Ex-Boxer's Ear Bitten Off in Pub Brawl'.

But this was a different class of court case. It wasn't only the sex that caused much of the excitement; the presence at the centre of events of one of the brothers who owned the famous Roches Stores department stores, which had started in Cork but now had stores around the country, also added to the excitement.

When Werner Braun of Killowan, Blarney, County Cork sued Stanley James Roche of 'The Cottage', Oysterhaven, County Cork in 1972 claiming that he had 'debauched' and 'carnally known' his wife Heide Braun, it was one of the most sensational cases of its kind to come before the courts.

Because Werner Braun was not only putting the details of his private life in a very public forum, he was also suing one of Ireland's richest men for damages for stealing his wife. The case shone a light into the once private world of this merchant prince and led to a change in Irish law following the howls of outrage from liberals, appalled that such an out-dated statute could be involved in so-called 'modern Ireland' – a country which they believed was at last beginning to emerge from the long shadow of de Valera and Archbishop John Charles McQuaid.

Criminal Conversation had long been a favoured legal manoeuvre by husbands whose wives had been seduced by other men. But it was a double-edged sword – they might get large sums in compensation, they might even ruin their adversary, but the lurid details of their private lives would also be splashed across the newspapers of the day.

Among the more famous cases was Massey v the Marquess of Headford which went to trial in 1804. Charles Massey was a Protestant clergyman who married a pretty young lady named Miss Rosslewin. She had an affair with the Marquess of Headford, when he was stationed with the Army in Limerick. He was 50 and she was in her early twenties, but with his enormous income of £30,000 a year she managed to find him very attractive.

The lovers eventually eloped to England. Massey sued for £40,000 damages – an enormous sum in those days – and the case was marked by the scurrilous speeches of the lawyers for both sides, as often happens in such cases. The jury brought in a verdict awarding £10,000 to Massey, who went on to enjoy the Marquess of Headford's money and another three wives before his eventual death.

Even more sensational was the case of Valentine Viscount Cloncurry v Sir John Bennett Piers for Criminal Conversation in 1807. Cloncurry, who built the beautiful Lyons Demesne in west Dublin (which was restored by the aviation millionaire Tony Ryan in the 1990s) and Piers had been childhood friends in Westmeath. When Cloncurry returned from 'the Grand Tour' (a leisurely tour of Europe undertaken by most young aristocrats in the nineteenth century) he employed an Italian artist called Gabrielli to paint four famous murals in the newly-constructed Lyons Demesne.

Around the same time someone in their aristocratic circle had a wager with Sir John Piers that he couldn't seduce Cloncurry's beautiful young wife Eliza Morgan. However Piers was equal to the task and made short work of the seduction – but Gabrielli, watching from his perch as he painted the murals, saw some of the carry-on, while Cloncurry himself became suspicious when his wife disappeared among the box-hedges in the walled garden arm-in-arm with the dashing young Piers. It is still not known whether or not Cloncurry was in on the wager.

'Sir John Piers is an infamous wretch, he is determined on my ruin,' said Lady Cloncurry, admitting her seduction.

'Piers, don't drive Lady Cloncurry to infamy, quit this place and God bless you,' Cloncurry is reported to have said when he confronted his noble friend, who was out shooting rabbits on the estate at the time.

But attitudes seemed to have hardened considerably when Lady Cloncurry gave birth to a 'spurious offspring' and Lord Cloncurry sued Piers for 'crim con'. He won his case and was awarded £20,000 in damages, enough to ruin his former friend who had already fled to the Isle of Man. Ruined and ostracised, Piers eventually returned to Ireland and hid himself away behind high walls at his famous house of Tristernagh so that Cloncurry's bailiffs couldn't get at him. Such stories were the stuff of legend.

By the 1970s most people were unaware of this ancient legal statute, but two high-profile cases were about to whet the public appetite for sex and scandal.

The first case involved a promiment member of the Irish senate.

'The defendant in this case is Mr Patrick McGowan, who lives for most of the time in Lifford (County Donegal). He is an hotelier, a member of the Senate and an unmitigated blackguard,' declared Mr Ernest Wood SC in the High Court on 5 June 1970, opening the case of Brolly v McGowan.

'Lest you should be in any doubt of the reality and the gravity and the shamefulness of the defendant, let me tell you at the outset that he is living with the plaintiff's wife openly, with a child of the union he formed and that he has made the plaintiff's wife his captive woman,' continued Mr Wood, one of the most famous advocates of his generation.

Daniel Brolly was a 'ganger' with the Board of Works who had fathered five children with his wife, Anne Mary (Annette) Maxwell, during the 16 years of their marriage. When his wife, described in court as 'this dazzled woman', got a job hanging curtains in the Inter County Hotel owned by the businessman and well-known Donegal politician Senator Paddy McGowan, things took a dramatic turn for the worst as far as Brolly was concerned.

The affair began in the spring of 1969 and by May of that year Brolly began to hear whispers and became concerned about his 34-year-old wife's behaviour with the Senator. According to himself he was 'deeply in love' with Annette and decided to go to Senator McGowan's home in Ballybofey to plead with him to leave his wife alone.

When he appealed to the Senator to 'send my wife back to me', he was laughed at. According to Wood, Brolly was subjected to 'the sort of threats that the big man in the town can make to the little man who is only a ganger'. Eventually the local priest intervened and one night brought Annette Brolly back to her husband at 1.30 a.m. But she only stayed a week before bolting again. Brolly discovered in mid August 1969 that his two youngest children were on holidays with Senator McGowan in a caravan on the Donegal coast. On 5 October that year his wife told him she was expecting a child.

'I was terribly shocked. I went to Senator McGowan and said could nothing be done about this because it was terrible for my youngsters to have to bear this burden,' declared Brolly. 'He sniggered at me and he rang my wife and told her what I had said.'

'I wanted the youngster – there is a word for it and I don't know what it is – I wanted the baby taken away. It was going to be a very sore slap to my young children.'

Although Brolly later conceded that he wanted his wife to have an abortion, he said he didn't really know the name of the procedure or fully understand the significance of it at the time.

He admitted that when his wife came in late one night in November he struck her on the face. The following May a child was born to Senator Patrick McGowan and Annette Maxwell. The court heard that when Brolly and Annette married in 1953 he was 31 and she was 17.

Brolly denied that he had sex with his wife in a car outside a dance hall five months before their marriage – or that he had sex with her against her will when she was just 16.

'He had never heard of her having expressed a wish to enter a convent, and he did not tell her that if she did not marry him he would slander her through County Donegal. Neither did he tell her that she was pregnant and would not be accepted in a convent,' said the court report at the time.

'I suggest,' said Mr Vincent Landy SC appearing for Senator McGowan, 'that this innocent 17-year-old girl told you she did not intend to remain your wife.'

'No,' replied Brolly, 'I knew she was going to throw the book at me to save Mr McGowan. She is prepared to tell a string of lies to protect him.'

Brolly then admitted shouting abuse at Senator McGowan in the chamber of Donegal County Council on 16 February. The Senator was chairman of the council and as he was coming out he 'sniggered' at him.

Brolly then hit him over the head with an iron bar.

'Did you injure him?' asked Mr Landy.

'Unfortunately not fatally,' replied Brolly.

'Your object in going to the council was to blacken Mr McGowan and put him out of public life?'

'I don't know if you are married, but if you were in my shoes maybe you would do the same thing,' replied Brolly.

This highly entertaining case was due to go on for several days but after the first day's evidence Senator McGowan, a small butty man who looked an unlikely Romeo, decided to settle the action for Criminal Conversation brought against him by Brolly. Without admitting liability he agreed to a settlement of £3,900.

Despite severe criticism at the time, both religious and political, Senator

McGowan went on to have a long and productive political career and was a member of the Irish senate at the time of his death.

The public appetite for scandal had certainly been whetted by the case and it was no surprise that two years later Werner Braun and his legal advisors should go to Mr Ernest Wood SC to help them embark on a similar case against Stanley Roche, which was heard before Mr Justice Butler and a jury in the High Court in Dublin in the balmy summer days of June 1972.

Heide was very much the star of the show. She looked every inch the femme fatale in her smart suit and her cheerful white-banded trilby-style hat. Her style was more suited to the winners enclosure at the Curragh Racecourse than the austere surroundings of the Four Courts. Her former husband, Werner Braun, with his slicked-back hair and his stiffly-collared white shirt, put on the dour front of the 'wronged husband'.

Of Stanley James Roche there were no photographs. And 35 years later we still know little or nothing about the businessman who along with other members of his family controlled the Roches Stores chain (although in recent years the chain has become a highly profitable property company rather than the retailer it once was).

But for a few brief days around the summer solstice of 1972 newspaper readers were treated to one of the most lurid court cases carried in an Irish newspaper. It also introduced to many for the first time the idea of a different moral code that had broken out of the strict Irish concept that chastity and sexual fidelity were 'moral' and anything outside that was immoral.

The scandalous message that emerged from the Braun v Roche case was that there was far more going on in the little seaside village of Oysterhaven than most people would have believed. Because it seemed that while Heide Braun was having a torrid affair with Stanley Roche, her husband Werner was having an affair with Stanley Roche's wife Carrie. At least that was one of the allegations bandied about during the two days of sensational evidence. The mere possibility of 'wife swapping' on the southern coast was enough to excite newspaper editors. But when you added 'three-in-a-bed sex' and an 'outraged husband' in the form of Werner Braun to the mix, it was in many ways a breakthrough in Irish court reporting.

Stanley Roche's family was extremely rich, but in a patrician sort of way. They were 'old money', but they had earned it in trade rather than as part of the landed gentry. They lived a good lifestyle but they did not generally flaunt their wealth, preferring to stay in business and spend their leisure time in the various sailing clubs dotted along the Cork coast, mostly the Royal Cork Yacht Club, said to be the oldest sailing club in the world, where they mixed easily with all classes of people. But they remained very 'Cork' – they rarely mixed in Dublin society. They kept to themselves. While they might have a great deal of money they made sure it was all very 'low key', and they most certainly avoided getting involved in scandalous court cases.

'The man (Stanley Roche) with his wealth has not merely debauched Mr Braun's wife, but has corrupted her. Mr Braun's only vindication is the damages in your hands,' said Mr Ernest Wood SC opening the case before Mr Justice Butler and a jury in the High Court in Dublin.

While the scandalous evidence that unfolded over the next two days told the troubled story of Werner Braun and his beautiful wife, Heide, it revealed little or nothing about Stanley Roche or the privileged and wealthy background from which he came and which was now reluctantly in the public gaze. His lawyers were obviously instructed that on no account were they to divulge the family secrets of one of the country's richest but most retiring clans – a family that had built a retailing empire which carried their name, but which revealed almost nothing about itself outside the confines of their own homes or the boardroom.

But the Brauns enjoyed no such luxury. Their life and promiscuous times were revealed in all their lurid detail in the stuffy atmosphere in Court No 4. It was even suggested during the opening day in court that there was something very different about the Brauns – because they were married in a Registry Office as opposed to a church.

'I don't know if religion has anything to do with this case,' declared Judge Butler when the matter of their religion became an issue. But then he felt compelled to reveal to the jury that in the 'pleadings' – documents handed in to the court before the case commenced – both Heide and Werner Braun had declared themselves as Catholics. Presumably they were a very different strain of Catholic to the members of the jury, who were far more likely at that time to be the more traditional Irish variety.

Heide Braun met her future husband Werner when she was a 15-year-old

High School student in Ladenburg, Germany where they both lived. When she was 17 she 'got to know him better' and began working in his office as a secretary.

'Within a few weeks you were having sexual relations with her?' suggested Mr Oliver Gogarty SC for the defendant in the case, Stanley Roche.

'It was certainly more than a few weeks,' replied Werner Braun.

'But did you have sexual relations when she was seventeen or seventeen and a half?'

'We first had intercourse when she decided to come to England with me,' Werner Braun replied.

In any event the two of them started going out together and quite soon they formed a sexual relationship, even though Werner Braun was 15 years older than Heide. Then the company he was working for decided to transfer him to Cardiff in Wales, and he asked Heide to go with him. He told her that if after three months she didn't like it, he would pay her fare back to Germany.

So they moved to a place near Shrewsbury in the English West Midlands. Some time later her residency permit came up for renewal, but the Home Office refused to let her stay on. She and Werner talked about going back to Germany, but in the end they decided that Heide would return to Germany, but then come back to England where they would marry – which they did in August 1960.

They lived for a time at Stratford-on-Avon and then he was transferred to Holland. But Werner had a row with his employer and they moved back to Ladenburg and lived with her mother. It was there that their first baby was born, a daughter. But already Heide was getting restless. She claimed that during this time she felt that both she and her husband 'should have their own lives' before they got too old. It was the 1960s and she was young and caught up in the sexual revolution. She said she asked him at this stage to separate. He refused to give her a divorce.

He then got a job in Amsterdam and they moved to Holland in August 1963. Their son Owen was born in June 1964, but six months later Heide developed tuberculosis (TB). She later claimed that when she recovered and left hospital she told her husband that she no longer loved him. He 'accepted' it, but was upset. While they continued to live together she had a succession of affairs. Unfortunately he found her lovers' letters and one night he got 'very violent' and beat her.

'No wife of mine is going to fool around and make a idiot of me – I won't stand for that,' he told her.

'I want a divorce,' she pleaded.

'You can have one, you can go, but you can't bring the children,' he replied.

'You know I will not leave without them,' she answered.

So they remained in Holland until July 1968, having constant rows according to her. One of the problems was that she didn't want to have sex with him, and if nothing else, Werner was a red-blooded male. When a woman who lived across the road from them in Amsterdam and who did some typing for him, Marjelina Tonino, was in the office one day with Werner, he tried to put his hand up her skirt. He asked her to go to bed with him, but she declined.

Another night when Werner and Heide were drinking with her friend Ans Dobbe the three of them went to bed together. Werner and Ans had sex while Heide was in the bed with them.

'It was enjoyable,' said Dobbe, who lived in Dusseldorf and had a child.

But then in 1968 the Brauns decided to move to Ireland to start a new life. Werner set up an import agency in Cork and Heide got involved in various different ventures. She met Carrie Roche, the wife of Stanley Roche, one of the owners of Roches Stores.

Heide was stylish and ambitious. Although she was the mother of two young children, she wanted a career of her own and her new friend Carrie encouraged her – using her husband's many connections, of course. Both were very interested in clothes and Heide opened a boutique in their home at Killowen, near Blarney in the early summer of 1968. It was during that same summer that the 'spark' was kindled between Heide and her friend's husband, Stanley Roche.

Although the boutique closed after six months because she wasn't doing enough business, Stanley Roche introduced her to Christy Kelleher who had established The Blarney Woollen Mills and was a friend of his. Heide began making high fashion designer dresses but most of the firm's business was with visiting American tourists who wanted Báinín hats and Aran sweaters, rather than the fashionable clothes she was making.

Heide regarded herself as a 'director' of the Kelleher family firm, but that too came to a premature end and her services were dispensed with. At this stage Heide was pregnant with the couple's third child, and according to Werner they were happy. But then tragedy struck. Their third child, born in April 1970, was very ill at birth and only survived a few hours.

'It may have been the loss of this child that left her in an unsettled state,' said Ernest Wood SC later when all these matters came into the very public arena of the High Court in Dublin.

Three months after their child died Heide met Stanley Roche 'casually' one day. His wife was at their holiday home in Spain for a month and he was on his own. Stanley asked her out for a drink and she agreed. As it happened they picked a public house in the small village of Towers near Blarney. While they were having their drink Heide expressed her disgust at the décor. As it also happened Stanley Roche had just acquired a financial interest in the pub – so he asked her to do it up. He told her not to spare any expense and she didn't. Even her husband liked the idea. She had been sad and restless since the death of her baby and this interior design job gave her something to do.

But unknown to Werner the pub was another project of Stanley Roche's. By now the wealthy businessman, with his yachts and a fleet of cars, was smitten with Heide and they became lovers within a short time of their first drink together. After the pub was finished Stanley Roche took Heide on as a 'consultant' to his store in Cork. They began to go away on 'business trips' together with such regularity that finally Werner Braun began to suspect that there was something going on between his wife and the wealthy merchant prince.

First they went on buying trips locally in Cork, but then they began to go further afield. Stanley, who had a fleet of cars, several yachts and no shortage of money, bought his new lover a trendy Triumph Spitfire as a 'company car'. It was bright yellow and she loved it, but the first time she turned up at Killowen in her new toy she and Werner had a row about it.

'It's essential to have a good car to impress clients in the places I am going to,' she told him, dismissing the Mini he had bought her as a

Christmas present the previous year as if it was nothing.

'Get rid of it, if you like, keep the money,' she said dismissively.

Before Christmas, Heide and Werner were having a drink and awaiting the arrival of Stanley Roche, who was to join them. Werner told his wife that he had got an anonymous Christmas card alleging she was having an affair with Stanley Roche. He asked her about it.

'Well, I can imagine where it comes from. Why don't you show it to Stanley Roche when he comes?'

He did. The card said that Werner Braun was 'a pimp' and Roches Stores was 'the best place for turkeys'. It also said that Werner Braun 'would be well off after the bank strike' (the long bank strike which took place in 1970) – implying he knew about his wife's infidelity.

Stanley Roche read the anonymous card and said, 'I received anonymous letters and things before and I just burned them'.

They both assured Werner that their friendship was purely 'platonic' and that there was nothing going on. Although Werner remained suspicious, given his wife's previous affairs, he was reassured for a while.

'Not only at that stage was he (Stanley Roche) a liar, but he was too cowardly to admit his guilt,' maintained Ernest Wood SC.

Werner brooded about his wife's previous affairs – 'but I forgave her because I thought it was all over'.

But as time moved on it was getting more difficult for him. He seemed to like Ireland and he wanted to settle at last. His business was going relatively well and he wanted to stay with Heide, if only for the sake of their children, who were now growing up and bringing a bit of stability to his life.

That December Werner Braun went to Germany on business, telling his wife she was to stay in Killowen with their children. But he had her watched and when he got back from the trip he was told that she too had been away, leaving the children in the care of their 'nanny' who was also privy to Heide's secret affair with Stanley Roche. Christmas was a difficult time and by January his suspicions were confirmed. He knew for certain that his wife was being unfaithful to him and having sex with Stanley Roche. Werner Braun had decided to play private detective.

'On a certain date she was in Cork. I asked her to be back at 2 p.m. and she was not. I went to Roches Stores, where she said she was going and the man in the parking lot said she was not there. I went down to Kinsale to Mr Roche's cottage and there she was. She was having lunch with Mr Roche and a friend of ours, a girl who had come over from Holland with us and looked after the children.'

'If I want to see my wife I don't want to have to come to your cottage,' Werner told Stanley Roche. 'I know what is going on. I won't tolerate you carrying on with my wife.'

But Heide turned on him. 'I love Stanley,' she told him.

'I'm very disappointed,' he said, as he prepared to leave.

'If it's any consolation to you, I haven't had sex with him,' said Heide.

'That is so,' confirmed Stanley Roche.

But by now Werner believed that they were having an affair and on 16 January Heide told him she was going to Germany to see her mother.

'I'd like to get away from things and consider where we're going. I might feel differently when I get back.'

But Heide Braun never came back.

'She told me that I had been mean to her and she wasn't coming back,' he said later, revealing that she had finally told him she was leaving him via a telephone call.

The couple later arranged a meeting in the room in the Imperial Hotel in Cork where Heide could meet with her children. By now Werner Braun was incensed by her behaviour and when he got to the room that Sunday she was out, but he went up anyway and that was when he searched through the drawers and found the contraceptives and what he described as 'a pornographic book'.

After he was carted away by the Gardaí, Heide Braun sat down and had a serious look at where her life was going. The following morning while her husband was still in Garda custody she drove to Killowen, collected her belongings, piled them into the car and drove away forever. She moved into 'The Cottage' on Stanley Roche's extensive farm at Oysterhaven near Kinsale. After that she only spoke with Werner to arrange visits with the two children.

When the case was finally called before the High Court in Dublin on Wednesday 21 June 1972 Mr Ernest Wood, who was instructed by the venerable Cork solicitor David Goldberg, was not about to let Stanley Roche escape lightly. The legal strategy, which dug up the old statute of Criminal Conversation, was clear: this is a very wealthy and private man and we will embarrass him as much as we can in public.

The charge was that Stanley Roche had 'debauched' Heide Braun at various times between August 1970 and January 1971 'at places known and unknown' but particularly at Mr Roche's cottage at Oysterhaven; at another of his homes, Waldin at Grange Heights, Douglas, Cork; at the Intercontinental Hotel (later Jurys) in Dublin; 'at an unknown residence at Kinsale; at Killowen; at an unknown place in Limerick city or county; and at an unknown place or places in Germany'.

Ernest Wood SC was up for the task.

'This is an action for Criminal Conversation, or crim con as it is sometimes known,' he told the jury in his plummy barrister's accent as he opened the case for the plaintiff, Werner Braun.

'Moreover it is an action by an outraged husband against his wife's lover – because Mr Roche has admitted having debauched Mrs Braun . . . he could hardly do otherwise, since Mr Roche has set up in style with her . . . he has lived with her and called her Mrs Roche . . . and she has borne him a child.'

And having set the tone he then told the jury that Roche's defence would be that Braun did not suffer any damages as a result of his wife running away with another man.

'It is a very sad case,' he said in a mournful tone. In previous legal proceedings over the custody of the Braun children it was suggested that because Werner and Heide had both been guilty of what was described as 'serious adultery', the jury would be told that neither side could have suffered any more damage than the other.

'That,' continued Mr Wood, 'is a false defence.'

He pointed to Roche, sitting in the courtroom.

'This man, with his wealth has not merely debauched Mr Braun's wife, but he has corrupted her. Mr Braun's only vindication is the damages at your hand.' In other words, Mr Wood was arguing that the only way in which the jury could right the wrong inflicted on Werner Braun was through the amount of money they decided to award him in compensation.

And so the case commenced.

On the other side Mr Oliver Gogarty SC for Roche was low key, soothing in tone and did everything he could not to provoke the witnesses, either for himself or the plaintiff, Braun. But of course his brief was to downplay the more sordid elements of the case he was asked to defend. His line of attack was the reputation of Werner Braun.

He went back to when Heide was a young secretary of 19 years and she was first romantically attracted to Werner.

'I suggest you invited her to come with you and to live as man and wife, but not married?'

'That is correct,' said Werner, admitting to what was considered, in respectable Cork circles, a heinous state of affairs in the early 1970s. But when Heide Braun came into the box Mr Ernest Wood was back on the attack.

'Do you have an account in Roches Stores?' he asked her.

'I do not,' she answered.

'Does Mr Roche not give you money for clothes?'

'He does not.'

'Can I put it to you that at the time you became Stanley Roche's lover he was living contentedly with his wife and children, a happy family and this had all come to an end because of you?'

'That is true,' answered Heide.

'Is it not true that since you became lovers he has effectively pensioned off his wife?'

'He has given her what she wanted,' said Heide.

'Is it not true that you have disgraced your husband?'

'That is not true.'

'Is it not true that he is now known in Cork, as a result of this affair, as a pimp, living on his wife's immoral earnings?'

'It's his own fault,' she replied.

'Are you not even prepared to apologise to him for what has happened, not even prepared to say sorry for the disgrace that you have brought on him?'

'No, I am not sorry,' answered Heide.

When the story of the 'threesome' in a room at their home with Ans Dobbe was raised, a slightly scandalised Judge Butler intervened.

'What do you mean you were there?' he asked incredulously when Heide told the court that she had seen her husband having sex with her friend.

'I was in the room,' she replied.

'Did you mind?' asked the judge.

'Not very much,' she replied.

But Werner Braun's barrister, Ernest Wood, was sceptical.

'You saw him committing adultery and took no action against him?'

'I did not, as I did not take action before when he was beating me, that would have been reason enough, I didn't do anything because of the children.'

'Do you not appreciate that if you had undeniable proof of his adultery that you could divorce him and retain the children?' asked the judge.

'I did not know, but I thought he could have the children as I was guilty of adultery too, and he had proof of this, and he tried to use them against me.' Then she mentioned two more women with whom her husband Werner told her he had sex.

'So he boasted to you, did he?' asked Mr Ernest Wood SC.

'He did not boast. He just mentioned in the conversation that he did not mind having sexual relations like he did with Una and Gerda: that he preferred this to emotional involvement.'

Mr Wood: 'When did he tell you this?

Heide Braun: 'After he talked to Mr Roche and myself.'

Mr Wood: 'Who was the next one after Una?'

Heide Braun: 'He just mentioned Mrs Roche.'

Mr Wood: 'You know she is sitting in court, don't you?'

Heide Braun: 'Yes.'

Mr Wood: 'Do be careful. Did you in the Guardianship of Infants Proceedings instruct your counsel to make the case that your husband had committed adultery with the first Mrs Roche.'

Heide Braun: 'That is right, after he told me.'

Judge Butler: 'It was not mentioned by your counsel when he was listing the infidelities of your husband. Mrs Roche was not mentioned?'

Heide Braun: 'No.'

Ernest Wood SC then showed Heide Braun the anonymous Christmas card her husband had received in December 1970 and asked her to describe the scene, which consisted of a picture of Father Christmas and a man sitting in a car.

'I suppose it occurred to you when your husband showed you the card that the sender was referring to the car that had been given to you?' he asked.

'I don't think that is true,' replied Heide. 'He was referring to the car my husband was driving around in sometimes, which was Mr Roche's Jaguar.'

Mr Wood: 'You told us yesterday that you and Mr Roche had agreed to tell your husband that this was a platonic friendship and that there had been no physical intimacy?'

Heide Braun: 'Yes. I had asked Mr Roche not to say it. He wanted to say we were lovers but I asked him not to, because of the children. I was not certain what was going to happen.'

Mr Wood: 'When did you agree on this course?'

Heide Braun: 'When we started loving each other.'

Mr Wood: 'And when was that?'

Heide Braun: 'In June 1970.'

Mr Wood: 'So, when your husband showed this card to Mr Roche you had been lovers for a time?'

Heide Braun: 'Yes.'

Mr Wood: 'Would it be unfair to describe this as a brazen falsehood?'

Heide Braun: 'On my part. I found it necessary to protect my children. I know it was wrong.'

Mr Wood: 'And a brazen lie by Mr Roche.'

Heide Braun: 'In my opinion it was not because he did not want to. I begged him to.'

Mr Wood: 'So may we take it that you were the strong partner in the new union?'

Heide Braun: 'I don't know what you call strong or weak. In what connection?'

Mr Wood: 'That Mr Roche would act on your bidding.'

Heide Braun: 'He was acting on my bidding about the children.'

Mr Wood: 'Did it occur to you that you were destroying Mr Roche's own marriage?'

Heide Braun: 'No. We were discussing this and he was considering his children. His marriage was destroyed before this.'

Mr Wood: 'He and his wife and children were, at the time when you became his lover, living together as a family – they ceased to do so after his association with you?'

Heide Braun: 'They did.'

As the cross-examination came to an end Mr Ernest Wood SC put on his best severe face and faced Heide Braun.

'Do you recognise now you have disgraced him?' he thundered.

'I did not,' she answered.

'You don't think it is a disgrace that he was regarded in Cork as a pimp – living on his wife's money?'

'It was his own fault,' she said, and those were the last words that Heide Braun would ever utter on the subject.

For Stanley Roche, then aged 44, the embarrassment of talking about his life bordered on mortification, yet he too met the disapproval of the 'hidden Ireland' honestly and without any trace of outrage at the predicament he found himself in.

He said he and his wife Carrie had been married for 19 years and had two teenage boys, Peter aged 17 and Nicholas aged 18 at the time of these events in 1972. His first child with Heide Braun was a son, Morgan, who was born in April 1972 and his birth certificate described him as 'son of Stanley Roche and Heidemaire Roche'. Stanley and Heide later had a girl, Ondine.

Heide Braun had been a friend of Stanley's wife for about two years and until 1970 he had only known her casually, to say 'Hello'. But then in August of that year his wife went to Spain on holidays and he asked Heide out for a drink. He admitted in cross-examination that they began a sexual relationship 'very early on' after their first meeting.

He said he and his wife Carrie had made a joint decision to end their marriage. He admitted that Heide Braun was certainly one of the reasons for the break-up and his decision to leave the family mansion. He and Carrie had finally become legally separated before the trial, early in 1972. He told Mr Wood he was neither ashamed nor sorry for what had happened.

'Do you not recognise that because of your behaviour Mr Werner Braun is regarded as a pimp in Cork?' asked Mr Wood.

'I don't recognise it,' he replied.

'Are you not ashamed of yourself?' asked Mr Wood.

'I am not,' said Mr Roche, and that too was his final word on the issue that would become a cause célèbre in the Ireland of the 1970s.

Judge Butler then told the jury that Criminal Conversation was a very old legal statute that had been abolished in England when civil divorce had been introduced. But because Ireland did not have divorce, the statute had survived in the Irish legal system. He also told them that although such cases were now very rare, the plaintiff in this action, Mr Werner Braun, had every right to avail of the law.

'You are to put all emotion out of your minds and view the evidence in this case coldly and dispassionately,' he said. 'You have heard it admitted here in this court that a wrong has been done to Mr Werner Braun. His wife was seduced and taken away from him and indeed was kept from him. In our law because of that he is entitled to damages.

'In this country a wife is regarded as a chattel, just as a thoroughbred mare or a cow and you are concerned merely with compensating Mr Braun for the value of the loss of his wife and the damages to his feelings.'

But he told the jury that the court was not concerned with morals or breaches of what he called 'the normal moral conduct in Ireland' at the time.

'But if you find on the facts that this was a marriage only in name and before Mr Roche came on the scene Mrs Braun was loose and unfaithful and that Mr Braun had also been unfaithful to his wife and guilty of the sexual perversion described of him, then the damages should be very nominal indeed.

'If that is the case then what Mr Braun lost was hardly worth losing and his feelings were such that they could hardly be hurt any more.'

The judge also cautioned the jury just because Mr Stanley James Roche was a wealthy man, as described in court, he should not be punished because of it. His wealth was not relevant in the case, unless of course the jury were convinced that he had used that wealth to take away another man's 'chaste and dutiful' wife.

'If he has done that, then that would have accentuated Mr Braun's outrage.'

In any event it took the jury just 90 minutes to find that Mr Stanley James Roche had indeed 'debauched' Mrs Heide Braun and was guilty of Criminal Conversation and her husband Werner Braun had suffered damages as a result of his wife having an affair with the wealthy businessman.

They awarded Braun damages of IR£12,000 which at the time would have been the price of a fine house in Cork. There was shock and disapproval at the verdict, but the jurors were just upholding the law as it stood. They were doing the job they were asked to do without prejudice and in accordance with the rules of the court and the evidence presented to them.

It was a trial that opened the eyes of many people living in Holy Catholic Ireland – opened their eyes to another way of life of which they knew little or nothing about and in the main didn't want to know anything about either, although it would only take a few years before the events described in such lurid detail would become common enough.

But most of the outrage was reserved for Mr Justice Butler's vivid depiction of the legal standing of a wife in Ireland in 1972 as 'a chattel' just like 'a thoroughbred mare or cow'.

The women's libbers, as they were known, were just beginning to assert themselves in Ireland. They were incensed by this blunt depiction of the legal realities of life. They vented their fury on the judge who had spoken so plainly and the jury who had made the award in favour of the rather dishonourable Braun.

As for Stanley Roche and Heide Braun, they returned to the obscurity which they craved. Stanley Roche and his brothers, William and Raymond, continued to run the business in the manner to which they had become accustomed – quietly, without fuss and with great success, amassing a huge fortune in the process.

Over the years their flagship stores in Cork, Dublin and Limerick expanded. They then turned them into shopping centres, in the process knocking down the historic Frascati House in Blackrock, County Dublin, once the home of the Duke of Leinster and the birthplace of the patriot, Lord Edward Fitzgerald. All that is left of the once historic house is a few blocks of granite strewn around the car park.

In the early years of the new century they got out of retailing altogether and Roches Stores became a property company selling space in its strategically-placed shopping malls to large outfits like Marks & Spencers and Debenhams. After the court case Stanley Roche and Heide moved to a new home near the village of Belgooly in Kinsale in west Cork where he spent the rest of his life remaining active in the day-to-day running of the family company and enjoying his other major passions – his family and sailing.

He married Heide Braun shortly after the traumatic events in the Imperial Hotel in Cork which led to the complete collapse of Werner Braun's marriage. He had two sons with his wife Carrie, Nicholas and Peter, and two children with Heide, Morgan and Ondine. He also helped to raise her two children from her marriage to Werner, Bronwyn and Owen.

Stanley James Roche died in Cork on 7 July 2008 and was described by the great and the good as 'a pillar of Cork society' and one of the last of the city's remaining 'merchant princes' – which of course he was.

In the meantime the law of Criminal Conversation was eventually struck from the statute books, but not for another decade after the tumultuous events of Stanley Roche's case. And not everybody wanted to abandon it simply because it was outdated. In Dáil Éireann Eileen Desmond asked the Minister for Justice, Gerard Collins, if he would abolish what she called 'the discriminatory' statute.

'I have already publicly stated that I am in no doubt that, in so far as the law in this matter applies differently to men and women, it should be changed,' said the Minister.

But he couldn't make up his mind whether it should be simply abolished, or a new law should be brought in, as recommended by the Law Reform Commission, which would make both men and woman accountable to a new type of action for adultery. It was proposed that whatever compensation was awarded in such cases would be put aside in trust for the children of the marriage.

Eventually it fell to Seán Doherty TD as Minister of State at the Department of Justice in 1981 to bring in the legislation which struck down the law of Criminal Conversation after several hundred years on the statute books. The new statute stated, 'After the passing of this Act, no action shall lie for criminal conversation, for inducing a spouse to leave or remain apart from the other spouse or for harbouring a spouse'.

Among those who contributed to the debate in Dáil Éireann on the new legislation was a young Labour party TD named John Horgan, who would later become the first press ombudsman in the country.

'As a person who has had some connection with the newspaper industry may I say how disappointed I have been at the editorial approach taken by some newspapers in relation to these cases,' he said, referring to the McGowan and Roche cases.

'They have made what was always a difficult and unpleasant situation a thousand times worse by focusing public attention on an unfortunate two or three or four people and, of course, any children, for the purpose of selling newspapers . . . there are limits beyond which I felt good taste would not allow them to go, but in many cases involving this cause of action, newspapers went beyond those limits.'

Chapter 6
Goldin's Disappearing Act

There were 1,700 hysterical people packed into the City Hall in Cork and the atmosphere was hot and steamy as hypnotist Paul Goldin astonished and enthralled the audience with an act that was a fast-moving mixture of illusion, drama and farce. Members of the audience clamoured to be called on stage where Goldin almost instantly put them into a trance. Then the ringmaster of this amazing human circus commanded them to do his bidding to the delight of the sweating, baying crowd.

One moment they were normal, rational human beings, the next minute they were frantically chasing leprechauns around the stage as Goldin exerted his mind-control techniques with dazzling speed and verve. Earlier some of them had even been let out onto the street in search of a phantom friend. All the mayhem ensured a packed house the following night.

Yet despite the calm assurance with which he went about his task, playing the audience in the palm of his hand, that famous mind occasionally wandered as the entertainer went over the details of the 'great escape' routine that he had planned for the finale of the show. The detailed planning had been done in the months, weeks and hours before the show . . . now there was no going back. Although he was booked to play before 3,000 people the following night in the Orchid Ballroom in Bandon, it was a date he would not keep. Because Paul Goldin, the master of illusion, was about to disappear from Ireland that night for his planned rendezvous with his latest lover, an alluring woman with the scent of danger who was about to become a fugitive from Irish law.

Of all the people in the City Hall that night, only one trusted helper knew that he had this date with destiny. 'Monsieur' Paul Goldin, as he was known, was about to pull off the greatest conjuring trick of his career. After about four hours of his amazing performance he suddenly collapsed in a heap on the stage and the massive crowd let out a collective gasp of amazement. Was it a trick? Was it part of the act? As they clambered onto their seats for a better look at the drama unfolding on the stage before them, the murmur from the crowd rose to a crescendo.

Goldin's eldest son David, who was helping with the act, seemed genuinely shocked as he frantically tried to revive his father who was in a strange trance – a trance that seemed even deeper than that experienced by the people he had been hypnotising on the stage just moments before. Then a troupe of stagehands came out and surrounded the prone figure with a screen shielding him from the audience. Suddenly the lights went up and ushers pushed through the milling crowd bawling repeatedly, 'Please leave in an orderly fashion – the show is over, the show is over'.

But even as the crowd spilled out onto the pavements outside City Hall the real drama was afoot inside. His Bentley car had already been shipped to England prior to its departure to a secret destination, and a member of the hypnotist's entourage had already collected his luggage at the Silver Springs Hotel outside Cork.

When he was spirited through the side door of the theatre seemingly semi-conscious, it was the last the public would see of Paul Goldin for the foreseeable future. He never turned up at the Orchid Ballroom in Bandon the following night, Sunday 24 January 1971.

When Paul Goldin was next seen it was on a beach in exotic Honolulu in the Hawaiian islands. Once again the love of a beautiful woman had thrown his careful, almost spartan life into disarray. With two former wives and countless lovers already behind him, Goldin now embarked on another great romantic adventure, this time with a married woman who disappeared from Ireland with her young children, much to the consternation of her estranged husband and the judges of the High Court.

Not only were his audiences missing the great theatrical spectacle of Goldin in action, but more seriously for him and his lover, the High Court in Dublin had issued a bench warrant seeking the arrest of his lover, Maeve O'Brien, and the return of her four children who had disappeared without trace, adding greatly to the already heightened drama that the affair had generated.

'Cork Gardaí confirmed last night that they had been searching for Mr Goldin, but said they could not reveal who had asked them to launch the search,' said *The Sunday Press*, under a story headlined, 'The night the magician did not make it'.

'It was not a member of his family, that is all we can say,' concluded the story mysteriously.

But before the story ended there would be much more said about Paul Goldin – by his deserted wife Patricia (Trish), the mother of his young son Ricki (5), by Patrick Murrough O'Brien, who was the estranged husband of his mistress Maeve O'Brien, by his business associates and indeed by many of those who had followed his amazing career since Paul Goldin arrived in Ireland years before and almost overnight became the highest-paid entertainer in the land.

Ronald Gold – or Paul Goldin as he would later become – claimed to have been born into a Jewish family in Paris in 1929. He told interviewers that his grandfather was Russian and his great-great-grandfather was an illegitimate son of the Tsar. Like many of the stories he would tell during his 80 years on this earth it was a good story, even if it was highly improbable and impossible to prove one way or another.

According to his story, his father Charles, a French psychiatrist, fled from Paris to London with his English mother Minnie (Elbury) at the outbreak of the Second World War in 1939. There the Gold family, Ronald (10) and his brother Jack (9), settled into the city's Jewish community. Even then real life was a carefully planned illusion for the man who would become Paul Goldin. His brother Jack later became an acclaimed film director, producer and writer. His credits include the film *The Naked Civil Servant* and the first and last episodes of the television drama *Inspector Morse*. Jack says he was born in London in 1930 and there is no mention in his various biographical details of his family emigrating to Paris and later having to flee from the onslaught of the Nazis, or indeed of any 'French connection'.

Jack Gold appears to have come from a conventional London Jewish family of that era. So did his elder brother Ronald Gold (aka Paul Goldin). But there was a very good reason why he wanted to disguise his true identity, especially in Ireland. It emerged at Paul Goldin's funeral that in true showbusiness tradition he had shaved a few years off his age.

Ronald Gold was, it appears, born in London in March or April 1927, which made him four years older than his brother Jack, and not one year older as he claimed in his biographical material. Ronald Gold said he studied to become a doctor in London but, according to several interviews he gave he grew disillusioned with medicine in his final year. He claimed he left medical school to attend colleges in Paris and the University of Hawaii where he took an MA in behavioural psychology.

This differs from a written version in a pamphlet he put out shortly after coming to Ireland which only recently came to light for the first time. Oddly enough all his qualifications came from obscure institutions in far-flung parts of the world and always remained shrouded in mystery. But there is no doubt whatsoever about his qualifications that became a lifelong trademark: he had an enormous ego and an amazing flair for two very important aspects of showbusiness – hypnotism and publicity.

Gold was already developing his hypnotic powers in a half-lecture, half-entertainment show he ran at lunchtimes to earn money to put himself through college. Always hungry for attention, he was on a soapbox at London's famous Hyde Park Corner with all the other eccentrics one Sunday morning around 1950 proclaiming his grandly-titled spiel 'Powerful Strategies with Predictable Outcomes', when a passing theatrical promoter stopped to listen and saw the potential for a stage act in a variety show he was touring.

It was a moment that would change the young Jewish medical student's destiny.

He was soon touring the north of England working men's club circuit, the staple diet of variety artists of all makes and sizes. According to himself he bumped into the likes of Harry Secombe and the young Ronnie Wood, who would later become more famous as one of the Rolling Stones (another wanderer who would use Ireland as his adopted homeland).

Ronald Gold, now renamed Paul Goldin, was at the bottom of the bill, living in boarding houses and moving from town to town. But he was getting paid and more importantly he was learning the cruel trade of a journeyman entertainer, developing the tricks of the stage and finding out the hard way what would please the audience and what would have them booing and baying for the next act on the bill.

Then, as chance would have it, he bumped into an Irish actor and theatrical manager Frank O'Donovan, who much later became known throughout Ireland as 'Batty' Brennan in RTÉ's first 'soap', *The Riordans*.

O'Donovan immediately saw the potential for a hypnotist show in Catholic Ireland where touring theatrical groups were still a great source of entertainment and revenue and where superstition and an almost pagan belief in the 'dark arts' were sure to draw massive crowds.

O'Donovan offered his new 'find' the enormous sum of a guaranteed £100 a week and 4 per cent of the takings at the door to venture across the Irish Sea and take his act around the few theatres, the new 'ballrooms' that were springing up in the oddest of places and the 'fit ups' in the parish halls of rural Ireland.

But the one word he could not use to describe himself was 'hypnotist' because that would alienate the church and that would mean he would never work in Ireland.

'The French psychologist with the Gallic charm and the Sixth Sense – Monsieur Paul Goldin,' as he was billed, was an immediate sensation and such were the crowds that he bought himself a brand new Morris Minor car out of his first week's takings. People were clamouring to attend his shows and find out more about his amazing stage act and his almost supernatural powers.

Shortly after arriving in Ireland he produced a booklet printed by the *Limerick Leader*. It was grandly titled 'The Sixth Sense' by Paul Goldin with an introduction by Frank O'Donovan.

'This little booklet written by Paul Goldin is the result of numerous requests received from various member of the public who feel that by knowing in fuller detail the workings of their subconscious mind they may derive even fuller enjoyment from their everyday lives,' wrote Mr O'Donovan. But it is the last page with the heading 'A Few Facts concerning Paul Goldin' that is truly fascinating.

'Paul Goldin was born in the outskirts of Paris and studied psychology at the Cité Universite, Paris. He qualified at the age of 19 and as he was too young to commence medical practice, he was advised to take up teaching psychology. The advice was taken and it was found that he was an excellent lecturer.

'Apart from his knowledge of psychology, he is an expert linguist and is able to lecture in French, Italian, German, Spanish and French . . . he likes making friends but he hates being pointed out in public as "The Great Paul Goldin".

'His immediate ambition is to eventually settle in the Irish Republic and make friends with people who will accept him as he is and not because he is a well-known stage personality.'

The one problem with this CV is that the Cité Universite in Paris is a university residence for students who want to study at other third-level colleges. It does not run courses or award degrees. It was just the first in a long line of showman's 'patter' that Paul Goldin would dispense during his very successful career.

The hypnotist Derek Cobbe who knew Paul Goldin when he was doing shows in the National Stadium in Dublin in the late 1950s describes him as 'suave, debonair and sexy', but concluded, 'he could no more speak French than I could'. Even when he was crooning at the audience in a fake French accent he would often slip back into London cockney – but by then the audience was too enthralled to notice.

'There was a good reason for the French accent,' says Cobbe. 'You have to remember that there was still a lot of anti-British feeling in Ireland at the time – people wouldn't take being made fools of by an Englishman. The only reason they would let themselves be hypnotised and made to do all these silly stunts was because they believed Paul Goldin was really a Frenchman – and the only Frenchmen they knew at the time were English and American actors who appeared in films and talked the way Paul Goldin did.'

Derek Cobbe says that it is the voice that really hypnotises people and Goldin had it down to perfection. He also remembers those 'dark eyes' boring into the audience. It was a deadly combination and women swooned over him. Many either fell madly in love with him or left the theatre literally 'terrified' by his powers.

'He was a pure showman – Mrs Duffy of Duffy's Circus said he was a "consummate showman" – and he planned everything down to the last detail. By the time people came up to the stage many of them were in a state of self-hypnosis and he just took it from there,' says Derek Cobbe, who later became an artists' manager, newspaper editor and finally a clinical hypnotist.

Although he returned briefly to London to collect his wife and three young children, Goldin soon became an adopted Irishman. Over the years he would become one of the highest-paid and most successful entertainers in the country. From then until his death 50 years later he remained a household name in his adopted country, although in the process he moved from hypnotist/entertainer to a behavioural psychologist and businessman who claimed he could cure everything from stammering and smoking to more complex psychological matters such as sexual dysfunction and even drug addiction.

Along the way he would love and leave his fair share of women. His affairs, both public and private, made him a notorious figure in the 'priest-ridden' republic – so much so that some people would cross the street when they saw him coming.

'I was the devil to some of them,' he would later admit.

He didn't always endear himself to the Gardaí either.

'He used to drive them mad,' remembers one showbusiness promoter from that era.

'There'd be people running around Dame Street – outside the Olympia Theatre – looking for leprechauns. There was chaos – the traffic would be brought to a halt. It was great fun, but you wouldn't get away with that kind of thing these days.'

His 'guinea pigs' were programmed to shout, 'I've found my leprechaun' at 10 a.m. the morning after the show. When they did it in workplaces and shops it caused a stir and added to the myth and the 'word of mouth' advertising campaign for his next show.

Moving from one grand theatrical gesture to the next, he was, in real life, a rather reserved man who enjoyed an odd glass of wine but did not live the life expected of an Irish showbusiness 'character'. But for the trail of lurid headlines when his private life spilled over into the public domain, he could have been just another anonymous businessman of Jewish descent who was doing rather well for himself.

Even today little is publicly known about the early years of his private life. His first wife Miriam is described in one profile as 'an Italian who died of cancer'. She bore him three children, Joanna, David and Bobby. As he criss-crossed the country in the 1950s and 1960s, Paul Goldin discovered that there was a 'hidden Ireland' where the teachings of the Catholic Church did not rule. He not only fell into the life of a showman with big headlines and even bigger cars, but he also fell into the arms of a string of beautiful young women, several of whom it is said bore his children.

Even during the 'Holy Season' of Lent when the theatres were closed because of strict religious observance, Paul Goldin turned to the cinemas and did his show from the cinema stage, much to the envy of other performers who had to go over to England or America to try and make a living.

In the early 1960s Miriam left him because of his constant philandering and took the younger children with her. By early 1964 Paul Goldin was divorced from Miriam and after a whirlwind romance had remarried, this time to a beautiful former TWA air hostess Patricia (Trish) Smyth. He met Trish after a show in the Shannon Shamrock Hotel outside Limerick where she was staying on a stopover flight from New York.

'Any girl would have been attracted to him and a lot of girls were,' she said. 'Not just because he seemed to promise the sun, moon and stars, he could have any girl he wanted without that, it was just his personality.

'He always looked after me very well, and really he led a fairly quiet sort of life for someone so wrapped up in showbusiness. It's a notorious game for drink and general high living, but Paul never drank,' she said. Although the couple had married on 18 March 1964 in the County Judge Court in Miami, Florida, Smyth's Irish-born parents were not happy with either this sudden development or the fact that they had not been invited to the wedding. But using his legendary charm Goldin won over his new father-in-law, and to keep everybody happy the couple were married again at the Burt Oak Registry Office in Middlesex, England, in August 1965.

After their marriage the happy couple travelled three times around the world, doing shows on cruise ships and entertaining in exotic locations from Hawaii to Las Vegas and Miami. They enjoyed the life of a glitzy couple with plenty of money and a taste for the good things in life and nothing much to tie them down. Any time Paul Goldin needed big money he came back to Ireland. He was sure to fill the halls and the new 'singing' lounges that were springing up around the country towns. There was always room on the bill for a hypnotist and Goldin had an exclusive franchise. Along the way there was the odd hiccup – like the 17-year-old hospital ward maid who fell into a three-day coma after attending a Paul Goldin show where she had been a 'guinea pig' in his stage act.

In the controversy that followed, Goldin's first thoughts were to protect his franchise, which meant reassuring parish priests around the country who controlled the 'parish halls' that were so vital to his act. He claimed that his act had been vetted by the 'leading ecclesiastical authorities' of the day. Although the girl recovered, there was a widespread belief among the God-fearing congregations that the incident highlighted the perils of dabbling in the occult which, unlike the teachings of the Catholic Church, could not be fully understood. But of course the whiff of danger was always good publicity and Goldin milked the drama for what it was worth.

However he was also looking for other outlets for his talents. One such scheme, Educational Motivation Systems (E.M.S.), appeared in the early 1960s. An accompanying booklet sets out a system promising a 'new way of life'. The scheme was what is known today as 'pyramid selling'. The booklet begins with an acknowledgement, 'I should like to publicly express my appreciation to my dear wife, Patricia, for her intelligent and devoted assistance – Paul Goldin'.

The basics of the operation were set out with diagrams and sought to entice people to bring in 'fellow workers, relatives, friends, card club members – just anyone'. Goldin's associate in this venture was one Seán Higgins, a businessman from Stillorgan, County Dublin who would reappear later in his life when unhappily the two men fell out rather spectacularly. The venture had its head office, the E.M.S. Corporation, in San Francisco and branch offices in New Cavendish Street in London, Upper Fitzwilliam Street in Dublin and even Mumbai in India. All were, of course, accommodation addresses but they looked rather grand on the prospectus that he distributed after his shows. In January 1965 he and Trish's son, Ricky Goldin, was born and Paul appeared to settle down to married life.

In November 1968 the entertainer, his wife and their young son moved to a large house called 'Woodlawns' on Grange Road, Raheny. Goldin rented the property for IR£75 a month from a religious order. Always the flamboyant showman, his distinctive silver Bentley car became a regular sight in the area. Ricky would later look back on an idyllic early childhood home through rose-tinted glasses.

'I remember we had a gorgeous home, 15 acres of land. The parents were doing really well. I was like Little Lord Fauntleroy. I had an electric car when I was six years old and I used to drive down my driveway and it took a full minute. Across the street was a family with nine children and a farm and I used to help to slop out the pig pen and stuff like that. I remember once I got stabbed in the leg with a pitchfork by accident. I still have the scar. I didn't want to tell my Mom because I thought she'd be angry with me, but of course she wasn't.'

Idyllic as it might have seemed to little Ricky, family life didn't exactly suit Paul Goldin's temperament and soon there was another affair, this time a steamy encounter with a married woman.

Whether he had tired of a life of constant travelling through the small towns of Ireland or whether the exotic nature of his stage show had worn a bit thin over the years, it is clear that Paul Goldin had now decided to re-invent himself as a 'behavioural psychologist' to cure addictive personalities of obesity, smoking and even stammering. It was a welcome break from the road and it also gave him time to develop a new show which would revitalise his career.

Where better to start the new venture than in his big rambling house in Raheny.

In February 1969 Paul and Trish Goldin opened their first 'health clinic'. Using a 'system for the control of obesity' which he had developed in Honolulu, Hawaii, with Dr Maurice Silvers, the 'Weight and Figure Control Centre' was tapping into the new fad for dieting and slimming that had arrived with the Swinging Sixties, and its figure-hugging clothes and short skirts.

Initially his partner was Seán Higgins, the gentleman from his previous venture, E.M.S., who also went under the name John J. Higgins but was now styling himself Seán Spencer of Stillorgan Grove, Dublin. Higgins/Spencer agreed to invest in the new venture but eventually the two men fell out over money. There were several acrimonious court cases and injunctions in the High Court in Dublin as a result of the dispute.

Paul Goldin alleged that Seán Spencer had agreed to put up IR£2,500 for his share in the partnership, but hadn't honoured the agreement. Spencer for his part alleged that Paul Goldin was attempting to 'swindle' him by taking money out of the business for his personal use.

He also alleged that Goldin had brought Mr Ivor Noyek of the well-known Dublin timber merchant family into the business and was allowing him to buy a share on behalf of his latest lover.

'Mr Goldin was not Irish and informed me that he did not like living in Ireland,' Spencer told the court in a further attempt to blacken Goldin's name.

But one of the office girls had a different story.

'Mr Spencer began to abuse Mr Goldin, saying he was wanted by police in several places, including San Francisco, Hawaii and India,' said Una McCabe of Howth in an affidavit read out in court. 'Mr Spencer also named certain people whom he alleged Mr Goldin had swindled. After Mr Spencer left she phoned the Gardaí and gave them a list of items removed by him,' stated a report into the ongoing series of legal cases.

At the centre of this dispute was a woman called Maeve O'Brien who was a 'friend' of Ivor Noyek. Paul Goldin had become acquainted with them and employed Maeve O'Brien at the princely sum of IR£30 a week – a considerable wage for that time. Seán Spencer was appalled that a secretary should be earning this kind of money from the business while he was a shareholder and was getting very little in return. But in the end it was Spencer/Higgins who got the bullet. He was pushed out of the business and Maeve O'Brien became Paul Goldin's 'right-hand woman' in the new venture.

She was a good-looking and fun-loving mother of four who was said to be part of the racing set. Certainly she was comfortably off and ran with a smart set, attending the races, hunt balls and parties in Dublin. She was separated from her husband Patrick Murrough O'Brien, a businessman who was living in Fermoy, County Cork, and three of their four children were in boarding school, giving Maeve O'Brien plenty of scope for a fun-filled social life.

While Trish Goldin looked after little Ricky in the house in Raheny, Maeve O'Brien was running the office and making sure the money came flowing in.

'When she came in first I smelled that she was trouble,' recalled Trish some time later. 'I was friendly with her for Paul's sake, but she was sickeningly friendly with me. Before she joined us she worked for Noyeks, the timber merchants,' she added rather disparagingly.

But like a lot of his enterprises the clinic was before its time and Paul Goldin sold the franchise to Maeve O'Brien to run from 'Tara', her grandly-titled five-bedroomed house in Willowbank Drive, Rathfarnham, Dublin. Or at least that's what he told his wife Trish.

It should probably have been clear to her by now that Paul Goldin, the man who preached 'mind over matter', had little or no self-control in the presence of beautiful women and was already in the throes of a torrid affair with Maeve O'Brien. Coincidentally Trish's father, who was originally from Belfast, fell ill in America where he now lived. Trish and Paul dutifully travelled to the United States with their son Ricky to be at his bedside. They spent five weeks in her parents' house at Hunter Avenue, Valley Stream, New York. As far as Trish was concerned everything was fine in their life, apart from her sick father.

At 8.30 a.m. on 27 October 1970 Paul Goldin got up as usual, had his breakfast and told his wife he was going to take flying lessons at a nearby airfield and walked out the door. He never came back.

It was a disappearing trick he was to perfect and play with faultless timing on several occasions after that. Trish became very worried about him and he was listed as a 'missing person'.

But as Trish would later learn in a phone call from a friend back home in Ireland, Paul Goldin was only missing from her. After he left the house that morning he boarded a plane and returned to Ireland and the open arms of his lover Maeve O'Brien, moving into her house at Willowbank Drive in Rathfarnham.

'Our marriage was good all the way to last August and if they did have "something going" I just never knew about it – he was always home at nights,' Trish would later tell *The Sunday Press* reporter John Kelly when her marriage publicly fell apart.

When Trish returned to Ireland with her young son in November that year she discovered that the lease on the house in Raheny had run out. Not only did she have no husband, but she also had no home. She rented a flat on Merrion Road and tried to pick up the pieces of her life – even visiting the lovers' new address, but finding nobody home.

As Paul Goldin prepared for a series of sell-out shows in the Cork area in the New Year of 1971, it was quite clear to him that his second marriage was truly over, his personal life was a shambles and the only way he and Maeve O'Brien could make a 'go of it' was to flee the country. For one thing, a picture of him and Maeve O'Brien clasping each others' hands like star-crossed lovers appeared in the social columns of the *Evening Press* on 18 November. Goldin even told the well-known columnist Terry O'Sullivan that he had been divorced in Hawaii and he and Maeve – now going under the name Maeve Dunne O'Brien – were going to get married.

'He was telling people that we were divorced in Reno, of all places,' said Trish. 'But we were never divorced and he could hardly remarry under the circumstances, could he?'

Armed with the story from the *Evening Press* and the evidence of friends, she headed for the Dublin District Court to seek a 'restraining order' to prevent him marrying his latest lover. Trish was seeking a declaration that she was the lawful wife of Paul Goldin and 'seeking an injunction restraining him from denying expressly, or by implication, that she is his wife and from representing himself to be free to marry'.

Mr Paul Carney representing Trish argued that under Article 4 of the Irish Constitution the family was recognised as the 'fundamental unit of society' and the court had a duty to protect it. Mr Justice Kenny, who by now had been involved in a whole series of court proceedings involving Paul Goldin, refused to grant the injunction.

'If the marriage to your client is valid, won't his marriage to the other person be invalid?' he pointed out, although this of course wasn't of much help to Trish Goldin who was trying to ensure her husband provided for herself and her son and didn't further deny his marriage to her.

It was at this point that Paul Goldin began planning his dramatic exit – stage left in Cork.

Before setting off for the highly-publicised tour, Goldin had his Bentley car secretly shipped to Honolulu. Accompanied by his son David from his first marriage, who was now working as his personal assistant, he set off for Cork for a series of sell-out shows and the disappearing act of a lifetime. Simultaneously Maeve O'Brien and her four children disappeared from the house in Willowbank Drive, much to the consternation of the children's father, Patrick Murrough O'Brien, who was increasingly concerned about his estranged wife's plans. It appears she had taken her elder children out of a convent in Chapelizod, west Dublin, run by the Sisters of St Joseph of Cluny that Christmas and never sent them back to school as she began her preparations.

In the second week of January 1971 Patrick Murrough O'Brien began to get suspicious about the disappearance of his wife and children. He sought an order in the High Court under the Guardianship of Infants Act to establish their whereabouts and to compel his estranged wife to produce them. The first part of the hearing was in secret to protect the children. At this hearing Maeve O'Brien gave an undertaking that she would not leave the jurisdiction. But almost immediately she too disappeared.

Dramatic newspaper reports of the disappearance of Paul Goldin from the City Hall in Cork that Friday night in January 1971 set off alarm bells in a number of households. Almost immediately Trish Goldin went to the District Court in Dublin to get an order for custody of the couple's child, Ricky. But of greater concern was the whereabouts of Maeve O'Brien and her children.

On Monday 25 January 1971 Mr Justice Kenny lifted his ban on publicity in the case in order to enlist the help of the public to try and find the exact whereabouts of the O'Brien children.

'This is a case in which your lordship after a full hearing of the matter and having considered all the implications involved, in particular having regard to the interests of the children, granted custody of the four children, the subject of the proceedings, Grace, Sheelyn, Stephen and Michael O'Brien, to the mother, Maeve O'Brien,' said Mr Liam Hamilton SC, opening the proceedings on behalf of Maeve's estranged husband Patrick Murrough O'Brien.

'Your lordship granted custody in spite of the fact that your lordship was satisfied that Mrs O'Brien had been living with Mr Goldin and was in love with him. Your lordship however, made it quite clear to Mrs O'Brien that the interests of the children demanded that they remain within the jurisdiction of the court and conditional upon Mrs O'Brien giving to your lordship a specific undertaking that she would not take the children out of the jurisdiction without your lordship's express permission. And in addition your lordship made it a condition of her obtaining custody of the children that she hand her passport into the care of the court.

'In pursuance of this undertaking, Mrs O'Brien did in fact hand in her passport. However, my lord, it appears from the information at the disposal of my client, Mr O'Brien, that Mrs O'Brien has within the past week obtained a further passport from the Department of External Affairs based on a representation that she had never previously been the holder of a passport and had never before been out of the country.

'This passport, in addition to covering Mrs O'Brien, covers the younger son Michael and was based on a letter alleged to have been written by the father, Murrough O'Brien, that he consented to the child being taken out of the jurisdiction and it was on that basis the passport was entered.

'I have to inform your lordship that Mr O'Brien states categorically that he never wrote that letter and never authorised Mrs O'Brien to take the child out of the jurisdiction.

'It has also transpired that in July last year Mrs O'Brien obtained passports in respect of the three elder children, Grace, Sheelyn and Stephen and these were also obtained on a letter alleged to have been written by Mr O'Brien giving permission to take the children out of the jurisdiction. He states categorically that he never wrote such a letter.'

It seems Maeve O'Brien and Paul Goldin had been planning their flight long before his wife Trish or her husband Patrick realised what was going on. Maeve had been to the United States embassy in Dublin looking for a visa for the three children to travel there. But when her husband found out about the applications he went to the Embassy and told them that he had a court order that they were not allowed leave the country. But Embassy officials, though sympathetic, told him that she would be able to obtain a visa in another city where there was an American diplomatic consul.

The O'Brien family flight from Ireland to join Paul Goldin was planned for Sunday 24 January – after they had been ordered not to leave the country, but before the authorities could stop them – because the order had been obtained in secret to protect the children and therefore nobody but the officers of the court knew about it.

'We have further reasons to believe, my lord that the date of intended departure was yesterday,' Liam Hamilton SC told the hushed High Court in Dublin.

'Upon becoming aware of the date, my lord, Mr O'Brien made inquiries and ascertained that the children had not been living in Rathfarnham for some time and that two of them had been staying with Mrs O'Brien's brother, but that they were collected on Friday and have not been seen since.

'Mr O'Brien has reason to believe that Mrs O'Brien's association with Mr Goldin has continued and there has been a certain amount of publicity in the case with regard to Mr Goldin's vanishing from Cork. Taking all these circumstances into account we have reason to believe that if the children have not yet already been taken out of the jurisdiction, that there is such danger and that they will be taken out of the jurisdiction.

'And we are asking for publicity on this matter in the hope that it will receive publicity so that if anybody becomes aware of the whereabouts of the children, that we will be notified so as to take the necessary steps to prevent their being taken out of the jurisdiction.'

A clearly annoyed Judge Kenny said that Maeve O'Brien had 'given her word of honour' that she would not leave the Republic of Ireland.

'I am making an order that the children should be produced in this court tomorrow – and if they are not I will commit Mrs O'Brien to prison,' he said. But of course Maeve O'Brien did not turn up in court the following morning, nor did her children. They were already on their way to Honolulu with her lover Paul Goldin. Her barrister Mr Henry Barron SC said that he had no instructions on the matter and could be of no assistance to the court.

'Last Monday you lifted the ban on publicity in the hope that this would lead to the children being found, clearly Mrs O'Brien and her children have gone abroad in spite of the solemn undertaking and oath that she gave to this court,' said Liam Hamilton SC.

'I now ask for a bench warrant for her arrest in the event of her being brought back to Ireland. I anticipate that the necessary steps will be taken by the Department of External Affairs to insure that wherever she is, the attention of the authorities will be drawn to the fact that she has succeeded in entering on the basis of a fraudulent misrepresentation that she was not the holder of an existing passport and that the passports issued in respect of the children were issued on the basis of forged documentation.'

An order was made for the immediate arrest of Maeve O'Brien. It transpired that the quiet five-bedroomed house at Willowbank Drive had been a hive of activity in the previous weeks. People had been calling and valuables had been removed. Apart from organising a bogus passport Maeve O'Brien had been seen at the local supermarket buying what were described as 'light clothes' for her sojourn in a sunnier climate than Ireland in January.

'It's sad about the children,' lamented a neighbour, 'they're lovely children – they'd often call to see us.'

But Maeve O'Brien was not looked upon so favourably.

'She was quite a nice person really, but she could be very temperamental,' said the same neighbour.

There was a steady stream of people still calling to the house, most of them looking for Paul Goldin. Some of them had paid him up front for the various treatments he provided and were anxious to find out where he was. Another caller to the abandoned house was Trish Goldin, who was seeking some news of her husband, the illusionist, but found none.

'She came several times to ask if we had any idea where they'd gone – naturally she's very upset,' a helpful neighbour told reporters. But over a gin and tonic in the Tara Towers Hotel the glamorous Trish, who was pictured with her five-year-old son Ricky, was more angry than upset when she sat down with the journalist John Kelly.

'Don't paint me as a distressed, deserted wife – I'm not distressed any more, I'm just very angry. I am angry that Paul deserted Ricky and me for a married woman and four strange children. He left me virtually nothing,' she said. 'Paul loved a challenge. Getting out of the country this way and maybe taking Mrs O'Brien and her children with him was a real challenge. But as soon as anything stopped being a challenge Paul usually tired of it. That's how it was with his health clinics even.

'Ricky misses him a lot – and this was his first birthday that he didn't even get a card from him. I think that hurt him most of all. But I have to make excuses, like telling him that his father is far away in a place where the dates are different, so that he would not know when to send the card.'

She added, 'I am not going to chase him. I'm determined to get custody of my son and that's all. I plan to go to Florida to see if there's any chance of settling there for a few years. But first I have to get my affairs sorted out here. I'm a one-man woman. That's all. I always thought our marriage was working. I always thought that we'd make it work. And then suddenly, this comes up.'

She told the journalist that the last few months had been 'nightmarish' but she would survive.

'A little older – a little wiser, eh?'

But then she thought of her son.

'Ricky is as much his boy as he is mine and it is to both of us, but especially Ricky, that Paul owes his responsibilities. He'll have to live up to them.'

Although Paul Goldin had a string of lovers around Ireland, a string of affairs around the world and four wives, he never lost his taste for good-looking women. Life in Hawaii didn't have the same attraction for the lovers as the land they had fled. Goldin could never resist the limelight and within a year he had slipped quietly back into Ireland. By mid 1972 he was hiding out in Kinsale, County Cork along with his fugitive lover Maeve O'Brien and her four children. They were sent to the local school in Kinsale using the name Gold – Paul Goldin's real name. Although the couple were making no real effort to hide from the authorities, they certainly were not trying to advertise the return of the O'Briens, especially as there was a warrant out for the arrest of Maeve O'Brien for lying to a judge and disobeying a court undertaking.

But secretly Paul Goldin was trying to make some much-needed cash. He couldn't advertise as himself, so he resorted to his real name, Ronald Gold, and advertised a new hypnotism show. But the public didn't make the connection that it was Paul Goldin in another guise – and as far as the Irish public was concerned there was only one showman worth seeing.

The result was that tickets didn't sell. According to reports there were also 'numerous misrepresentations' about the new show. Some of the sponsors became alarmed when they discovered that the person behind this latest showbusiness venture was actually Paul Goldin. *The Cork Examiner* newspaper, for one, felt it important enough to point out in its own paper that it was not one of the sponsors.

As a result the shows were a disaster and according to a report 'a certain amount of money trouble' had arisen. Paul Goldin and Maeve O'Brien had been unmasked for who they really were.

Once again matters were put in the hands of Mr Justice Kenny in the High Court in Dublin. He appears to have taken a lenient view of Maeve

O'Brien breaking her word and the warrant for her arrest was lifted. Then he was asked to rule on what should happen to the four children, now that they were back in Ireland. Their father, Patrick Murrough O'Brien, said he was solely concerned about the welfare of his children and if the court allowed it he wanted them to return to Mount Sackville Convent in Dublin, where the nuns had indicated they were willing to take them back. He added that he had 'no confidence' in the ability of Goldin or his wife Maeve O'Brien to care for them. Returning them to the convent Judge Kenny said he was not making an order as to who should get custody of the children – that was a matter which would be decided later in the family court.

But there was one further twist in the secret life of Paul Goldin and Maeve O'Brien. On Wednesday 19 March 1975 the following notice appeared in the personal columns of *The Irish Times:*

'Paul Goldin and his wife Maeve proudly announce the birth of their daughter Sarah-Anne. A baby sister for Grace, Steven, Sheelyn and Michael. Buíochas le Dia.'

Had they married in Hawaii or Las Vegas? Nobody knew. But the mercurial hypnotist was never one to let the publicity and the intrigue die down.

That was the last that was heard publicly of Maeve O'Brien or her children.

Once more Paul Goldin was back doing shows, travelling around the country, lining his pockets with ready cash and looking for the next big venture and once again falling into the arms of another lover. As well as his talent for showbusiness there was one thing Paul Goldin understood and that was how publicity worked and he understood it better than anybody. The media, he knew, was always a sucker for such dramatic gestures.

In 1979 to relaunch his career Paul Goldin announced that he would jump out of an aeroplane at 760 metres over Ipswich Airport in the United Kingdom. Luckily for Goldin the police stepped in and refused to allow the stunt to go ahead. But the acres of publicity did wonders for the new tour that was underway. Paul Goldin was not only back on the boards, but backing him in business and in love was a new woman.

Helen Breen had always been fascinated with showbusiness – ironically ever since her mother took her to a Paul Goldin show in her home town of

Mitchelstown, County Cork when she was just a seven-year-old child. It was a story that they liked to tell together and a succession of reporters doted on it. *The Sunday Press* gave it the full treatment back in 1993. Whatever else it's a good story, so a decade or so later they re-told it during a joint interview with Sarah Caden for the *Sunday Independent.*

'I remember it well, we were sitting in the front and all the people were keeping their eyes down and wouldn't talk to Paul,' said Helen, describing how her mother had brought her along to one of his shows when it came to her home town.

'I asked her are you married and she told me she wasn't,' remembered Paul. 'And I said, if I come back one day would you marry me and she said she might, and that was that.'

But 10 years later, as a 17-year-old, Helen was visiting her aunt in Dublin when she met Paul again, introduced to him by a friend of her aunt's, the comedian Hal Roche.

'I didn't think anything of him, but after that I became very interested in psychology and I used to send away for all the books Paul had advertised in the papers.'

She also became fascinated by the whole showbusiness scene and after leaving school decided to become a publicist and promoter. She shared a cramped office in Parnell Square in Dublin with Jackie Johnston, who managed the star of *Phantom of the Opera*, Colm Wilkinson. She was learning the business, and she was learning about life.

She became romantically involved with a tragic and now forgotten figure, Bob Lynch who, in some ways, was the 'missing Dubliner'. He had been in a duo with fiddle player John Sheahan and they played in the famous Abbey Tavern in Howth, where The Dubliners had recorded an album. After one of the periodic rows between leading personalities Ronnie Drew and Luke Kelly, who never really liked each other, the hot-tempered Kelly left the group to go solo. Bob Lynch and John Sheahan joined The Dubliners in 1964, seamlessly fitting into the new set-up. Lynch sang 'The Kerry Recruit' on their *Dubliners* album.

However after about two years Luke Kelly decided to come back and Lynch left (or was dropped from the band) just months before The Dubliners went to the top of the British charts with the song 'Seven Drunken Nights'.

It opened up an international career for the band that was to last for decades and brought them and their earnings to another level.

Lynch's relationship with Helen Breen ended before he emigrated to Canada. But after a few years he came back to Dublin, dabbled in the folk scene and opened a small electrical shop in the city. Tragically he hanged himself some years later, something that is not often talked about even among Dubliners fans.

'His suicide was a shock,' said John Sheahan later. 'He was always a very happy fellah – always cracking jokes. We drifted apart. I had lost contact with him for the previous five or six years before he died.'

By that time Helen had met up with Paul Goldin for a third time – probably due to her work as a showbiz promoter. What started as a business relationship was turning to love and their lives became completely intertwined. Helen Breen began to book venues for him and organise his publicity. It wasn't long before he had moved on from his third wife and moved in with his much younger lover.

Helen Breen also had a colourful past, or so it seemed. One interviewer even came away with the impression that her mother was the last surviving daughter of Lady Mount Cashell of Kilworth in County Cork, a famous landed family who once owned 11,000 acres of Cork and Tipperary. If there was a relationship, it was pretty distant by the time she was born.

The fifth Baron Mount Cashell, Charles William Moore, was born in 1828 and although he had a number of daughters, he didn't have a son or heir. He ended his days in a lunatic asylum as a result of losing the family fortune and becoming embroiled in a costly and damaging court case over the upkeep of his daughter in a Swiss sanatorium. When he died in 1898 the title passed to his first cousin, Edward George Augustus Harcourt Moore, sixth Baron, who died unmarried in 1915 and the title Mount Cashell of the city of Cashel died with him.

Blue blood or not, Helen Breen's mother was far from happy with her daughter's new Jewish lover and was made even unhappier when the pair, with typical showbusiness flair, got married in Las Vegas in 1981.

'I understand her reservations now, but not at the time,' Paul Goldin told Sarah Caden in the interview with the *Sunday Independent*. 'Helen's mother saw her only child marrying someone in showbusiness, Jewish, English, divorced, children. I had no home. I was travelling all the time. She had no idea what I had to offer her daughter.'

It was probably Paul Goldin's best assessment of himself after a lifetime in showbusiness where he had made and seemingly lost a fortune. But the marriage was to tide Paul Goldin through the last and most stable part of his life. Always in search of a new scheme, most of which would cost him dearly, he decided to follow in the footsteps of the famous British entrepreneur Freddie Laker and set up a company to run cheap student flights to the United States.

At the time, in the 1980s, there was a huge market as thousands of students went to America each summer on working visas to try to earn enough money to last another year in college in recession-hit Ireland. But once again he was getting into a venture he knew nothing about. Not only did he lose all his capital, but he was also fined $500,000 by the United States authorities for breach of aircraft-leasing regulations.

Goldin had now withdrawn from the parish hall shows and repositioned himself in the lucrative business of psychologist and expert in mind-control techniques – a man who could cure smoking, stammering and any other sort of psychological ailment.

There was the Ideal Weight Clubs Limited, the Weight and Figure Control Centre, the Health and Figure Control Centre and various other enterprises which were eventually sold or dissolved, going the same way as other enterprises like RP Gold Ltd and EMS Ltd. As one venture would quietly wither away, a new one would open up. And every so often a disgruntled client would take a court case or cause a stir in the newspapers, but Paul Goldin, the man with the piercing dark eyes, appeared to have the survival instincts of a very agile cat.

After years of 'research' when he disappeared from the limelight, the new Paul Goldin that emerged was no longer just a stage hypnotist – although he would never fully abandon that lucrative profession – but a 'behavioural psychologist' and hypnotherapist. He announced that after years of research he had developed a cure for stammering.

With over 100 clients paying IR£500 each for a 'Six Day Freedom Course' Paul Goldin was soon reaping the rewards of his so-called 'scientific endeavours'.

As the journal *The Phoenix* later reported, 'Wherever he studied his stammering therapy, Goldin's courses to alleviate and cure the speech impediment have run into flak from dissatisfied customers. Despite grandiose claims of a 100 per cent success rate, by the middle of last year a distressingly high number of Goldin's ex-patients were not only still stammering, but also asking for their money back.'

Of course there was a 'no cure – no fee' guarantee, but the loftily-titled 'Institute of Applied Psychology' declined to make refunds and the still-stammering customers had to go the Office of Consumer Affairs or the courts to seek recompense.

One group of six disgruntled customers launched an embarrassing court case against the 'hypnotherapist' in the Dun Laoghaire District Court. They sued Paul Goldin and his Institute of Applied Psychology regarding its promise of a 'complete and perfect cure in six days or guaranteed refund'.

Vincent Scallan BL representing Michael O'Donoghue of Adare Drive, Coolock, Dublin said six people had participated in the course but were not cured and did not receive a refund as promised. Paul Goldin, who had long challenged the medical establishment, now found himself confronted by Margaret Leahy, a lecturer in speech pathology in Trinity College Dublin. Leahy said that up to 500 hours of therapy was needed to treat speech impediment, and a six-day course could not possibly cure the ailment.

'Strategies such as head nodding and slow rhythmic speech work in the short term in some cases,' she declared. 'But relapses are common in the vast number of cases where intensity alone is a method of treatment.'

She said she saw one of the plaintiffs, a Mr Joseph Dowling, who had a 'moderate speech deficiency', but while the techniques he learned on the course were of benefit to him initially they did not work in the long term.

The case was heard on 9 March 1988 and disgruntled customers told District Justice Hubert Wine that they had paid IR£500 to attend Mr Goldin's 'stammering course' – a fee of IR£300 and an additional IR£200 for hotel accommodation.

But Paul Goldin was not without his supporters. An English woman, Julie Anne Crawley from Bournemouth who came to Ireland for the course, said she had suffered from stammering for a number of years and had tried hypnosis and acupuncture before without success.

'I'm very happy with my cure and would recommend it to others,' she said. Another client, Peter Lismore of Belfast, said that after 12 years of stammering this had stopped after he took the six-day course with Mr Goldin. Adrian Hardiman BL, now a member of the Irish Supreme Court, was the young barrister representing Goldin. He said he would show tapes of Goldin conducting the course to District Justice Hubert Wine, who adjourned the case for a month because there was such a large number of witnesses. When the case resumed on 4 May 1988 the judge was told that it had been settled for 'undisclosed damages' and that was the end of the matter.

It might have seemed like another bout of bad publicity – but the skilful Goldin seemed more than able to cope with such setbacks. It certainly didn't stop the crowds flocking to his Monkstown home, 'Beau Parc' – so much so that the well-heeled neighbours complained to the planning authorities. Goldin was so overwhelmed by clients queueing up to see him in this residential neighbourhood that he eventually had to sell up and move to a large property in the millionaire belt of Rathmichael in the foothills of the Dublin mountains.

Neither did it put a stop to his ability to tell wonderful tales.

In a 1988 interview in *The Irish Press* he claimed that while in Russia he had developed a cure for drug addiction. This, he said, came about when he began treating injured Russian soldiers returning from the war in Afghanistan. Many of them were morphine addicts from their time in the war or as a result of medication. He set about gradually reducing their dosage but used his mind-control techniques to make them think they were still getting the same amount of drugs. At the end of four weeks they were happily taking saline injections that contained no morphine and they were 'cured'. But Irish hospitals were unwilling to let him start similar programmes here for drug and alcohol addiction.

'They all had their own programmes and just weren't even willing to give mine a try,' he lamented. 'That was two years ago, but things are slow to change. I have got people off tablets that they had been taking for years. Using this principle instead of taking the full tablet I make them take half the prescribed one and a Smartie. They may end up Smartie addicts but they drop their dependency on drugs which is much more important,' he joked.

But given that he had also claimed in 1978 that he was employed by the CIA – in the aftermath of the horrific Jim Jones massacre in Guyana – to 'de-programme' survivors of the atrocity, the 'drug cure' claim probably wasn't so outlandish.

Jim Jones was a cult leader who moved his followers from California to the jungles of Guyana after coming under investigation by a member of the US House of Representatives, Leo J. Ryan. When Ryan travelled to Guyana and tried to lead disgruntled followers from Jones' camp on 18 November 1978, Jones had him shot. His followers then lined up and hundreds of them killed themselves with poison – the adults squirting a cyanide-based cocktail into the children's mouths before they drank it themselves. Only two people didn't drink the poison. One of them was Jones who was found dead from a gunshot wound. The coroner said he believed it was 'self administered', but there was a conspiracy theory that when it came to killing himself Jones refused to drink the poison so he was shot by the camp guard who then shot himself. A few survivors escaped into the jungle and a small group, including Jones' son Stephen, survived because they were away playing a basketball match.

In all 913 people died, including 276 children. Of the handful who survived, most of them hid or got new identities when they returned to the US. There was never any evidence that they were 'de-programmed' on the orders of the CIA. Although there is a large body of investigative material about the mass suicide and its aftermath, there is no reference to Paul Goldin apart from his own claims to have been involved.

But it had all the hallmarks of a classic Paul Goldin story – there were no records of it ever happening, the CIA were unlikely to confirm it, it happened a long way from Ireland and journalists were all too willing to believe it in the interests of 'good copy'. Indeed he was seldom out of the newspapers or the courts for one reason or another.

The next time he was involved in litigation Paul Goldin was claiming damages for serious injuries he received in a car accident. Accompanied by his friend, the British investigative reporter Roger Cook of the Cook Report, he treated the courtroom like a stage show.

As he was awarding 'undisclosed damages', Judge Diarmuid O'Donovan recalled going to see Goldin 'performing his hypnotic act as a junior counsel in Roscommon many years ago' and how a colleague with him had to go on stage to have Mr Goldin release his hands which he imagined under hypnosis were handcuffed.

In 1992 a journalist for *The Irish Times,* Mary Russell, went to the Olympia Theatre in Dublin to see the latest revival of his stage show, which once again was playing to packed houses. It was his first show in the city in eight years.

'Wearing an evening suit and with a French accent that slipped somewhat as the show progressed, he chatted to the audience, dispensed plenty of throw-away lines and reassured his victims with all the ease of an old pro. He wasn't going to hypnotise them, he said. He was just going to demonstrate the power of the mind.

'The line-up on the stage was a mix of teenagers and twenty-somethings. "You'll be all right," Goldin told them, "as long as you're wearing clean underwear." It was a bit like that all the way through.

'Later, when the men, convinced they're members of the Chippendales, start stripping, the audience shrieks with excited anticipation, but we never get to see their underpants – Goldin has his limits.'

The new Paul Goldin was moving into gracious old age. But not without another scheme. 'Stress' was the new buzzword and of course he'd been studying it deeply for the previous eight years.

'I've been engaged in the study of neuro-linguistics. I'm supposed to be an authority on that sort of thing,' he told the sceptical reporter.

'People can't make up their minds about Paul Goldin,' the article concluded. 'Can he really stop you smoking and drinking? Can he help you become thin? Is he really French?

'At the beginning of the show he told us about someone he had levitated at the previous night's show. The audience listened in awed silence. The thing is, if you believe that, you believe anything.'

But Paul Goldin had people who believed in him – his family. His and Helen Breen's daughter, Katie Jane, was already being groomed to inherit her father's empire. Born with a silver spoon and golden good looks, she was a school friend of the one-time Miss World, Rosanna Davidson. Of course their fathers, Paul Goldin and Chris de Burgh, had a shared showbusiness heritage.

Over the years Paul Goldin had churned out hundreds of business ideas, many of which failed. But now with Helen Breen and Katie Jane concentrating on the business side of the venture there was a new and more professional approach which began to pay dividends. A combination of good public relations organised by Katie Jane's mother, her own marketing skills learned at the Dublin Business School, and of course Paul Goldin's well-known Irish 'brand' name all helped. The clinics specialised in techniques for solving the ailments of the modern world – stress, smoking and weight. But there was also the modern need for positive thinking so there was talk of Katie fronting a television show to boost the clinic's performance.

There was also, happily, a reconciliation between two of Paul Goldin's wives, Trish, the mother of Ricky Paull, as the actor and soap star was now known, and Helen, the mother of Katie Jane. After her acrimonious split with Paul Goldin, Trish had emigrated to the United States where her son Ricky became a child actor working mostly in television commercials.

'My mother was very protective, she was one of the good mothers you know, looked out for me, very much so. I missed my Dad, but Trish compensated a lot, she was both Mom and Dad,' he said.

At the age of 16 he made his Broadway debut in a production of *On Golden Pond* and his stage career was born. He later played in *Grease* on Broadway for two years and came back to Ireland to play in *The Pirates of Penzance* on the Olympia stage, a place his father worked so well over the years.

'It was first on my list to go back and set foot in that theatre because of what it means to me,' he said at the time. His engagement to *Baywatch* star Yasmin Bleeth, with whom he lived for five years, got acres of coverage in the world media. The couple got engaged at Christmas 1996 while he was home in Dublin doing the show. But their romance didn't survive doing a film together.

However the relationship between father and son had improved with age.

'His father was the internationally famous hypnotist Paul Goldin,' reads the official biography on his fan website 'but his mother Patricia deserves all the credit.'

'I have homes in New York and in LA but I love the idea of being in

Ireland for the holidays,' he said while promoting his appearance in the Olympia at which he planned to recreate his father's show using a professional hypnotist who would use his father's techniques.

'I feel quite comfortable here.'

'My father never tried out any hypnosis on me or anything – I always thought of him as being an entertainer primarily. My mother Patricia is coming over for opening night. She gets on very well with my father's wife Helen and we will probably spend the day at dad's. My father says that I am physically more powerful than he is and so I am planning to recreate his show in LA or on Broadway.'

Ronald Paul Gold (otherwise Paul Goldin) of Old Conna Lodge, Ferndale Road, Rathmichael, County Wicklow, described officially as 'a psychologist', died on 13 February 2007 at the Blackrock Clinic in Dublin.

He came to Ireland without a penny and it seems he happily checked out with very little either. After all the big houses, the Bentleys, the round-the-world cruises, he was a showman until the last. Easy come, easy go. At a time when plumbers and prison officers were leaving millions behind them, his estate came to just €27,754.

The afternoon of his death the RTÉ radio presenter Joe Duffy did a show in tribute to him, which brought a 'surge' of goodwill towards a man who while not gone was largely forgotten in the new modern Ireland.

'Even in dying, Paul Goldin got our attention,' said one radio critic.

His simple death notice did not refer to his wives, but to his sons and daughters starting with the youngest, Katie-Jane, and remembering the others – Joanna, David, Bobby, Ricky and Sarah.

At his funeral service in the Unitarian Church on St Stephen's Green, Miriam Ahern, the estranged wife of the former Taoiseach Bertie Ahern, read a eulogy written by Paul's daughter Katie Jane:

'My idol, my hero, my inspiration and my heart – I will miss you always. You will stay in my heart forever.'

As his son Ricky called for a last round of applause to 'send him on his way', two of his wives, Patricia and Helen, sat together mourning a man who had brought so much into their lives. Old friends from showbusiness, Dickie Rock, Red Hurley and Twink, either sang or spoke of the man they remembered as 'charming, witty and charismatic'.

But perhaps one of Dublin's last remaining Jewish 'cantors' and a long-time friend of Paul Goldin, Mitchell Wax, left a fitting epitaph for this charming scoundrel and man of many and varied talents:

'Those who never loved and were never loved – never lived. Those who loved and were loved – never really die.'

Chapter 7
The Ambassador's Daughter

Upon walking into the drawing room of Tassagart House, the first thing a discerning visitor noticed was the Picasso painting hanging on the wall. Hotel tycoon Jim Mansfield dismissed it with the wave of a hand, as if to say such trophies as your very own Picasso were of little consequence to a man like him.

He'd come up the hard way, from urchin to owner of this beautiful house outside Dublin not very far from the farmer's cottage near Brittas where he grew up. He started work as a farm-hand at the age of 14 before going to England to make his fortune. He then returned to Dublin to become the Tsar of Citywest.

From the plush interior of his elegant Rolls Royce he could survey his empire of hotels, apartment blocks and golf courses that stretched along the Naas Dual Carriageway.

Across in Weston, near Celbridge, he had his own airfield and his private jet flew in and out taking the tycoon and his sons on business trips throughout Europe. Rather unfortunately, in late September 2006 the jet was detained in Belgium shortly before take-off to Weston when a man boarded it with heroin worth €10 million destined for a Dublin criminal gang.

Jim Mansfield, who would later declare 'there are no drugs in my business', said he knew nothing of this. He didn't even know his jet was in Belgium at the time.

Further down the road near the village of Johnstown he had acquired the one-time stately home of the Earl of Mayo, Palmerstown House. His son, Jim, had been very friendly with the previous owner, an elegant woman who was once a great beauty. Jim Jr persuaded his father to buy the place from under the nose of another developer. Little did they realise what a can of worms they had opened.

* * *

Anne Moen Bullitt, who as a child in the 1940s was known in the international press as 'Little Annie Bullitt', was the daughter of a famous American diplomat and writer, William C Bullitt. By the late 1990s she had gradually retreated to just three rooms of Palmerstown House where she lived in the perpetual half-gloom that no sunlight was allowed to penetrate.

In the end psychiatrists declared that she was unfit to run her own affairs. The once-famous millionairess was carted off to a home – a Ward of Court – leaving behind her Picasso painting, her Ming vase, her evening gowns by Dior and Givenchy from Paris and even a pair of duelling pistols presented to George Washington by a favoured general at the end of the American War of Independence.

These items would become the subject of a protracted legal dispute between Anne Bullitt's Trustees and self-made millionaire Jim Mansfield.

So where did this incredible collection that included paintings, jewellery, haute couture gowns from the great Parisian designers, personal papers of the famous psychiatrist Sigmund Freud, love letters from writer Eugene O'Neill and even John F Kennedy's doctoral thesis come from?

To understand that, you have to delve into the fascinating past of the woman who was known at various times in her life as Anne Moen Bullitt, Anne Moen Biddle, Anne More O'Ferrall and Anne Moen Brewster – and three of those names came from her four husbands, the first lasted such a short time she never conferred on him the distinction of adopting his surname.

Whatever you choose to call her, 'Little Annie' was born the only daughter of two famous American parents. She travelled the world meeting some of the greatest figures of the twentieth century, lived in Palmerstown House outside Dublin for many years and remained largely anonymous outside the 'racing set' where she was admired. She had the distinction of being the first woman in Ireland to hold a Trainer's Licence.

Anne's mother was born Louise Mohan in San Francisco, California of Irish extraction in 1895. Louise's parents divorced while she was still a child and her mother moved to Nevada where she took her stepfather's name, becoming Louise Bryant. She was first an illustrator and later a journalist. Moving to New York Louise fell in love with another journalist, John Reed, and they lived in a community of artists, writers and political activists in Greenwich Village.

Described by her biographer, Mary V Dearborn, as the 'queen of Bohemia' she was a colourful and well-connected figure, writing, acting, travelling and posing nude in the early 1900s for a celebrated portrait.

Louise Bryant and John Reed married in late 1916 but in keeping with their loose lifestyle both had lovers. Louise had a stormy affair with the hard-drinking playwright Eugene O'Neill, author of *Long Day's Journey Into Night*. When her husband went to Russia in 1917 to report on the Bolshevik Revolution, she soon followed him. It was this experience that informed Reed's book *Ten Days That Shook the World* – which was later made into the film *Reds* with Warren Beatty playing Reed and Diane Keating playing his wife Louise.

Reed died of typhus in Russia in 1920 and was buried beside the writer Maxim Gorky in a plot located between Lenin's tomb in Red Square and the Kremlin that contains the last remains of some 200 famous figures from the twentieth century.

Louise later turned up in Paris where she enjoyed the fast life of the pre-war set, the dancing and drinking and the endless round of dinners with the rich and famous.

It was there that she encountered William C Bullitt, an American writer and diplomat, who in his lifetime would meet and become friends with some of the greatest figures of modern history, but whose biography would bear the half-hearted title that appeared to sum him up: *Close to Greatness.*

William Christian Bullitt Jnr came from a patrician family in Philadelphia. He graduated from Yale in 1913 and became an influential journalist and writer before he was sent on a secret mission to Russia in 1919 on behalf of US President Woodrow Wilson.

At the time a cruel civil war was raging in Russia between the Communist Bolsheviks (or 'Reds') under Lenin and the 'White' Russians, comprised of an alliance of anti-Communist groups. Bullitt soon recognised that the dreaded Reds would win the war and negotiated a deal with their leader Lenin whereby the United States would recognise him and his Soviet government.

It was a deal that could have changed the course of world history, but Wilson and his ally, British Prime Minister Lloyd George, repudiated the deal and continued to throw their support behind the doomed White Russians.

It was a blow that Bullitt would remain bitter about for the rest of his life.

Disillusioned with politics he resolved to find some exotic place where he could 'lie in the sand and watch the world go to hell'.

But he was never content to sit around watching things from the sideline for very long.

Instead he pursued Louise Bryant across Europe before settling in Paris where they joined the ex-pat community which included figures such as F Scott Fitzgerald and Ernest Hemmingway. Louise and William agreed to marry although some of her friends were shocked by her choice of second husband.

'After Jack Reid to go to something so superficial, very rich and very society' was very strange, according to her friend, the feminist Sara Bard Field.

Although William Bullitt had turned his back on the 'blue bloods' of his home town, Philadelphia, he could not let it be known that he was about to marry the daughter of an Irish working man. So he had Louise Mohan Bryant change her name to Louise 'Moen' Bryant for the wedding announcement.

'For all the scores he had to settle with Philadelphia society, he was still a highbrow when it came to the importance of a good name, and he preferred an Anglo-Saxon ancestry to immigrant Irish,' say his biographers Will Brownell and Richard N Billings in *Close to Greatness*.

It is ironic that their only daughter ended up living in Ireland many years later.

William C Bullitt married Louise in 1923 and their only daughter Anne Moen Bullitt was born in Paris on 24 February 1924.

Still bitter about Woodrow Wilson's 'treachery' Bullitt embarked on a collaboration with Sigmund Freud, the founder of psychoanalysis, on a psychological study of Wilson, his one-time friend, which was so controversial and critical of the American president that it wasn't published in the United States until the 1960s.

Indeed many scholars disputed the authority of the book, claiming that Freud had not really participated in this study of the American President at all. However papers handed over to Yale University after Anne Bullitt found them in a trunk in Palmerstown House included much material relating to the book, such as letters from Freud which proved that he had indeed taken an active part in writing the critical study.

Even more importantly, Anne Bullitt, according to Freud, proved one of his great psychoanalytical theories. When the inventor of psychiatry asked her if she loved her father, the young Anne Bullitt replied, 'My father is God'.

'That child is very articulate,' Freud is reported to have concluded. 'You know I have developed a theory that male children's first love is their mother and females' their father. But this is the first time a child has confirmed my theory.'

In 1926 her mother Louise contracted a condition known as Dercum's Disease. She began drinking heavily; whether it was to kill the pain or the disappointment of her failing marriage to Bullitt remains an unanswered question.

'I want you to know one thing,' she wrote to her husband, 'I have lived too long with unconventional people to be suddenly made into a bourgeoisie.'

Bullitt now turned his attention to fiction and his first novel, *It's Not Done,* was published to literary derision – yet sold 150,000 copies, a remarkable feat for an unknown writer. Ernest Hemmingway said in a letter to F Scott Fitzgerald, describing the people he encountered in the fashionable watering holes of Paris, 'Also Bill Bullitt, or Bull Billet, a big Jew from Yale and fellow novel writer'.

By the end of the 1920s, Bullitt's relationship with his wife had completely broken down. He divorced Louise in 1930 and was given sole custody of Anne.

'I never have news of Anne. It is difficult for me to work,' Louise wrote to friends from Paris where she was a lonely, sick alcoholic with nothing but memories of the past as she moved from one rented apartment to the next, waiting for the cheque to arrive from Bullitt, who was prepared to give her a generous allowance as long as she stayed away from him and their child.

The details of Louise Bryant's life are well known because around this time a group of researchers from Harvard began to classify the voluminous papers she and John Reed had kept.

As Anne moved about the cities of Europe and America, educated and reared by a succession of governesses, she continued to believe that her parents were deeply in love throughout their lives.

'Once I was playing the Eighth Symphony of Schubert, the 'Unfinished' symphony, and I noticed my father was crying. I asked him what was the matter and he said the piece reminded him of my mother, as it had been one of her favourites,' she said in a newspaper interview, remembering the precocious child she had been.

In 1933 William Bullitt was appointed the first United States Ambassador to the USSR by his friend, the American president Franklin Delano Roosevelt. The appointment was not popular in diplomatic circles. But Bullitt got the job because of a long-standing friendship with prominent Soviet figures and it was his reward for cementing the deal that allowed the two great powers to restore diplomatic relations for the first time since the Russian Revolution.

He sailed for Europe in November of that year accompanied by his daughter Anne, now nine years old, and her West Highland terrier Pie-Pie. It was a strange life for a young girl, living in a suite in the National Hotel in Moscow while the Embassy was being built, her father being cheered in the streets and at the Opera, and the endless parties in Moscow where the diplomats drank the finest wines and dined on the choicest caviar as more than nine million peasants died in the countryside from starvation and brutality.

Eventually her father sent her back to Philadelphia to continue her schooling, but she was a frequent visitor to Europe, meeting him in exotic locations from Odessa to Istanbul.

Her mother Louise Bryant died suddenly in 1936. Later the same year William Bullitt was appointed as US Ambassador to France, taking up residence in the finest foreign embassy in Paris, with his daughter by his side.

Anne was growing up a lonely figure, adoring her father from afar. In one letter thanking Roosevelt for having himself 'and Anne' to the White House he noted, 'I did not realise how lonely she felt, alone in America. And I am deeply grateful that she will not be'.

In 1940, as Europe was inflamed in the Second World War he turned down the job of US Ambassador to London in succession to Joseph

Kennedy, father of JFK, Bobby, Edward and the rest of the Kennedy clan. Bullitt was determined to remain in America to 'shepherd his daughter's introduction to society', according to his biographers.

'Anne was 17, a graduate in June of the Foxcroft School, and while she would have preferred going to college – she was accepted at Vassar for the fall of 1941 – her father was insistent, though for an unusual reason. "You'll do parties for a year," he ruled. "If you don't, you'll spend the rest of your life wondering if you should have. If you do, you'll realise how empty and meaningless they are".'

He also vetoed her attempts to follow somewhat in her mother's footsteps by becoming an actress.

So she did what is probably the next best, or worst, thing: she made a bad marriage. In February 1944 at the age of 19 the socialite Anne Moen Bullitt married Caspar Wistar Barton Townsend, a 24-year-old Army Staff Sergeant in Washington in what one newspaper described as 'a surprise ceremony'. According to *Time* magazine, when her father was asked about the happy event his reply was, 'What?'.

It was the first of four marriages for Anne, none of which seemed to be particularly happy or lasted very long. Freud probably had it figured out – in her eyes none of her husbands ever matched up to her father.

In May 1947 Anne Bullitt was already a divorcee when she married Nicholas Duke Biddle, the son of one of her father's lifelong friends in Washington DC and scion of yet another famous family in Philadelphia. Her husband was an attaché in the American Embassy in Spain and once again she moved back to Europe, this time as a diplomat's wife rather than a diplomat's daughter.

While her husband was busy with Generalissimo Franco and other important matters, Anne Bullitt developed an interest in bloodstock and persuaded him to buy a large farm outside Madrid where she started to breed horses.

Then in 1952 her husband Nicholas Biddle resigned from his job to go into business on his own. He had a considerable private fortune and decided he and his wife would move to England where he could pursue a career as an investment banker in London and she could dabble in horses, finding good mares to bring back to their Spanish estate.

They rented a large house in the country for the weekends and in keeping with her lifelong interests they began to mix with 'the racing set'.

That was how she came to meet Roderic More O'Ferrall and his colourful brothers Francis and Rory at Lingfield Races in the summer of 1954.

The More O'Ferralls were an ancient Irish family who claimed to be the descendants of the Gaelic chieftain Rory O'More. The family 'seat', Kildangan Stud near Monasterevin in County Kildare, had been a castle of the FitzGeralds but had passed to a rich merchant family called Reillys from Cavan and then by marriage to the More O'Ferralls.

After the introduction at Lingfield, Anne Bullitt bought a filly from Francis 'Frank' More O'Ferrall who ran a bloodstock agency. When he decided to run her at The Curragh on 26 May 1954, she and her husband Nicholas decided it would be 'rather fun' to come over to Ireland.

She had been to Ireland, she claimed, with her mother 'when I was little' but had no real recollection of the land of her impoverished Irish great-grandfather.

Although she only came for the weekend, it was long enough for Anne Bullitt to finally find a place to call home.

They had a glorious day at the races and that evening they were invited by the colourful horseman and trainer Patrick J Prendergast to join him and his guests for dinner at his house, Rossmore Lodge, near Newbridge, County Kildare. Frank More O'Farrell and Major Collen were among the guests that evening and much of the dinner-table talk was about horses and 'horse dealing', buying and selling horses and what various mares and sires were worth.

She got on so well with 'Darkie' as PJ Prendergast was known, that the following day he took Anne and her husband to Castletown Stud near The Curragh where they looked over a few horses and she and 'Darkie' decided to buy a mare together.

If there was one thing the Irish landed gentry had, and particularly the racing set, it was a good eye for someone who had plenty of money and was prepared to spend it.

'You buy a half share with me and then if anything happens, and for some reason you want her and you do not want me to have her, you can always pay me back what I put into her and that is that.' According to Anne Bullitt, this is how Darkie explained their business arrangement to her. Originally she had intended bringing her Irish horses to Spain where she and her husband maintained an estate. But it didn't work out that way – Darkie Prendergast had plans to keep them nearer home.

Eventually Anne Bullitt ended up spending over £20,000 on horses, which was a considerable amount of money at the time, considering that the newly-fashionable Ford station wagon, named The Squire, was then retailing for £420. The principal horses acquired by Anne and Darkie were War Loot, Persian View and Fine Flower. The mares eventually had a number of foals, which were said to be very valuable.

Anne Bullitt enjoyed the conviviality of Ireland far more than her husband. A banker and diplomat, he was more at home in the salons and boardrooms of London than the windswept plains of Kildare.

With divergent interests, Anne Bullitt's second marriage soon faltered and came to an end, although she remained on good terms with her second husband for the rest of her life.

Her partnership agreement with Darkie was never written down, but it was sealed over a fine dinner in the Dolphin Hotel in what is now Temple Bar, Dublin, an establishment frequented by the Irish racing set when they were wining and dining important clients. The hard-drinking natives preferred it to The Shelbourne, which was patronised by the more refined Anglo-Irish and English visitors.

Travelling between England and Ireland, Anne Bullitt began spending weekends at Kildangan Stud where she was becoming increasingly friendly with the aristocratic owner and one of the main 'movers and shakers' of the Irish racing scene, Roderic Charles Francis More O'Ferrall.

Born in Ireland in 1903 and educated at Eton and Oxford, Roderic More O'Ferrell did a short spell with a trainer in England before he came back to Kildangan Stud in 1927 and took out a trainer's licence. He had considerable early success as trainer to Count John McCormack, a world-wide celebrity who had made a fortune as a recording artist and singer and who lived nearby at Moore Abbey, which he had rented from the Earl of Drogheda.

McCormack's horse, Beaudelaire, trained at Kildangan and won the Irish

St Leger in 1931. But the Count terminated his racing interests the following year after losing a great part of his fortune investing in 'the sport of kings'. Roderic assumed ownership of Kildangan when his father Dominic died in 1942.

His younger brothers lived in England. Francis (Frank), who lived in Sussex, owned the Anglo Irish Bloodstock Agency and among his customers was Darkie Prendergast. The youngest brother, Rory, married Lady Elveden, a daughter of the Fourth Earl of Listowel and widow of Lord Elveden (Arthur Guinness), only son of the Second Lord Iveagh who was killed in action in the Second World War.

In the early 1950s after the expensive restoration of Kildangan and major improvements to the gardens, Roderic More O'Farrell was very amenable to the idea of a rich American divorcee who loved the social life and the prestige of his house and stud farm.

Guests were greeted by 'Dinkin' the Butler. The rooms were done up beautifully, with Roderic's aristocratic friends helping out. The salon was decorated according to the exceedingly good taste of Ann, Duchess of Westminster, a frequent guest, who would later gain considerable fame as the owner of the great racehorse Arkle, winner of the Cheltenham Gold Cup for three successive years in the 1960s.

Roderic was extremely hospitable, according to guests, although sometimes there was a 'camp' atmosphere about the house, especially when a distant cousin, Edward More O'Ferrall from the Longford branch of the family, was staying. They called each other 'Rod' and 'Ed' and although Edward was by no means from the same social background as his wealthy cousin, Roderic nevertheless included him as one of the 'family'.

Anne Bullitt was staying for increasingly long periods at Kildangan, where guests at his 'house parties' might include Lady Haddington, the Earl of Iveagh, the Marchioness of Dufferin and Ava and many more, from the Mayor of Bombay, Sir Sultan Chinoy, to well known politicians and statesmen.

Conversely Roderic More O'Farrell moved in the highest social circles in England – staying with the Earl and Countess of Derby for Royal Ascot week, or at the Northumberland castle of his business partner Sir Percy Lorraine, a former British Ambassador to Italy and Turkey and a 'formidable' poker player, who bought a half stake in Kildangan in 1950. Roderic was also on very friendly terms with the English Catholic aristocrat, the Duke of Norfolk.

Anne Bullitt was certainly smitten by More O'Ferrall and his international circle of friends. Roderic was as at home in the highest social and political circles in London or Rome or New York as he was in County Kildare. For someone like her, who had spent a lifetime wandering the globe and meeting all the 'best' people, there was the attraction of his reputation, his home with its beautiful gardens and his horses.

But there was a secret side to Roderic More O'Ferrall that was known to only very few and Anne Bullitt was warned about it.

During 1954 her friend and business partner Darkie Prendergast, who she later admitted said 'a lot of things', mostly scandalous, about other people, had watched her become friendly with the aristocratic Irish family. Darkie loved a bit of salacious gossip but there was more than that about some of the disturbing things he had to say about the More O'Ferrall family and Roderic in particular.

'He said Roderic was very peculiar. He kept telling me a lot of things about Roderic, he said that Roderic was a fairy and a sadist,' she would later tell the High Court in Dublin.

'He said that Frank (Francis) More O'Farrell was completely dishonest, that Roderic More O'Ferrall was extremely queer and that Rory was all right, because he had married a wife who had a lot of money.'

'Paddy,' she replied, 'I think you are exaggerating.'

To which he said, 'I know what I am talking about.'

But, as she observed, 'one really did not pay so much attention as he said things about so many people.'

Darkie Prendergast was apt to pass colourful remarks about everyone, regaling Anne Bullitt with tales of the racing set and even scandal about his own wife, 'saying awful things about her'.

But despite the things he was saying about her friends she enjoyed the company of Darkie. On her travels she kept up a correspondence with him signing her 'friendly and affectionate' letters to him 'with love Anne'.

With her 'film star good looks' and her money, there was a dangerous chemistry about Anne Bullitt and her wild-but-charming Irish business partner Darkie Prendergast that led to a lot of gossip around the paddock at The Curragh and the Phoenix Park.

It was a tight circle. Darkie was buying horses through Frances More O'Farrell and his company The Anglo Irish Bloodstock Agency and they were being kept at Kildangan, the home of Roderic More O'Farrell. Darkie was getting fees and a half share of the horses.

Anne Bullitt began to get an uneasy feeling that she was picking up more than her fair share of the bill for the whole operation.

She spent her time 'travelling' abroad between October 1954 and January 1955. But when she came back to Ireland in the New Year her affairs were about to get very complicated and not a little murky. On Saturday 29 January 1955 the following announcement appeared in *The Irish Times:*

Mr Roderic More O'Ferrall and Miss Anne Bullitt: The marriage has taken place of Mr Roderic More O'Ferrall, eldest son of Mrs More O'Ferrall and the late Mr Dominic More O'Ferrall D.L of Kildangan, Co Kildare, and Miss Anne Bullitt, only child of the late Mrs Bullitt and the Hon William Christian Bullitt, former American Ambassador to France and Russia. The ceremony took place in the Cathedral of Our Lady of Guadalupe, in Mexico, where Mr Bullitt has been staying recovering from an operation. The Right Rev. Msg. Baudelio Pelayo, Dean of the Cathedral officiated and Nuptial Mass was celebrated by the Rev Oscar Chavez.

The sudden Mexican wedding, which also involved a civil ceremony, came as quite a surprise in Irish racing and social circles.

For her wedding Anne bought herself an impressive diamond necklace produced specially in Paris for her by Cartier. What she paid nobody now knows but it was later said that it 'perfectly matched her society lifestyle' and her elegant designer outfits.

If Darkie had made salacious remarks about Roderic More O'Ferrall before she married him, the new Mrs Anne More O'Ferrall soon discovered at Kildangan that this was not just idle gossip.

There were two sides to her complex and brilliant husband and one of them was very unpleasant according to her later evidence.

In February 1955 she had a conversation with Darkie when he was ill in bed at home. She said that Darkie said to her on that occasion that as she was now married to Roderic More O'Ferrall, he wanted her to know that if at any time she felt that Mr More O'Ferrall objected to her ownership of mares in partnership with him (Darkie), she must remember that all she had to do was to pay him back any money he had invested in them and the mares would be hers.

'That is so nice of you,' she told him. Things would not remain so nice between them for much longer.

Within months of her marriage she told Darkie that she might have to leave Ireland. She was now a valued client of his and their partnership had accumulated some very high-priced bloodstock. Most of the two-year-old fillies had been bought rather cheaply with Anne Bullitt's money and Darkie's equine expertise, but had risen considerably in value when their progeny went into training with Darkie and began proving themselves on the racecourse.

But now Darkie was worried about her domestic situation in Kildangan. So worried, she would later say, that he even suggested that she could lose her life.

'I had been beaten up several times by Mr (Roderic) More O'Ferrall, and Mr Prendergast said that he thought he would do almost anything to me if I stayed there.'

Although he continued to act, in public at least, as if he was a 'friend' of Roderic More O'Farrell, within weeks of the marriage Darkie had been urging Anne Bullitt to leave her husband and Kildangan, for her own safety.

Later, in the summer of 1955, she was ill in bed in Kildangan and under the care of Dr O'Connell. The doctor sent for Mr Prendergast.

'You must tell me what is the matter – I know something awful is the matter – that it is something more serious than the flu – something awful has happened, I am sure it is Roderic, you must tell me,' Darkie said to her. On 11 July 1955 she arrived back at Dublin airport from a trip to London. She was met at the airport and brought to Mr Prendergast's house.

'I told him that I thought I would have to leave Kildangan and I said if I left Kildangan it might be awfully difficult for me to stay in Ireland, and if I don't stay in Ireland what will we do with the mares?'

'There's no problem about that,' he replied, telling her that all she had to do was pay him back any money he had invested in the horses belonging to their partnership 'and you can do what you like with them after that.'

She thanked him.

'I was most grateful to him for being so kind and I hoped I would not have to leave Ireland. He said he would help me in every way he could so that I would not have to leave Ireland and that I could count on his help at all times,' she said.

But when she started to make arrangements to leave Kildangan and take her horses with her Darkie's attitude changed.

Afraid for her own safety and no longer able to live in the rambling mansion, she moved around various hotels wondering what to do. She begged her father to come to Dublin to help her decide her next move. She also wanted his advice about a house that was advertised in *The Irish Times* on 24 September 1955. It was Palmerstown House, 'a valuable stud farm' standing on 697 acres which was being sold by the auctioneers Ganley's.

Palmerstown House, according to the architectural historian Mark Bence Jones, was built in Victorian 'Queen Anne' style as a tribute to the Sixth Earl of Mayo who was Chief Secretary for Ireland before becoming Viceroy of India. There he had the misfortune to be assassinated by an escaped convict in the Andaman Islands in 1872. Although the stately pile was burned down in 1923 it was rebuilt by the Seventh Earl, who was a member of the new Irish senate where he served until his death in 1927.

The house was then sold to a local vet, W J Kelly, who had lived there since.

The day after this advertisement appeared in the paper William C Bullitt arrived in Dublin from Washington and booked into the Shelbourne Hotel where his daughter had taken up residence.

On Monday 26 September Anne Bullitt sent for Darkie Prendergast. He drove up to Dublin to meet her and she told him that her husband Roderic was going to the Newmarket Sales which together with an important race meeting at the same venue would last for at least a week. She was going to take all her belongings from the house while Roderic was away and she asked him to have transport ready the following Thursday to remove the horses owned by them from Kildangan.

She was leaving the house for good she told him. He agreed that he would help her in any way he could. But on the drive back to Kildare he began to have second thoughts, although he kept them to himself for the time being.

On the Tuesday she phoned him at home and asked him if he could fly to England to watch her filly Atlantida, which Darkie trained, running in the prestigious Cheveley Park Stakes at Newmarket the following day. She alleged that her husband or his brother would try to stop it winning. Darkie told her he had too much to do at home and could not travel. In truth he probably felt that at 10/1, Atlantida wasn't worth the trip.

So she went herself.

In any event the six-furlong race for two-year-old fillies was won for France by Midget, trained by Criquette Head, with Anne Bullitt's horse trailing in fifth. After watching the race she stayed overnight in London and came back to Dublin the following morning. By the time she arrived back at the Shelbourne Hotel on Wednesday 28 September, Darkie Prendergast had already phoned looking for her. He spoke to her father William Bullitt and said he would ring back at 11p.m.

When he did, he told her he had changed his mind about removing the mares from Kildangan.

'I don't think it's the right thing to do, to interfere in a dispute between a husband and wife,' he told her.

'Paddy, do you really mean that?' she asked, feeling betrayed.

'I don't want to be mixed up in your divorce from Roderic,' he answered.

'You had six months to think about that,' she replied, reminding him that it was he who had been telling her to leave Roderic and Kildangan. She went and got her father, who spoke 'very strongly' to Darkie. When she got back on the phone they both exchanged angry words. Prendergast, who was a colourful character, said later that Anne Bullitt 'flew into a violent temper and used abusive language' to him. He replied that he was going to ring Roderic More O'Ferrall and tell him what she was planning to do – that she was going to take all the mares from Kildangan in secret while he was away.

As the argument raged back and forth, Darkie said he could no longer continue to train for her if she spoke to him like that. She replied that after what he had done to her that night she did not want him to train for her ever again.

After putting down the phone she went to the writing desk and wrote to Brigadier Boylan notifying him and the Turf Club that Patrick J Prendergast no longer had any authority to act on her behalf. By 30 September she had taken her things from Kildangan and removed the horses to the establishment of Mr Michael Dawson.

Inevitably the dispute between Patrick J Prendergast and Mrs Anne Bullitt More O'Ferrall ended up in the High Court before Mr Justice Dixon in December 1955, where Anne broke down crying as she related details of her troubled marriage to Roderic More O'Ferrall and the collapse of her once-friendly relationship with Darkie Prendergast.

Anne Bullitt revealed that she had spent about £30,000 buying blood-stock in Ireland and she had been advised in her purchases by Darkie Prendergast who knew far more about horses at the time than she did. The question for the court was did Mr Prendergast have a 'half share' in three mares and two foals which were the subject of the 'partnership' agreement – a verbal agreement never committed to paper.

'Mr Prendergast was to have a half share – naturally, if you are going to get a half share in anything you must pay for it,' she maintained in her evidence, suggesting that the partnership was maintained with her money. She also insisted that her agreement with him was that if at any time she wanted to terminate the agreement she only had to repay him the money he invested, not half of £30,000 which is what the horses they owned were now supposed to be worth.

After a long and scandal-ridden court case, Judge Dixon decided that a mare and two foals were part of a partnership and Mrs More O'Ferrall was entitled to re-purchase Mr Prendergast's interest in them by paying all monies expended by him. Mr Prendergast was ordered to pay half Mrs More O'Ferrall's costs.

The case was a huge scandal at the time, especially the references to domestic violence and Roderic More O'Ferrall. To outside observers it seemed like neither side had come out as a winner. The judge had more or less dissolved their partnership on an equal basis, something they could easily have done themselves.

In early 1956 Anne Bullitt, with the help of her father, had negotiated the purchase of Palmerstown House and stud. Not many people wanted a big pile like that at the time, there wasn't much money around and the 'rates' for such houses were astronomical. The upkeep of estates with servants, gardeners and grooms was vast and had she not bought the house it could quite easily have been left to fall into ruin like many other great houses.

For Anne it was a place to finally put down roots, and that's what she did.

When she bought Palmerstown and its estate it was probably the biggest stud farm in Ireland. And she was determined to make it one of the best. She employed Tommy Shaw, who was known as 'the quiet man of racing' because he abhorred publicity of any kind, as her private trainer. With his hard work and Anne Bullitt's growing knowledge of breeding and racing – which was acquired by long hours studying the Stud Book – they proved a formidable team. The resident stallion, 'Milesian', sired 38 of the 74 horses that carried Anne Bullitt's colours to victory between 1958 and 1964.

1963 was probably her most successful year, when her horses won the Ladbroke Gold Cup at Epsom, the Ebor at York, the Duke of Edinbugh Stakes at Ascot and the Beresford Stakes at The Curragh. Even more remarkable was that these winners, ridden by the stable jockey Liam Ward, were bred at Palmerstown.

Anne Bullitt had confounded the racing establishment. But after these successes there was shock in the racing industry when she handed in her licence in 1965 to concentrate on the bloodstock end of the business.

In 1967 Anne Bullitt married for the fourth and last time. Her husband Daniel B Brewster was a US senator who would later stand trial for accepting bribes. He was found guilty, but the decision was eventually overturned. The marriage ended in divorce just two years later in 1969.

When her father died on 15 February 1967, William Christian Bullitt was almost a forgotten man. A diplomat who had been literally embraced by both Lenin and Stalin, a friend of successive American presidents and other world figures, a best-selling author and collaborator with Sigmund Freud, he was buried in Philadelphia without much fanfare. The only dignitary of real importance was Richard Nixon whom he had supported in his failed

1960 presidential race against John F Kennedy.

His biographers concluded, 'Bullitt came close to greatness, for he had the promise of greatness; that he failed to realise that promise was a tragedy.'

It's probably a harsh epitaph, given that he was a man of his time. Whatever else he ended up as an important footnote in the history of the early twentieth century.

For the next 30 years his only daughter continued to live at Palmerstown House, but with each passing year her name and her own place in history began to fade. She had allowed her breeder's licence and insurance to lapse, but she was still a glamorous figure at the races. As her eyesight deteriorated, she retreated to a three-room apartment in the huge and increasingly gaunt Palmerstown House. She never allowed the curtains to be opened, living in the semi-darkness, the gloom lit only by artificial light.

She kept up with events, watching as the other great house with which she was associated, Kildangan Stud, changed hands, eventually ending up as the Irish residence of Sheikh Mohammad of Dubai, one of the world's most powerful racing figures.

In 1961 following the death of his business partner Sir Percy Lorraine, Roderic More O'Farrall sold a half share in Kildangan to 24-year-old Lord Elveden, or Benjy Guinness as he was known, around the same time as he became the last Guinness to be appointed chairman of the family brewing firm, Arthur Guinness & Co, and inherited a brewing empire valued at £87 million Sterling.

Even better for Roderic he was, in a way, keeping Kildangan 'in the family' because Lord Elveden – who would later become the Third Lord Iveagh – had spent many happy summers at Kildangan. His mother, Lady Elveden, was married to Rory More O'Ferrall, Roderic's younger brother.

But the enormous costs associated with a house like Kildangan and the upkeep of the stud farm and its 400 acres had taken its toll. In the late 1970s and early 1980s secret overtures were made to Taoiseach Charles J Haughey to see if the Irish State would take over the place. But just as a deal was on the verge of being signed-off, Haughey's government collapsed. So in 1985 when Michael Osborne, who was Roderic More O'Ferrall's 'go between' in these negotiations, was asked by Sheikh Mohammed of the kingdom of

Dubai to find him a stud farm in Ireland – Kildangan was the obvious answer.

When he died at noon, 29 October 1990 at the age of 87 Roderic More O'Ferrall and his second wife Patricia Laycock, who had previously been married to another racing figure – the Earl of Jersey, were now only tenants of the stately home and gardens that he had lavished so much money and attention on during his lifetime.

'Roderic was the most charming and kindest of men and was much loved in return,' said his 'Appreciation' in *The Irish Times.*

As the 1990s wore on, Anne Bullitt too was struggling with the huge costs of keeping up Palmerstown House and its massive estate. When her financial advisors came to see her they had to read the documents to her. She was, however, 'an independent and determined lady'. By that they meant that even at the age of 75 she wouldn't let anybody push her around, resisting their attempts to persuade her to sell the estate. So in 1997 her 'advisors' agreed to sell Palmerstown House and estate for IR£8.2 million to a developer. But while they were doing this deal Anne herself went behind their backs and 'to the consternation of her advisors' agreed to sell the house and lands to Mr Jim Mansfield of the Citywest complex for IR£10 million (€12.7 million).

Whatever else had gone she never lost her appetite for a good deal.

And there was no man better able to spot a deal in Dublin than Jim Mansfield.

The self-made millionaire had worked for a local farmer near Saggart in west Dublin and then in a gravel pit before buying his own lorry and going into business for himself. He married a local girl, Anne and had three sons, Tony, Jimmy and PJ.

'When I got married first I left the house every morning at 4 a.m. and didn't get back until 11 p.m.,' he says of his early life.

It is said that one of his great money-making schemes was to buy old but still reliable JCBs, re-paint them in the traditional canary yellow colours and either sell them on at a huge profit or rent them out to busy contractors. Mansfield came back to Ireland and bought Tassagart House and 160 acres in west Dublin for €1.3 million in 1990. Over the next ten years he restored the house and set about building the Citywest complex.

In the process he acquired thousands of acres of land – making multi-millionaires of small farmers whose families had been in the area for generations. The singer Paddy Reilly who owned an eight-acre field beside his property was paid €35 million for the parcel of land.

'I started with 35 rooms, I don't know where to stop,' Mansfield told reporter Aine Coffey. His acquisitive streak and his determination to get his own way led him into constant battles with planners as they tried to restrict the onward march of his empire.

His son Jimmy Mansfield was friendly with Anne Bullitt through their shared interest in racing. When he heard that her legal advisors were planning to sell Palmerstown House, the Mansfields approached Anne Bullitt and offered her a deal.

She signed – it was a deal that led to a decade of litigation. Palmerstown House was to be the 'jewel in the crown' of the Mansfield golfing and hotel empire and no expense was spared in restoring the house and filling it with antiques.

It was later alleged in court that Jim Mansfield agreed to buy Palmerstown House with a €500,000 deposit – but her solicitors claimed that money never went to Anne Bullitt's estate and was retained by the company used by Mr Mansfield to buy the property.

Anne Bullitt's decision to sell to Mansfield also led to a serious rift with her advisors and trustees – mainly a distinguished New York lawyer and estate planning expert called Robert M Pennoyer and solicitors from the Dublin firm of Arthur Cox.

They arranged for her to be seen by a psychiatrist in July 1998. 'To say she was uncooperative was an understatement,' according to her lawyers. Ms Bullitt told the psychiatrist in her best French and in most undiplomatic terms what to do with himself.

'The psychiatrist's interview was terminated in a very peremptory manner,' said her lawyers in their best 'legalese'.

Sadly it was the beginning of the end. The developer who had been 'gazumped' in the sale of Palmerstown House sued for breach of contract. There were further court hearings and in the year 2000 Anne Bullitt had the ignominy of being made a 'Ward of Court' by the President of the High Court in Dublin – which means that the day-to-day running of her life was taken out of her hands and transferred to an officer of the Court.

She left Palmerstown House for the last time and was taken into care. Jim Mansfield believed that not only had he bought Palmerstown House but he had also acquired some of its valuable contents, including a Picasso painting, the Ming Vase, the Japanese screen and the George Washington pistols that would become the subject of a protracted dispute.

When Anne Moen Bullitt died in the Kylemore Clinic, Church Road, Ballybrack, County Dublin on 18 August 2007 there was little indication that she had once been such an international beauty, an heiress with a taste for designer clothes and the daughter of a very famous mother and an important American diplomat. Her death went largely unremarked, a testament possibly to the fleeting nature of fame.

Her Will, dated 1987, states, 'I direct that my funeral service shall be held at the Church of the Holy Trinity on Rittenhouse Square in Philadelphia, Pennsylvania, and that it be a traditional Anglican funeral as set forth in the Book of Common Prayer published during the reign of King Edward VI. I further direct that my remains be buried in Woodland Cemetery, Philadelphia, Pennsylvania, next to the grave of my father and that my grave be marked with a stone cross identical to the other crosses in the family plot inscribed solely with my name and the dates of my birth and death.'

She left her Raoul Dufy painting of a white horse to her nephew Nicholas Duke Biddle and IR£30,000 to her friend Challoner Chute if he should survive her. The rest of her Irish estate, which came to over €11 million, she left to the William C Bullitt Foundation.

In December 2007 the 100-carat diamond Cartier necklace which had been a wedding present for herself as she was about to marry Roderic More O'Ferrall was sold at auction by Christie's for £602,500 Sterling, more than double the estimated price.

But there were certain things that Jim Mansfield firmly believed were his and he was prepared to go to court to fight for them. When the case was called before the High Court in Dublin on Thursday, 19 February 2009 it had been rumbling on for years in the background. Robert M Pennyoyer, a prominent New York attorney and a Trustee of Anne Bullitt's estate, was seeking a declaration from the court that valuable items were part of her estate and not the property of Jim Mansfield who claimed he had acquired them when he bought Palmerstown House.

Pennyoyer was also claiming that a deposit of €500,000 which was to be paid to Mrs Bullitt as part of the sale of the house had been retained by Mansfield's company, Bridford Developments.

Mansfield denied all the claims.

The case was opened on behalf of the Plaintiffs – Mrs Bullitt's estate – by Mr Bill Shipsey SC. With some colour he described the history of the Bullitt family to Judge Mary Laffoy and described vividly the items in dispute. But just when he had piqued public interest the case was suddenly adjourned after 30 minutes to 'facilitate talks' overnight between the two sides.

When it reconvened the following morning, Friday, the judge was told that it had been settled.

Judge Laffoy said that she was striking out the case 'with a little note of sadness' as she would have liked to have heard more about the relationship between William C Bullitt and Sigmund Freud. Presumably she has now learned all she needs to know about this fascinating man and the mysterious daughter whose life only came to light for many people because of a dispute over a Picasso painting and a Ming vase.

Chapter 8
The Man in the Silver Shadow

The elegant Rolls Royce left the Berkeley Court Hotel in leafy Ballsbridge that sunny Friday evening and glided noiselessly through the traffic until it reached St Stephen's Green where it came to a halt outside what was then Dublin's most expensive restaurant, Whites on the Green.

It was 15 June 1986, the eve of Bloomsday. The vintage Silver Shadow, then an uncommon sight in recession-hit Ireland, did not park in the normal fashion. It was more or less abandoned outside the restaurant as the three occupants got out, leaving the large car marooned in the middle of the busy street. As the traffic ground to a halt the handsome 'lads' strode up the granite steps and burst into the restaurant with the nonchalant air of men who were accustomed to creating a stir wherever they went.

As they moved about the room greeting their guests they gave off an aura of money and glamour but also lurking in the background was the powerful whiff of danger. The first two were the Hollywood actor Patrick Duffy, known at that time all over the world as 'Bobby', JR Ewing's younger brother who had just been 'killed off' in the hit television series *Dallas,* and his flamboyant friend, the Irish actor Daragh O'Malley.

The third man was James 'Danger' Beirne, a former Roscommon football star with a questionable past and an even more dubious future. Duffy and O'Malley were business partners in an exciting new venture that was to be launched that very night in the exclusive Dublin restaurant.

Waiting to greet them at the door of Whites on the Green was the firm's 'secretary' Hylda Queally, a one-time teenage Irish dance champion and former AIB bank official from Bearfield, 'a bend in the road', outside Ennis, County Clare. She was also Daragh O'Malley's girlfriend. In time she would go on to make a name for herself as one of the most powerful women in Hollywood, but right now she was just delighted to be present at this glittering event in Dublin.

Inside the sumptuously decorated restaurant, the plaything of millionaire property developer Peter White, a mixture of film people, media personalities and political hangers-on swilled brimming glasses of Bollinger champagne and chomped on puffed pastry prawns.

The excuse for the party was to greet Patrick Duffy who had arrived in the city amid a fanfare of publicity as he became the latest Hollywood star to trace his Irish roots. That Friday night the city's glitterati were out to play, eating and drinking in style and dying to share in a little bit of the promised Hollywood limelight. Eimear Haughey, whose father Charlie was then the leader of the opposition and a man with a permanent whiff of danger himself, chatted with Patrick Duffy, who had been flying around Ireland in a helicopter piloted by her brother Ciaran.

Her mother, Maureen Haughey, talked to Daragh O'Malley about his father Donogh and their college days together in nearby Earlsfort Terrace. O'Malley's father was a colourful Minister for Education with a taste for alcohol and excitement who died young at the age of 47 but left behind the legacy of free education in Ireland, while his mother, the beautiful Hilda Moriarty, was the inspiration for Patrick Kavanagh's haunting love poem *On Raglan Road*.

Among the other guests that night was PJ Mara, the smooth-talking Fianna Fáil sidekick of The Boss (Charles J Haughey) and his wife Breda, the LA film director Joseph Losey, a frequent visitor to Dublin, and the colourful theatrical impresario Noel Pearson who would get his own taste of Hollywood success with the film *My Left Foot*.

And of course there were media hangers-on who were there to drink for free and record the moment for posterity.

Although the two actors were the centre of attention, the man who owned the Rolls Royce, James Francis Beirne, otherwise known to his friends by the nickname 'Danger', was probably the most interesting man in the room that night. As he ordered more champagne and cajoled trays of food from the kitchen, Danger was about to pull off a IR£17 million financial transaction that would send ripples through the world of high finance from London to Lagos.

Improbable as it might seem and unknown to his guests that night, Danger who was introduced around town as 'a film producer', was actually in the middle of buying almost the entire world supply of Norwegian dried fish to sell to some very dodgy customers down in darkest Africa. Yet apart from the flashy Roller, his only assets were his friendship with Daragh O'Malley and a heavily mortgaged house in Castleknock, County Dublin which he'd bought for IR£20,000 the previous year.

Before the summer of 1986 was over, his Norwegian business associates would be left wondering where their millions were gone and how they had ever become entangled in his web of deceit and double-dealing. Such trivial details mattered little to James Beirne as he mixed with 'the great and the good' in Whites on the Green in Dublin that summer's night. To his guests and the media, he was a man of substance, a 'producer' at the centre of a film project that would bring some much-needed glamour and money to the humdrum streets of Dublin in the late 1980s.

'I found my visit to Ireland quite extraordinary. I don't know what it is about the Irish,' Patrick Duffy enthused to his guests that night, 'but they seem to have an active regeneration of their own patriotism and when they come back to their roots, as I have, they find it very special. It's a very spiritual thing.'

But as the American actor regaled the dinner party about his pilgrimage to Ireland, Danger's thoughts were far from spiritual. He was wondering how exactly he was going to get out of the restaurant and back into the double-parked Silver Shadow without being stuck with the bill for a long and very expensive evening.

According to legend, James Francis Beirne was born in the county hospital, Roscommon – the son of two well-respected teachers from the town of Elphin. He was educated at the local national school and later at Summerhill College in Sligo, the alma mater of such luminaries as Albert Reynolds and Ray McSharry.

A good scholar, the sharp-witted Beirne had what his friend Daragh O'Malley later recalled as 'sublime intelligence'. He was also an excellent Gaelic footballer.

'If you got past Danger you were entitled to your score,' maintained one seasoned observer of the county championship. Indeed it was his determination on the football field that earned him the nickname 'Danger'. Whoever thought it up certainly had a very prescient idea of the lifepath that James Beirne would take in the years to come.

In 1966 the 18-year-old Beirne was a member of the Elphin senior football team which was defeated in that year's county final. But glory awaited when he was selected for the Roscommon Under-21 football panel. After a most unexpected victory over Mayo and another over Galway, the little-fancied Roscommon team found themselves in the All-Ireland final in Croke Park, playing the defending champions Kildare for the first ever Tim Clarke Cup. Even the local newspaper, the *Roscommon Herald,* was sceptical of the team's chances especially as their star mid-fielder Dermot Earley, who would go on to become Chief of Staff of the Irish Army, was just 18 and still eligible to play minor football.

This scepticism seemed to be confirmed as Kildare pulled away in the first 15 minutes of the second half and were 6 points ahead going into the final quarter of the game.

'Out to mid-field came Dermot Earley, and the Keanes, Jim and Martin Joe, swapped places so often that the Kildare defence didn't know which way to turn. While they were making up their minds, the first Keane, Jim, took a pass from Earley, picked his spot and sent a sizzling left-footed shot to the corner of the net,' went the colourful description in the *Roscommon Herald* the following week.

This was followed by a second goal from Joe Finnegan and the result, as the paper noted, was 'this totally unexpected victory for Roscommon'.

Danger was a member of the panel but didn't get to play in the historic game, but that didn't stop him in later years, when memories had faded somewhat, of dining out on the story of that famous All-Ireland victory.

The bonfires that burned to welcome the team home to the west made a lasting impression. Young, ambitious and full of schemes, James Beirne couldn't wait to leave school and make his way in the world. But his parents were insistent that he should have a third-level education and he was accepted into the College of Dentistry in Dublin. He found the profession far too dull for a man of his talents. Although he spent a couple of years at college, he was not noted for his attendance at lectures and never finished the course. Real life was far too exciting.

His first big enterprise was a jeans manufacturing plant in Strokestown, County Roscommon. Like a lot of things in his life, it didn't work out. Maybe he was ahead of his time or like a lot of his future schemes he was more interested in getting rich quick by gambling on success rather than working hard enough to make the business work.

In the end the big losers were the banks and the investors. Danger quickly put it behind him and followed his star towards the bright lights of Dublin. A second venture in Dublin failed, but the factory mysteriously burned down and Danger moved on again.

In the 1970s he turned up in London where he teamed up with another Irishman to supply building workers, Irish navvies, to construction firms for what was known in the trade as 'the lump'. It was a simple process and very beneficial to the big building firms. Middlemen like James Beirne would supply enough labourers for a job on a daily basis. It meant the contractors always had the right number of men for a job. If they weren't up to it, the men didn't get picked to work the following day.

Better still the firm didn't have the burden of employing them, so there was no sick pay, income taxes or social security. That was left to Beirne and his associate to sort out. Needless to say the tax or the stamp was never paid, but he made a fortune as a contractor in human sweat.

'Himself and another guy were earning about £8,000 to £10,000 a week into their pocket "organising workers",' recalls a friend from those years. It was a fortune at the time.

'The lorries would pull up outside the Archway Tavern and other Irish pubs and Beirne and his associate would organise who was going where. You had to be tough, but he was that. He was making a pile of money. After the weekend the guy he was in business with would still have most of his share of the money, but Jim would be broke. He'd have gambled and drank it, living the high life around London.'

He was always just one step ahead of the tax authorities. As in his football days, he was a difficult man to catch. His 'associates' tended to be shady guys from the race tracks, the gambling dens, the Irish pubs and the late-night joints of Soho. They wore sharp suits and drove fast cars and hung out with beautiful women – London was still swinging and Jim Beirne stayed close to the action.

When the 'building trade' got too hot for him, Jim disappeared for a while. But it wasn't long before he turned up again. This time, improbable as it might seem, he was a gold bullion dealer. It was a trade worthy of his talents. But it all ended rather abruptly in 1983 when James Francis Beirne, as he was known on the charge sheet, was arrested and sentenced to three years in prison for obtaining 353 gold Kruggerand coins worth the considerable sum of £95,999 from a Jersey bank with a forged bank draft. Beirne believed that taking money from banks was a 'victimless crime' and it wasn't the last scam he would try.

The court was told that the defendant was 'under very extreme pressure' because of gambling debts and that he feared for his life because the money was owed to some very unscrupulous people. He didn't do the full stretch and when he got out of prison he decided that Ireland was a safer bet than going back to his old London haunts.

Within weeks of returning he was back at the race track. This time the softly-spoken Roscommon man was hoping for a change of luck. He would later admit that he was 'a ducker and diver'. In an attempt to stay ahead of the game he took out a bookmaker's licence and ran what was later described as an 'unprofitable' bookie business, with a shop in Dublin and a pitch at The Curragh, the glamorous headquarters of Irish racing.

He and his young wife Joan started a family. When their daughter was born the wayward James Beirne appeared to settle down to a normal kind of suburban home life in Maple Green, a nice little housing development in Castleknock, then a growing suburb of Dublin city. There was a slight hiccup in his new existence when he got involved in a serious card game back home in Roscommon. It was what one local described as a 'big game' which drew some serious punters. Thousands of pounds changed hands over the course of a night.

Of course Danger with his reputation as a high-roller and his insatiable thirst for a punt, got an invite to sit down with the big boys, including a well-known police detective. He survived the encounter without losing too much cash. But mysteriously the following Saturday night, as the card game progressed, a man in a balaclava suddenly burst into the remote farmhouse, grabbed the money, estimated at about IR£3,000 and took the detective hostage. There was a huge local scandal when Danger was arrested and questioned for hours. He never cracked and he was never charged with involvement in the robbery and abduction. But what he hadn't factored into his calculations was that another of the players was well connected to the IRA and Danger was now in danger from an organisation much more deadly than the police.

'He was a bit like the Scarlet Pimpernel', said one local businessman. 'You never knew when he'd turn up, but the stories about him were legendary.'

For a 'chancer' like him there was always another scheme and what better enterprise than the film business, awash with money and populated by dreamers and schemers in search of an elusive blockbuster and the glamour that came with it. And in Dublin there were always people on the lookout for a new business venture and a man who wanted to make it work.

As it happened Daragh O'Malley had just started the European Motion Picture Company in Dublin. Tall, debonair with a head of black hair and well-connected socially, O'Malley was laying the groundwork for the arrival in Ireland of his friend Patrick Duffy who was to have a half share in the company which planned to make a number of films, the first of which was to be shot largely in Ireland. When he wasn't at his desk, and that was quite often, Daragh O'Malley was strolling around Dublin and enjoying the conviviality of the Horseshoe Bar in Dublin's historic Shelbourne Hotel. It was a melting pot for all sorts – politicians, barristers, writers, businessmen, journalists and hangers-on. And among the companions he met leaning against the brass rail of the bar was James Beirne.

'I started the company with Patrick Duffy who had just been written out of *Dallas*,' recalled O'Malley. 'Duffy had an option to make three films for Lorimer Pictures and the first was to be called *Dillon*, which was to be shot in Ireland. We got a suite of offices in Harcourt Street. We met with accountants Stokes Kennedy Crowley (SKC) to organise the finance and we had a lot of money in an account with Barclays bank.

'Hylda Queally was my girlfriend at the time. We had met Patrick Duffy in the United States and she ran the office in Harcourt Street for us. Everything was going fine with the *Dillon* project – Duffy was coming over to Ireland and all that and we were really planning to make the film, which was a very exciting venture at the time.

'One night in the Horseshoe Bar in the Shelbourne, I met Jim Beirne. He told me he was in the fish business and had a few horses in training. He said he was looking for investments in Ireland and he mentioned that he wanted to open an office in Dublin. I told him he could have one of ours which wasn't in use at the time.

'I had no reason not to believe what he was telling me. He had the racehorse. It was trained by John Hasset in Limerick. It was called Fishy Business, which was typical of Jim. We became great friends and I recall we all went up to Ballinrobe to see it running – and I think it won.'

While Beirne was never part of the European Motion Picture Company he ran his 'fishy business' out of the same office suite and he hung out with O'Malley, who introduced him around Dublin as his friend.

'Jim loved it and you would have thought he was part of it the way he played it up,' O'Malley recalls. When Jim Beirne moved into the office it was 'like the League of Nations'. There were all sorts of people turning up. Among Beirne's associates was a man called Tom Forde who was involved in a successful television rental company with offices around Dublin. Many years later Forde was identified as an informant for the United States Drug Enforcement Agency in Miami.

Another caller was Peter Bolger, who appeared to be a respectable businessman living in Templeogue, Dublin with his schoolteacher wife. In reality he was a money launderer and conman known in the underworld as 'The Banker'. He too was to become a guest of Her Majesty's Prison Service after spending 10 years and a small fortune fighting extradition to Britain for a fraud conviction.

'Jim used to have these high-rolling bankers come in from Norway and other places. He would take them by helicopter down to Leitrim where someone would paint a landing pad in a field. But he never let them get out and meet real people. If they'd asked around, they would have found out what he was really like and what he was really worth,' remembers another associate.

What O'Malley and Duffy didn't grasp was that while they were all having great fun, James (Jim) Beirne was also using the film business as 'cover' to pull off his latest scam. They were young, brash and ambitious. O'Malley, who would later perfectly capture that ebullience as Patrick Harper in the *Sharpe* television series, loved the life and the limelight of Dublin in the 1980s. Danger's contribution to the company was to squire people who needed to be impressed around Dublin in the Rolls Royce, hand out big cigars and talk like a Hollywood producer. It was something that came very naturally to him.

Meanwhile Daragh O'Malley finally got his friend Patrick Duffy to come to Ireland to launch their joint venture and hopefully cement a deal with Lorimer to shoot a film in Ireland. Daragh O'Malley, Hylda Queally and the European Motion Picture Company were determined to make a big impression when Duffy arrived in the city and so Jim Beirne was roped in to become part of the team because his Rolls Royce car added that important air of Hollywood glamour to an otherwise depressed city. According to Hylda Queally, the 'office' was run on a shoestring and initially they operated from a phone box on Harcourt Street because there was a six-months' waiting list to get a phone installed by the Department of Posts & Telegraphs.

'When I wasn't around some Corporation workers would answer the phone and say in their best Dublin accents, "she is indisposed at this time",' she recalled. And that was why Patrick Duffy was so important. He had 'star status' at that time and everyone, including politicians, social climbers and bankers, especially bankers, wanted to meet him.

It is hard to imagine the effect that the series *Dallas* had on recession-hit Ireland. In a country where the roads were potholed, the cars held together by wire, the north of Ireland exploding and unemployment knocking on every door, the glamour, opulence and sexual chemistry of the series based in the oil capital of the world was high-grade escapism, the only narcotic that people could afford at the time. Duffy had Irish roots and he loved the good times that the Irish 'boys' showed him – with introductions to the Taoiseach-in-waiting Charles Haughey and a chance to visit his old ancestral home outside Kinnegad in County Westmeath.

Duffy's eventual arrival in Dublin that summer was heralded like a royal procession. Early in May 1986, Duffy and his producer pal Robert Lovenheim arrived in Dromoland Castle, County Clare. From there they flew by helicopter to Ashford Castle near Cong, County Mayo where they met up with Daragh O'Malley, amid 'well placed' rumours that the young O'Malley was being 'courted' by Haughey to stand against his 'Uncle Dessie' (O'Malley) in Limerick in the expected general election. As the excitement built, the party arrived in Dublin and eventually made their way to Whites on the Green for the glittering reception to announce the European Motion Picture company's first big venture. The film *Dillon* was based on a Michael Connolly thriller and it would star Patrick Duffy and be directed by Lovenheim. 'Preproduction won't begin until the autumn,' Hylda Queally gushed, confidently talking like a real film producer, 'and filming will begin in the spring of 1987.'

Once *Dillon* was in the can the Irish company proposed the rather bizarre follow-up of *Twenty Years A-Growing*. Maybe that was just a ploy to impress Haughey because it was a story about life on the Blasket Islands, one of which he owned, and the producers expected generous government grants and tax incentives. The night in Whites on the Green was a tremendous success – although Peter White now can't recall exactly who paid the bill for the lavish affair. Certainly at the time it was something of a mystery and some wondered whether it had been paid at all. But after the champagne went flat and the publicity died down and Patrick Duffy went back to LA, the European Motion Picture company went into a slow and unspectacular decline.

'One day I got a call from Patrick Duffy's agent Joan Scott,' recalls Daragh O'Malley. 'She told me he was putting the whole *Dillon* project on hold – he'd been written back into *Dallas*.

'"How can they do that? He's dead," I said.

'"That's the pictures business for you," she replied, and that's how it ended.'

But with a two-year option left on the offices O'Malley decided on a new venture and he established a talent agency called 'Limelight International'.

'It was the first in Ireland at the time. Hylda didn't have a clue about it (talent agency work), but that is how the fifth most powerful woman in Hollywood got into that side of the film business. She ran Limelight for two years. She was very good at it. We discovered Brendan Gleeson, who was a teacher, and Liam Cunningham, who was an electrician. Eventually I told her she had to go to LA – my mother was sick at the time and I didn't want to leave Dublin.'

Hylda moved to LA and has since become one of Hollywood's top agents. She was honoured with a US - Ireland Alliance's 'Oscar Wilde: Honouring the Irish in Film' award in 2009 for her outstanding work as an agent. This award was given to her by one of her clients – Kate Winslet. Queally also represents Cate Blanchett, Angelina Jolie and Katie Holmes.

As for Daragh O'Malley, the only money he made from the whole venture came from a libel action he took against a number of publications – including *The Sunday Press* – who had run a story with the headline 'Dallas Star and the IRA'. The story concerned the background to one of the men Patrick Duffy met, who had a connection to the IRA. While O'Malley wasn't mentioned by name, the European Motion Picture Company was.

So he employed other habitués of the Horseshoe Bar – Adrian Hardiman and Gerry Danaher – to sue on his behalf and he got a very nice settlement. Unfortunately for him he ploughed all the money he made from the libel action into a stage production of *The Rocky Horror Show* which failed spectacularly and swallowed up all his cash.

Patrick Duffy returned to *Dallas* when the scriptwriters put his death down as a bad dream and wrote his character back into the series. His one-time Irish companion, Danger was soon at the centre of his own high drama – and the script was something Hollywood would find just as difficult to dream up. The great 'Norwegian stockfish scandal' was about to unravel.

It had all started on 18 March 1986 when two senior executives, one a businessman, the other a banker, arrived at Dublin Airport from Oslo in Norway to clinch an important business deal with a mysterious Irish tycoon. They were met at the airport by businessman Thomas A Forde and taken by helicopter to an impressive stately home deep in the Irish midlands where a lavish weekend house party was in full swing in what they were told was the country manor of the Irish-born Hollywood film producer James F Beirne. With its battlements and old paintings in gilt frames and long rambling corridors, the castle was dark and mysterious and like nothing the Norwegians, who came from a more frugal place, had encountered before.

There they enjoyed drinks with 'associates' of the tycoon – Tom Forde, a prominent Dublin businessman, and Joe Grimson, a colourful Icelander, who had organised the deal. The 'big man', James Beirne, described by his friends as an Irish sporting hero, was in New York putting the finishing touches to yet another multi-million pound deal. He would, the Norwegians were informed, only have time for a brief meeting in Dublin later that weekend before he had to jet off to yet another exotic location.

As the party progressed and the drink flowed, the Norwegian executives were introduced to a Eugene Keaveney and given to understand that he was a high-ranking executive of the Northern Bank, then an offshoot of the Midland Bank, one of the biggest banks in Britain. The bank had its headquarters in Belfast, so it wasn't unusual they were told that meetings would be held outside Dublin. Had the Norwegians dug a little deeper they would have learned that Keaveney was, in fact, a branch manager of the bank in the nearby town of Carrick-on-Shannon, the smallest in the bank's entire network.

The Norwegians were hardly innocents abroad. When Keaveney told them that the man they were waiting to meet, James Beirne, was an old school friend who had 'world wide' experience in international banking and was a substantial businessman with assets sufficient to cover the IR£17 million business deal that was under negotiation, they should have been suspicious, very suspicious. But a combination of their exotic surroundings, the colourful Irishmen they were meeting and their own desperation for a deal seems to have overwhelmed them. Common sense was forgotten, as it often is, in the headlong pursuit of profit.

To understand what happened next, it is necessary to make a short detour into the history of Norwegian cuisine. Strange as it may seem, wind-dried herring, known as stockfish, are a prized delicacy in those parts. But with its small population (four million) and massive fish stocks the country produced far too much stockfish for its own people to consume. Oddly enough, the only other people partial to stockfish were Nigerians (population: over 100 million). Because it was relatively cheap and the dried fish didn't rot in the hot humid climate, there was a brisk trade in stockfish between the two nations. But then the notoriously corrupt Nigerian government officials began to impose import barriers and other restrictions on the stockfish trade because the scrupulous Norwegians wouldn't pay the required bribes. As the trade wilted, thousands of tons of stockfish began to pile up in the centre of the industry, Tromso, a pretty Norwegian town just over the edge of the Arctic Circle.

Unable to deal with the Nigerians and desperate to shift the stuff, the main stockfish producer, a company known as BJA, came up with an attractive incentive to move the dried herring 'mountain'. They offered a commission of 15 per cent of the value of any consignment of stockfish which could be shifted. This piece of commercial intelligence soon found its way to a convicted Icelandic fraudster named Joe Grimson, who just happened to be living in Dublin at that time and just happened also to be conveniently acquainted with Tom Forde and one Danger Beirne.

The seeds of the stockfish scam were sown. Grimson contacted BJA and said he had just the man to do the deal, a colourful Irish businessman and film producer called James Francis Beirne. He, they were told, was very 'well connected' meaning that he had less scruples than the Norwegians, was willing to bribe whoever mattered and take the risk involved in dealing with the cabal of officials and military men down in Nigeria who needed to be brought on board to make the transaction work. And that is how the Norwegians ended up in a remote location in County Leitrim getting assurances about James 'Danger' Beirne from a man they were led to believe was a high-ranking Irish banker.

Later the Norwegians were ferried by helicopter back to Dublin where they briefly met James Beirne at another lavish and crowded party in what they were told was his IR£4 million Dublin mansion – the location of which they couldn't later recall. They were also introduced to some of his more interesting friends, including the leading Irish actor Daragh O'Malley, some very pretty girls and also a man posing as Beirne's bloodstock advisor. Grimson, who was fluent in Norwegian, acted as spokesman for the group, offering to buy IR£17 million worth of the stockfish which would be sold in Nigeria in three separate consignments.

The negotiations were tough but the final agreement showed just how desperate the Norwegians were to do any kind of deal. The transaction was to be conducted in dollars, then the most negotiable currency in the world, and would be worth $21 million in all. The Irish consortium headed by Beirne would buy the 'stockfish' and export it from Norway to Nigeria in three shipments. Essentially there would be no cash payment from the Irish consortium until after the second consignment reached Nigeria. But the commission, the 15 per cent of the value of each cargo, would be paid 'up front' before each consignment left Tromso and set sail for Lagos, Nigeria.

The Norwegian company BJA and its bankers, the Tromso Sparbank, agreed to rely on the honesty of their Irish associates. Of course this was backed by the bank guarantees from the Northern Bank signed by Eugene Keaveney, the 'high-ranking executive' they had met in Leitrim. These 'promissory notes', as they are known in business, are a form of IOU to be paid at a future specified date. After taking legal advice, the promise of future payment was sufficient for the Norwegians and their bankers to believe that Beirne and his associates had sufficient funds to pay them when the debt fell due. On 25 March 1986 the Norwegian bank received a promissory note for $7 million worth of fish, signed by Danger Beirne and endorsed by the banker Mr Keaveney. They instructed Hambros Bank in London to pay Tom Forde, acting on behalf of Danger Beirne, $2.12 million by way of commission fee on the first consignment which set sail for Nigeria.

The bank draft for this amount was cashed in London the following day. On 5 May a second promissory note for $4.7 million worth of fish was signed in London by Beirne and endorsed by Keaveney. On 14 May a second commission payment of $1.3 million was paid to Forde again 'acting' on behalf of Beirne. On 26 May the Norwegians returned to Dublin to conclude the deal and were given the third promissory note to the value of $9.6 million.

They were collected by Rolls Royce and brought to James Beirne's offices in Harcourt Square. The paperwork was signed by Beirne and endorsed by Keaveney and then the Norwegians were brought next door to the headquarters of the European Motion Picture Company where they were formally introduced to Daragh O'Malley.

It was all very exotic and Irish – Norwegians didn't normally do business in this flamboyant manner.

Afterwards they all adjourned to the Horseshoe Bar in the Shelbourne Hotel to celebrate the conclusion of the deal. The celebration went on late into the night. As bottles of champagne popped, James Beirne must have believed that the deal was over the line. It was as if his horse Fishy Business had just won the Ascot Gold Cup instead of the 4.30 p.m. at Ballinrobe. But just as the third commission of over $1 million was about to be cashed, some bright spark in Hambros Bank in London raised an eyebrow. He was a very careful banker who had had dealings with senior executives of the Northern Bank before and could not recall any high-ranking official by the name of Eugene Keaveney.

He asked the Norwegians to check that Keaveney was indeed acting on behalf of the Northern Bank. A call was made to the Financial Controller of the bank at its Irish headquarters in Belfast who was somewhat surprised by this query. Keaveney was at the centre of a deal involving over $21 million plus more than $4 million in commission – and the controller had never heard of it or indeed the aforesaid Keaveney.

More surprising still, he further discovered that this gigantic transaction was guaranteed on behalf of the bank by the manager of its smallest branch in a rural town in the Republic. Suddenly alarm bells began to go off all over the place. The London bankers suggested that the promissory notes had been forged. Keaveney was suspended from his duties and an internal inquiry was ordered by the Northern Bank. As everyone scrambled to justify their actions, things appeared to slow down considerably.

The Norwegian company BJA stopped the second shipment of stockfish which was somewhere in the St George's Channel heading for Lagos, Nigeria. Then they began to look for assurances from the Irish consortium that the deal was above board. But Jim Beirne continued to string them along with assurances that he had the money and he would make the payment when the promissory note fell due. Initially he claimed there was 5.4 million 'Naira' (the Nigerian currency) in a bank in Lagos, but he was having difficulty getting the money out of the country. Then he told them that he would be able to pay $500,000 a week from his non-existent film business until the debt was cleared.

Instead of immediately contacting someone 'in the know' in Dublin to find out more about their Irish associates, – a number of detectives were well aware of James Beirne and his activities – the Norwegian businessmen and bankers seemed to simply cross their fingers and wait patiently for the first payment of IR£5 million ($7 million approximately) due to them, to be transferred electronically to their account in the Tromso Sparbank.

It did not arrive, as promised, by the close of business on Friday 18 July and they had a very bad weekend indeed. On Monday 21 July 1986 when a Norwegian bank manager, John Olaisen, and two executives from BJA flew in to Dublin to collect payment of the millions drawn on the account of James 'Danger' Beirne and endorsed by Eugene Keaveney on behalf of the Northern Bank in Carrick-on-Shannon, County Leitrim, it was a very different welcome from their previous visits to Ireland. Now there were no manor houses, no lavish entertainment and no helicopters or Rolls Royce cars to ferry them around.

When they finally arrived at the offices of the Northern bank in Carrick-on-Shannon in a rented car they were told the bank manager was suspended and there was no money in the account they were enquiring about. The bank would not honour the promissory notes as there was 'some doubt' about the bank guarantee and the authenticity of the signature of Eugene Keaveney.

It was just the first of many shocks that day. The trio left Carrick-on-Shannon and met with a solicitor in Dublin who made a few phone calls to contacts and pointed them in the direction of an address in Castleknock. When they made their way to the real home of Danger Beirne, the bankers were aghast to discover that the tycoon and film mogul lived in a modest suburban home on the outskirts of the city and not a castle or a IR£4 million Dublin mansion. The Tromso Sparbank rushed to get an injunction against James Francis Beirne restraining him from reducing his assets in the state below $7 million. Similar injunctions were taken out against his associates Thomas A Forde, c/o Irish Permanent House, Grattan Crescent, Dublin and Joseph Grimson, Cedarwood Gardens, Dublin.

'The background to this case was one of deceit,' concluded Judge Henry Barron when the bankruptcy proceedings came before him.

'It has all the hallmarks of a confidence trick.'

Beirne always insisted that there was five million Naira in a Nigerian bank waiting to be paid to him but it was denominated in the local currency and he couldn't get it out of Africa.

What happened to the $3.3 million the Norwegians had already paid in commission remains a mystery that has never been unravelled. By the winter of 1988, James Beirne was adjudged a bankrupt in the Bankruptcy Court in Dublin. The Norwegian bank, Tromso Sparbank, registered a judgement for $9.6 million against him and the debt carried an interest rate of 8 per cent until it was paid off – which of course it never was.

Judgements for smaller but still significant amounts were registered against Thomas A Forde and Joseph Grimson. The Norwegians also took a case against the Northern Bank which was eventually settled. The terms of the settlement were never disclosed.

As far as is publicly known no money was ever recovered by the

Norwegian banks or the firm BJA. The only consignment of stockfish to arrive in Nigeria was looted from the docks in Lagos.

The stockfish saga was over but it wasn't the end of Danger Beirne. He had another trail to blaze. There was a new fortune to be made and this time it was bound to work. This time it wouldn't be quite as colourful as Kruggerands or as boring as dried fish. The new project was a very different and much more valuable commodity than either. It was cocaine.

The first inkling of Danger's new career path and new friends came on 3 September 1992 when a man named John Francis Conlon, originally from Westport, County Mayo, arrived at Dublin Airport from Miami, Florida where he was then living. He was picked up outside the airport in a van driven by Eamon Kelly and the two men drove away towards the city. But unknown to them, Detective Inspector Martin Callinan had a fleet of vehicles, including a specially modified secret surveillance van, watching Kelly's every move from early that morning. Conlon was observed withdrawing IR£2,000 from a bank and the two men then proceeded to Jurys Hotel in Ballsbridge. Conlon got out of the van entered the hotel and was tailed to the fourth floor. He went into a hotel room, emerged soon after with a plastic bag and then rejoined Kelly who had remained in the van. Two Garda witnesses, Detectives Noel Clarke and Sean Butler, said they saw Eamon Kelly examining the contents of the plastic bag, in which it was later established were three heavily wrapped packages of cocaine, and then assist John Conlon in putting it behind them in a secret compartment of the van.

A short time after driving out of Jurys Hotel both of them were arrested. In custody John Conlon told gardaí he was working undercover for Scotland Yard. When the two men were later released on bail, John Conlon disappeared.

Eamon Kelly, a well-known criminal in the city, vehemently denied that he was aware that Conlon was carrying drugs. He said he had simply collected him from the airport at the request of a friend, named in court as James Beirne from County Roscommon. He said Conlon told him the bag contained money 'for a friend of Jim Beirne'.

In 1994 Eamon Kelly, then with an address in Furry Park Road, Killester, Dublin, pleaded not guilty to the charges but was convicted by a jury and sentenced to 14 years in prison by Judge Gerard Buchanan for possession of IR£500,000 worth of cocaine. John Conlon was re-arrested in London two years later. He was extradited to Dublin and pleaded guilty before Judge Cyril Kelly to the cocaine charges. He was sentenced to 10 years in jail.

Curiously Conlon again claimed to have been working for international intelligence agencies. Normally this could be dismissed as the delusional denials of a career criminal incapable of telling the truth. But it later emerged that prior to passing sentence in the Dublin Circuit Criminal Court, Judge Cyril Kelly took what was described as 'the unusual step' of allowing officers from the FBI and Scotland Yard to give mitigating evidence about Conlon in the judge's private chambers. What they said in this private audience with Judge Kelly is not known. It didn't save Conlon, who was given a prison sentence, but it gave an inkling of the circles in which Danger Beirne was now mixing. The spectre of the one-time GAA star, gold bullion dealer, film producer and fish broker was appearing yet again from the mists of time. Living in Paddington, London, Danger Beirne's new 'associates' were a colourful collection of criminals and drug dealers.

Among them was Charles Russell, a notorious London gangster and murderer, who had been convicted in the infamous 'handless corpse' case back in 1981. This involved the murder of a New Zealand-born drug baron called Martin Johnstone who was shot with a gun provided by Russell. Johnstone's hands were then chopped off and his face disfigured to disguise his identity before he was dumped in a Lancashire quarry. Russell was sentenced to 16 years in jail after a 121-day trial. He was released from jail in 1995 and very soon made contact with some like-minded people, including James 'Danger' Beirne and another associate, a handsome Peruvian drug runner with the unusual name of Miguel Urena-Wong.

The Irishman, the Englishman and the Peruvian met with an associate of Urena-Wong called Gilberto who ran a bogus shipping company out of Peru. They ordered a consignment of cocaine with a street value of £6.5 million which was hidden in a container of parquet flooring and dispatched to Europe. But Beirne and his new associates had come up with a novel plan to avoid detection by the British authorities. They didn't ship the container directly from Peru to Britain as they believed this might arouse suspicion. The consignment was supposed to go first to Estonia and then by a circuitous route back to London docks. But you just couldn't get a good shipping company in those days and instead the consignment was mistakenly off-loaded at Felixstowe in Britain in March 1997.

Customs officers became suspicious of the consignment. When they examined it, they found the cocaine hidden in the parquet flooring, 25 planks of which had been hollowed out to contain the drugs and then glued back together again. The customs officers replaced the drugs with rock salt and sent it on its way to Rotterdam and thence to Estonia. Fearing the ring-leaders might flee, the British police moved to arrest the 'conspirators'. They only managed to get three of them, including Danger Beirne who was arrested on the morning of 28 April 1997.

James Beirne was back in prison and protesting with much more vehemence than normal that he was innocent. By the time the gang was sentenced the case had gone on for years and the costs in lawyers' fees far outran the huge value of the cocaine they were trying to import. It took three trials and millions of pounds before they were finally sentenced. As he languished in Belmarsh Prison, Danger spent months, first at Southwark Crown Court and later at the Old Bailey, as the trials went on their wearying way.

The first trial collapsed after the jury could not agree a verdict after a record 16 days of deliberations. In the next trial the Peruvian deliberately revealed Russell's murder conviction and the case had to be scrapped. But the gang's luck finally ran out in the third trial in the summer of 1999. It lasted 10 weeks and cost an estimated £4.5 million. After six days the jury returned a guilty verdict. Russell was sentenced to 20 years in jail and Danger and his Peruvian co-defendant got 18 years each.

Of course it wasn't the last we would hear of James Beirne. The Scarlet Pimpernel of Roscommon was about to get romantic. In July 2000 the *News of the World* reported that James 'Danger' Beirne had married his 'pretty Russian girlfriend' Maria Issouponova, who was said to be originally from St Petersburg, inside top security Pankhurst Prison on the Isle of Wight.

'Beirne's wedding to his Russian bride – who is 20 years his junior – took place in the visiting room inside the sombre red-brick prison,' stated the report. 'Maria, who lives in a £500,000 flat in the posh London suburb of Hampstead, arrived at the prison in an ankle-length blue wedding dress and a large white lace hat.' The wedding, which took place in the play area for visiting children, took just 15 minutes and then the happy couple had a small iced wedding cake.

'His daughter and I will wait for him no matter how long it takes for him to come out, I love him very much,' the Russian bride was quoted as saying as she left the prison. Although Danger Beirne is not due to be released from high security prison until 2017, Her Majesty's prison now says 'our records do not disclose J. Beirne to be in prison custody'. As usual Danger Beirne had disappeared like a will o' the wisp on a Roscommon bog.

People say he's living somewhere around Strokestown with a new identity. Others have him in some far more exotic locations, but like a lot of things he has been involved with, nobody knows for sure.

'Jim – I haven't seen him in donkeys' years, but I hear he's living in North London', says Daragh O'Malley. 'He was one of the nicest people I have met in my life – a gentleman, a compulsive gambler, but a gentleman.'

One can only guess that somewhere Danger is sitting in a comfortable armchair dreaming of past glories on the football field and thinking up some thrill-seeking new scheme that will make him wealthy.

And of course this time . . . it is going to work.

Irish Family Feuds

Battles over Money, Sex and Power

LIAM COLLINS

When families fall out, the bitterness that emerges is matched only by the ferocity of their attacks on each other. Family feuds are far more vicious than disputes between strangers, as family members compete to crush each other completely and without mercy.

Cases include many rich and famous Irish families:
- Ben v Margaret – Duel at Dunnes
- The PV Doyle family 'hotel' war
- Comans and the 'Pub brawl'
- Enya, Clannad and the Brennan family feud
- 'Volkswagon vendetta' – the O'Flahertys' family secret

and many more family feuds over money, power and sex.

Frozen Blood
Serial and Psycho Killers in Ireland
MICHAEL SHERIDAN

Best-selling author Michael Sheridan describes a distinct and brutal pattern of killing women which has emerged in Ireland, one used by psycho sex killers.

To powerful and disturbing effect, FROZEN BLOOD examines the circumstances surrounding the murder and disappearance of several women. Young women such as Phyllis Murphy, who was raped and viciously killed, and Raonaid Murray, who was brutally attacked with a six-inch kitchen knife, murdered by men who have no inhibitions or feelings of remorse.

Why does an innocent child turn into a depraved killer? What are the common denominators among the tiny percentage of people who savagely kill? Why do they do what they do? Tracing the horrifying phenomenon of psychotic sex killers, FROZEN BLOOD provides terrifying profiles of killers active in Ireland.

Larry Cunningham

A Showband Legend

Tom Gilmore

Despite a number of heart attacks, a cancer scare and several attempts at retirement, showband legend Larry Cunningham is still singing in his 70s. His story is a *potpourri* of humour, success, shady deals – as well as sadness, death and murder on the music scene.

Larry Cunningham was the first Irish artist to make the UK Pop Charts – long before U2, the Boomtown Rats, Boyzone or Westlife. His 'Tribute to Jim Reeves' spent over three months in the British hit parade, sold more than a quarter of a million copies and culminated in his appearance on *Top of the Pops* alongside Cliff Richard and others.

When 'Gentleman Jim' Reeves walked off the stage at a dance in Donegal, Larry's singing of Reeves' songs stopped an angry mob from burning the place down. His first No. 1 'Lovely Leitrim' sold over a quarter of a million but the song has sad links to a bloody shooting in a New York bar. The gunfight and deaths, as well as two forgotten song verses, are recalled in this book.

Fascinating reading for those interested in Showbands and Sixties nostalgia, Country 'n' Irish music, the rise and decline of the Ballroom dances and Jimmy Magee GAA All-Stars Football charity.

Bainisteoir

The 10 Greatest GAA Managers

Finbarr McCarthy

Bainisteoir tells the individual heroic stories of the GAA's 10 most successful managers – based on personal interviews given to the author.

- **Dublin's** Kevin Heffernan – how he trained the Dubs' teams for victory.
- **Kerry's** Mick O'Dwyer – the secrets of his long run of success with the Kingdom – and **Kildare**, **Laois** and **Wicklow.**
- **Kilkenny's** Brian Cody –the 4-in-a-row, his research, 'player management' and training routines.
- **Cork's** Billy Morgan – dogged by controversy and his outspoken nature – yet **he** achieved great things down South.
- **Meath's** Seán Boylan – how he combined an outstanding run of success with the 'royal' county and his role of 'Healer'.
- **Clare's** Ger Loughnane – followed by controversy at both Clare and **Galway** but he's a great motivator and retains the will to win.
- **Tyrone's** Mickey Harte – outsmarted Kerry and motivated his players to success.
- **Kerry's** Páidí Ó Sé – straight-talking stewardship of the Kingdom, and later with **Westmeath** and then . . . **Clare**.
- **Cork's** Jimmy Barry Murphy – hurling success on Leeside with an Adidas controversy and Greyhound-racing hobby.
- **Armagh's** Joe Kernan – how he achieved three-in-a-row in the Ulster Championship.

Working On A Dream

A year on the road with Waterford footballers

DAMIAN LAWLOR

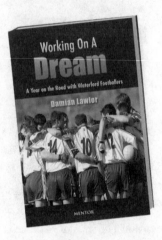

Far from the madding crowds of Croke Park, the inflated egos of star players and boardroom wrangles in the top counties, some GAA teams are fighting for their very existence....

Working On A Dream goes where no Irish sports book has ever gone before - a no holds barred, behind-the-scenes look at an intercounty GAA team struggling to survive at the lower end of the scale: Waterford senior footballers.

With access to all areas, the author, award-winning journalist Damian Lawlor, spent the 2009 season on trains, planes and in the dressing room with the Waterford players as they chase their goals for the year: climbing out of Division 4 of the national league and winning a championship game.

The tale that emerged is an honest, dramatic, sometimes tragic, sometimes comic depiction of what it's really like to be involved at the very grassroots of the GAA.

Tunnel Vision

Behind the Scenes at Great Irish Sports Events

Tadhg de Brún

Tunnel Vision takes the reader where no Irish sports book has ever gone before – behind the scenes at great Irish sporting events – from the Irish Open to the Heineken Cup to the All-Ireland Finals. Over 30 years with RTÉ Sports as event/floor manager has given Tadhg de Brún a unique insight into the stories and secrets at all the biggest Irish sporting events.

- Memories of the Irish Open – the golfers, their egos and their problems – and some very rewarding bets placed by the RTÉ crew!
- Snooker Finals at Goffs – the tension and the chaos; how Dennis Taylor was neatly put in his 'seat' after complaining about the facilities.
- All-Ireland Final days – the craziness *not* shown on TV; how the Kilkenny captain emerged from the victorious dressing room dressed in boots and gear and rushed off to church.
- The characters you meet on the road – the managers, players, caterers, cleaners, as well as the rakes of Liberty Square and the security man at the Brandywell. The comedy and tragedy of their lives as witnessed on great sporting occasions.
- Behind the great events of the Charlton Era, including an eventful trip by Tadhg and his crew to the World Cup in America in 1994.